MISMARKETING

MISMARKETING

Case Histories
of Marketing Misfires

Thomas L. Berg

NELSON

THOMAS NELSON AND SONS LTD
36 Park Street London WIY 4DE
PO Box 18123 Nairobi Kenya
THOMAS NELSON (AUSTRALIA) LTD
597 Little Collins Street Melbourne 3000
THOMAS NELSON AND SONS (CANADA) LTD
81 Curlew Drive Don Mills Ontario
THOMAS NELSON (NIGERIA) LTD
PO Box 336 Apapa Lagos
THOMAS NELSON AND SONS (SOUTH AFRICA) (PROPRIETARY) LTD
51 Commissioner Street Johannesburg

First published in the United States in 1970 by
Doubleday & Company, Inc.
First published in the U.K. in 1971 by
Thomas Nelson and Sons Ltd

ISBN 0 17 155034 X

Printed in Great Britain by
Richard Clay (The Chaucer Press), Ltd
Bungay, Suffolk

to . . . TOSHIKO

Preface

Strictly speaking, this book deals more with marketing misses than misfires. Shots were fired that failed to hit the mark. I have been motivated to analyse constructively some marketing mistakes in terms of the original forces and strategies that caused those operations to go astray. By so doing, I hoped I might provide a useful aid for teaching and learning in the field of marketing management and an incentive for others to study additional marketing failures on their own initiative.

I want to thank Michael Shimkin for leading me to Doubleday and to express my appreciation to Samuel S. Vaughan for editorial guidance and for patience over missed deadlines. My former mentors and colleagues, Ralph S. Alexander and William H. Newman, supplied friendly encouragement and psychological support at many moments when they were badly needed. Toshiko Betsumiya Berg, my wife, quietly suffered while I was engaged in the preparation of this book but bravely concealed the fact from me. No amount of kudos can repay my debt to her.

The Appendix acknowledges both the primary and secondary sources of information to which I am directly indebted. This book is my first attempt even to approximate the writing of history, and through this experience I have come to appreciate Barbara Tuchman's remarks about the sources she drew upon while writing *The Guns of August*:

> Through this forest of special pleading the historian gropes his way, trying to recapture the truth of past events and find out 'what really happened'. He discovers that truth is subjective and separate, made up of little bits seen, experienced, and recorded by different

people. It is like a design seen through a kaleidoscope; when the cylinder is shaken the countless coloured fragments form a new picture. Yet they are the same fragments that made a different picture a moment earlier. This is the problem inherent in the records left by actors in past events. That famous goal, *wie es wirklich war*, is never wholly within our grasp.

In this book, I have tried to tell the truth as I see it. Yet, I am fully aware that many may quarrel with the way I have related marketing history. I, alone, am therefore responsible for the interpretations that appear on the following pages.

Thomas L. Berg

Closter, New Jersey

Contents

CHAPTER I

Boosting the Batting Average in Marketing

The end of World War II marked the beginning of a period of rapid maturation in American marketing. With innovative boldness and daring unmatched in any other country, our marketers have contributed to one of the longest sustained periods of economic prosperity ever enjoyed. In just over two decades U.S. marketing successes have come to be envied and emulated by even the most anti-capitalistic of countries.

While marketing success stories have circulated and while it is recognized that many producers have become increasingly knowledgeable and skilful in resolving marketing problems and delivering customer satisfactions, these facts have tended to obscure the unpleasant fact of frequent failure. Hits are publicized; misses are not.[1]

The battlefield of distribution is littered with the corpses of marketing failure – discontinued products, aborted missions, scrapped programmes, records of sometimes staggering financial loss. Marketers misfire increasingly if for no other reason than that marketing opportunities and problems – and the attendant risks – have become more numerous and varied in the present age of affluence.

To maintain or improve our excellent track record, I believe we must learn to perform more penetrating post-mortems, calm examinations of misfires and mistakes. The purpose of this book, therefore, is to inquire into the nature of marketing failures and to see what lessons they may hold for marketing successes.

WHAT ARE MARKETING FAILURES?

(1) Whether we like it or not, failure is a pervasive characteristic of modern marketing; (2) marketing failures can, and do, appear in many forms; (3) the term 'failure' should be viewed as a relative, as opposed to an absolute, term.

Pervasive Characteristic of Modern Marketing

Marketing failures beset all kinds of firms – large and small, prestigious or unknown. New marketing students often make the dangerous mistake of assuming that sheer financial power can immunize a company from marketing failure. Although seasoned executives know better, student case reports on marketing problems repeatedly reflect this bias; there is an implicit assumption that a GE or GM or a P&G can do no wrong and that the small entrepreneur has a deck so stacked against him as almost to guarantee commercial failure.

Without in any way denying that financial strength and reputation are important marketing factors, any broad-gauge survey of marketing failures in a cross section of companies would almost certainly reveal such wide differences in size of firm as virtually to wipe out financial power and position as the determinants of distributive success. Marketing failures are ubiquitous; all types of companies live in fear of them. To illustrate: in reflecting upon the demise of the much-maligned Edsel, a marketing fiasco estimated to have set back the Ford Motor Company approximately $350,000,000, John Brooks was prompted to ask, 'How could this have happened? How could a company so mightily endowed with money, experience, and, presumably, brains have been guilty of such a monumental mistake?'[2] Similar questions might be levelled at many companies, for Ford certainly does not stand alone under the spotlight of failure. *Most* large companies have marketing skeletons in their cupboards.

Failure Assumes Many Forms

It has been widely observed that four out of five new products introduced on the market fail to achieve commercial success.

2

While the startling rate of new product mortality is a serious issue, it should not monopolize our attention, for there are less widely publicized kinds of marketing failure of equal seriousness. Marketing failures can occur in any substantive area of marketing strategy and in any of the procedural states of decision-making – from inadequate definition of the initial problem to errors and oversights in the execution and follow-through of selected courses of action.

A useful distinction might be drawn between 'partial programme' failures and 'total programme' failures. In cases of the first sort, a portion of an overall marketing plan may fail in its objectives and blunt the edge of strategy without totally wrecking the entire effort; e.g. a specific advertising campaign, a new price policy, a distributive tactic, a change in product design, or some other single decision area may deliver less than fully acceptable results. Or, a total programme may fail. Unsuccessful attempts to introduce new products into new markets, failure in introducing new products into established markets, inability to penetrate new markets with established products, and failure to maintain the position of an established product in an established market are examples of total programme failure. Such failures are more interesting and challenging areas of investigation than are partial programme failures. They enable us to observe the *interrelationships* between individual elements of the marketing mix and serve as a vehicle or springboard for the comparative analysis of alternative programmes and strategies.

'Failure' Is a Relative Term

The spectrum of marketing failure ranges from corporate bankruptcy to mild disappointment over results. Studies of business failure, conducted for many years by Dun & Bradstreet, repeatedly assert that the most important reason for company-wide failure is 'inadequate sales'. It is not unrealistic to infer from this that mis-marketing can be a major factor in corporate bankruptcies. The Edsel situation resulted in something less than a death blow to the company. Ford continued to prosper in other lines while Edsel floundered. This type of marketing is not so serious as to halt the

3

continuation of the company as a going concern. However, it is typified by complete withdrawal of a product from its market, by the cancellation of a large-scale programme, and by the abrogation of rather large commitments made in the past. Such failures may permanently or temporarily cripple a company with high financial losses even though the firm continues to live on. In less serious failures, a 'sick' marketing operation may operate in the black but at such low profit levels as to be adjudged unsuccessful. Since the word failure is seen to carry many meanings, when viewed in relative terms, it should be employed in the sense of 'falling short of expectations' or of 'not achieving objectives at acceptable cost'. Thus, a product or a firm need not be completely 'dead' before an autopsy is warranted. Serious failure, however, is usually the best kind to study, for such cases offer more opportunities to move along multiple and complex avenues of exploration.

WHY ANALYSE MARKETING FAILURES?

Autopsies of marketing failures should be of interest to marketing students and teachers, consultants, marketing research people, corporate sales executives, advertising agency representatives, media people, dealers, distributors, stockholders, consumers, and anyone else affected by or engaged in the marketing process.

But why study marketing failures? Wouldn't the study of successes teach us all we need to know? The answer is that *failure is a teacher* which is in some respects superior to success. The general educational value of the autopsy has been amply proven in the classroom over the span of several academic semesters. Executives who have gone through such post-mortems also confess to having absorbed profitable lessons from the experience. Despite our enviable record of successful marketing, we continue to create failures at a disturbing rate. This mismarketing cries out for explanation.

More specifically, autopsies of marketing failures can add to marketing efficiency in at least seven different ways:

1. By calling attention to the high social and economic costs of failure and revealing ways to reduce unnecessary expense.

2. By unveiling alternative courses of marketing action otherwise closed off by the dark door of 'experience'.

3. By developing a healthy tolerance of distributive failure through understanding its nature, causes, and cures.

4. By giving us positive guidelines for future marketing strategies and their tactical execution.

5. By adding to our knowledge of the dynamics of marketing action.

6. By augmenting our decision-making skills at specific stages of the planning process.

7. By providing a relatively inexpensive and simple form of research heretofore under-utilized in practical marketing – the historical method.

Cost of Failure

From the social viewpoint, marketing has long been subjected to criticism. Despite countless rebuttals, the real answer to the now classic question 'Does Distribution Cost Too Much?' is yes. Marketing costs are higher than they *need* to be. The responsibility for these costs and for increasing marketing efficiency must be jointly borne by the consumer, the marketer, and by other participants in the distributive process. Since we all have a direct stake in marketing costs, every marketer has a chance to repair the bent social image of marketing by reducing his failure rate.

From the corporate point of view, the manager certainly wants profits rather than losses. That objective is thwarted by mismarketing. From a strictly dollar-and-cents perspective, the price of errors is steadily going up. The prohibitive expense of marketing mistakes increases the urgent need to cut down on them. Note the following points:

(a) *It is becoming increasingly easy to make costly marketing errors.* With the inflationary squeeze on profits reducing marketing elbow-room, and with increasing competition from new products and new rivals (domestic and foreign) over smaller chunks of the market, the probability of failure has increased.

(b) *Both the short-term and long-term costs of errors are rising.* Because of the increased cost and greater market-penetration power of marketing services, more risk attaches to a given marketing move than was true a few years ago. 'It is little or no trouble,' say the editors of *Sales Management* magazine, 'to lay a $200,000-egg on one TV programme; and the coverage is better than ever. For its money, a company can now *look bad* before more people at one time than ever before.'

(c) *The costly cumulative effect of past errors is piling up on many firms.* External distribution systems, which may be used to illustrate this point, no longer have the slack to *absorb* bad decisions in many cases. Certain corporations' trade relations have reached the point of breakdown if one more egg is laid. Customers, particularly in big-ticket consumer durables and industrial goods classifications, are becoming more reluctant to forget a supplier's error. Corporate growth has often additionally meant a loss of contact between front office and field. 'The bigger, more complex a company gets, the more formal (or even non-existent) is the relationship between salesman and manager. The field force becomes stiff-legged. The salesman must stick to rules, pre-set prices, etc. This adds to the cost in two ways: (1) the salesman can't take it upon himself to *patch up* the error at customer level to any great degree, and (2) jammed communications between front office and field create an expensive *time lag* between the moment the salesman discovers something wrong and the time top management hears about it. Such time lags . . . mean just that much more time for the company to get in deeper and deeper.'

(d) *Marketing failures increasingly hurt the company as a whole.* With the growing internal importance of the marketing function in American businesses, management by crisis resulting from emergencies spawned by partial marketing failure leads to further mistakes in non-marketing areas. 'More and more company operations revolve around marketing. When to expand capacity, whether to engineer a new product or improve an old one, and whether or not new financing is needed are all typical non-marketing decisions that are coming to depend more and more on the marketing director. His estimates of markets, of future sales, and of customer desires *set the pace* for the entire corporation. An error by him has a much farther-reaching effect than does a misjudgement by other members of the management team.'[3]

6

Alternatives Obscured by Failure

What has worked once is worth trying again; what has once failed will fail once more – these are two of the most insidious and dangerous precepts in the conventional wisdom of marketing. The conservative alumnus from the 'school of hard knocks' typically responds to a new marketing proposal with, 'We tried it once and it didn't work. Why try it again?'

It is an understandable aspect of human nature that once burned we tend to shy away from flame when we see it again. But understanding this common reluctance can lead us to overcome a natural weakness. The tyranny of experience results in 'trained incapacity' and a kind of 'selective credibility' in decision-making. The fact that we are inclined to propagate 'proven' practices and to stifle those 'disproved' in the past often leads us to the premature rejection of legitimate alternatives. Yet, it is just as reasonable to presume that what failed in one situation may succeed in another as it is unreasonable to presume that what worked in one situation will work in another. What has failed in one market or at one time might very well pay off handsomely in other markets or at a more propitious strategic moment.

Marketers who sweep their failures under the rug and refuse to examine the dust and debris with care are doing themselves a tremendous disservice. They are failing to heed Santayana's famous dictum that those who do not understand history are condemned to repeat it.

Oscar Wilde once noted that experience is simply the name we give our mistakes. We obviously do learn by experience, but we often learn the wrong things. The famed school of hard knocks educates us only if our failures are closely examined for the real lessons they contain.

Healthy Tolerance of Failure

Two recognized enemies of success in marketing are over-pessimism and over-optimism. Fear of failure is the father of pessimism. It leads to a preoccupation with safe courses of action – an overly cautious stance towards risk-taking. It leads to

B

inflexibility – a preference to 'stick with our plan' at any price, even under changing conditions calling for new lines of attack. Fear of failure is probably the greatest single obstacle to delegation and decentralization in a business organization. Fear of failure inhibits creativity in the individual. The discouraging effect of consistent failure manifests itself in morale and motivational problems within the company and in strained relations outside. Fear of failure freezes the status quo – it inhibits action, sometimes to the point of do-nothing attitudes persisting over long time periods.

Over-optimism stems from a failure to fear failure. It expresses itself in empty and unrealistic bravado, a view of the marketing world through rose-coloured glasses. Fortunately or otherwise, learning theory tells us that pleasant experiences have a way of superseding the unpleasant ones in the human memory – further reinforcing our optimism in risk situations. A certain amount of optimism is an essential element in commercial success; it is perhaps an especially important characteristic to have in sales people. Certainly, actions with greater risks are often the ones with the greater pay-off. But optimism can be carried too far. The marketer needs to take calculated risks rather than blind risks.

How can we develop a healthy tolerance of failure? In part, but only in part, the answer lies in developing proper attitudes towards past mistakes. We do need to take courageous stands and to stick to sound commitments when generating and executing marketing strategy. But this alone is clearly not enough.

When still a struggling writer with a small stack of rejected manuscripts, Arthur Gordon got some advice from the then president of IBM, Thomas J. Watson, Sr:

> Double your rate of failure. . . . You're making a common mistake. . . . You're thinking of failure as the enemy of success. But it isn't at all. . . . Every one of those manuscripts was rejected for a reason. Have you pulled them to pieces looking for a reason? That's what I have to do when an idea backfires or a sales program fails. You've got to put failure to work for you. . . . You can be discouraged by failure – or you can learn from it. So go ahead and make mistakes. Make all you can. Because, remember, that's where you'll find success. On the far side of failure.[4]

Failure needn't be feared as much as it seems to be feared – provided the potential cost of any single error is not prohibitively high and provided that lesser errors are not repeated again and again. The realistic middle road between over-pessimism and over-optimism lies in the overcoming of ignorance – the common cause of both maladies. We must learn to understand the nature, causes, and cures of marketing failure. Formal dissections of marketing mistakes, if skilfully conducted in an orderly and systematic fashion, both comprehensively and in depth, can help to provide that knowledge.

Role of Failure in the Refinement of Strategy

Many guidelines for the generation of future marketing strategies and tactics are rooted in past failures. Someone once noted that British naval strategists ultimately became among the world's finest for the very reason that the British Navy suffered so many defeats – they became successful because of, not in spite of, the fact that they had been whipped so often. After every loss, the defeats were scrutinized to see what could be gleaned from them to help the Navy fight better some other day. The British learned two things: negative principles about what to avoid in future campaigns and positive maxims about what to stress in future naval operations. Their strategy was never permitted to be regarded as permanently fixed. New principles, concepts, methods, and procedures were successfully introduced as a progressively refined and changefully dynamic body of strategic doctrine evolved over time.

Altogether too many marketers seem to use a 'success formula' approach to marketing. Their pat formulas sometimes fail because they are statically over-generalized and over-simplified. They are often based on faulty premises, e.g. spurious reasons for past successes, or – worse yet – based on no recognizable premise at all other than 'intuition', hunch, or fear of experiment. Such inflexibility often gets marketers into serious rigid trouble. Marketers must view their operating methods not as jelled formulas but as bodies of doctrine and patterns of behaviour requiring progressive refinement.

9

Failure and Marketing Dynamics

The road to marketing failure is paved with good intentions. Things have a way of not working out as planned. Although the factors contributing to success or failure are precisely the variables that any prudent manager would ponder before taking action, the fact remains that unexpected developments can occur in a way to upset all preparations. Perception of change is one key to success; the inability to perceive and adjust to change may result in failure. In the wake of marketing headaches, executives sometimes sound like the knocked-out prizefighter who said, 'If I had known when the punch was coming and seen it thrown, I could have ducked.'

The details of marketing strategy rarely work themselves out spontaneously. Follow-through demands close monitoring to catch turning points in a stream of events. The time dimension in marketing is often critical. When discussing the failure of 'Analose', the antacid and analgesic product introduced some years ago by Bristol-Myers, a company executive noted, 'One of the toughest things that management has to do is to know when to quit, take its licking, and put the effort in other directions.' A critical decision is to determine precisely when to administer the *coup de grâce* to a faltering product or programme; too often the die-hard old college try is ordered at the moment that a more merciful euthanasia is most needed.

Failures and Decision-making

Arthur Nielsen, Jr, President of A. C. Nielsen Company, once recorded what he termed 'the 13 most common marketing errors'.[5] They are:

1. *Failure to keep product up-to-date* – first you must have a good product – suited to the market.
2. *Failure to estimate the market potential accurately* – to temper enthusiasm with regard to prospects of future sales.
3. *Failure to gauge the trend of the market* – to guide adjustments in the marketing programme – either up or down.
4. *Failure to appreciate regional differences in market potential and in*

trend of market – to make sound distribution of sales and advertising efforts.

5. *Failure to appreciate seasonal difference in your buyers' demand* – not only nationally but for various types of market breakdowns.

6. *Failure to establish the advertising budget by the job to be done* – any company which continues to set its advertising budget based upon sales alone is asking for trouble.

7. *Failure to adhere to policies established in connection with long-range goals* – to allow time for a significant trend to develop.

8. *Failure to test-market new ideas* – there is a big difference in what people say they will do – and what they actually will do.

9. *Failure to differentiate between short-term tactics and long-range strategy* – special promotions are no substitute for advertising.

10. *Failure to admit defeat* – to learn from our errors, and to change.

11. *Failure to try new ideas while a brand is climbing* – all too often, changes are made only after a competitor forces the change.

12. *Failure to integrate all phases of the marketing operation into the overall programme.* Co-ordination is the key word.

13. *Failure to appraise objectively your competitors' brands* – the tendency to (*a*) underestimate the resources and ingenuity of your competitors; while at the same time (*b*) overestimating the position or reputation of your own brand.

The interesting thing to note about this list is that, stripped of its specific content, most of these errors can be classified under one broad heading – *failure to get the facts and interpret them correctly*. If management fails to recognize problems and opportunities in timely fashion and fails to define its problems adequately in the first place, there is little hope of resolving issues soundly, of incorporating these solutions into appropriate programmes, of executing plans in a satisfactory manner.

A knowledge of marketing failures can contribute to the vital *diagnostic stage* of problem-solving and thus lead to a reduction in the number of poor decisions.

Failures Easy to Study

Hindsight is, as they say, 20–20 and it is easier than foresight. The past is known, or can at least be understandable. The historical case, the *fait accompli*, can provide a comprehensive picture of an event or process. Current appraisals of continuing programmes (sometimes prematurely adjudged successful only to fail at a later date) can provide only a partial view of the whole. Historical perspective permits a cool and objective detachment, whereas any analysis of current activity is often coloured by personal involvement and distorted in the heat of battle. Monday-morning quarterbacks, who delight in pointing out foibles, especially in others, are rarely in short supply. Therefore, it is easy to gain co-operation in data-gathering and interpretive phases of a post-mortem. Students appear to like the autopsy approach to the study of marketing management, partly because they can get more complete information and, therefore, more satisfying explanations for failures than for successes.

The theme thus far – for a sounder market future, look at past marketing mistakes. We have discussed seven reasons for analysing marketing failures. The next chapters develop this theme in greater detail. They will take us from the abstract to the concrete – from general principles to specific cases.

So, to conclude as we began, let's now take a closer look at some familiar American companies, presenting products and programmes that misfired in the market place.

CHAPTER II

The Case of the Impermanent 'Permanents'

In 1960 three giants in the chemical industry locked horns in a fight over a chance at three hundred million dollars in annual sales revenue. This is the story of that battle, which someone has already labelled 'the big hullabaloo in the anti-freeze market'. The origin and nature of the struggle were deeply rooted in automotive and chemical history.

A SHORT, CHILLY HISTORY OF ANTI-FREEZE

When the gas burner replaced the oat burner at the front end of buggies around the turn of the century, people quickly discovered that horses had at least one advantage over mechanical beasts. A horse's blood never boiled over in the summertime and seldom froze in winter. The circulatory system of the horseless carriage suffered in both respects. Fluids were quickly evolved to serve several essential functions for the automobile.

Since the high temperatures generated by the new petrol engines decreased operating efficiency and burned-out engines, means had to be found for dissipating excess heat. After early experimentation with air-cooled engines, American automotive engineers settled on water as the principal coolant. By making this key design decision, they thereby created a whole set of problems for themselves and others to solve. Radiators, for instance, had to be designed, hoses had to be installed, and special gaskets had to be created to seal engines and control coolant seepage and leaking. But the problems went far beyond design.

Regardless of engine design features, water has the distressing characteristic of freezing in cold climates. Since water expands when it freezes, cracked engine blocks and burst radiator cores were often costly results. To prevent such engine damage, motorists – without much guidance or help from car producers or anyone else in the early days – began to add various substances to lower the freezing point of water. Because there were no specially manufactured additives commercially available for this purpose, ordinary household items were used – such substances as sugar, molasses, table salt, glycerine, and rubbing alcohol.

But these crude additives produced undesirable side effects. Some reduced the heat-transfer potentialities of pure soft water. This, coupled with the fact that many motorists used tap water with natural minerals that created rust and scale deposits in the cooling system, caused engine overheating. Some additives, like salt, were corrosive. Others were fugitive – they would seep away and leak out of the cooling system and leave the engine unprotected. Some items were highly volatile and evaporated or boiled away. Some produced a magnificent, frothy foam, like the head on a good beer. Still others created toxic fumes. Most of the additives contaminated cooling systems in one way or another. Some homemade concoctions were incompatible and couldn't be mixed.

The early-day motorist never felt quite sure that he had adequate cooling or anti-freeze protection. Furthermore, conventional additives were terrible nuisances. Cooling systems needed frequent and inconvenient check-ups, solutions had to be strengthened from time to time during the winter, periodic draining and flushing of radiators and engine blocks were called for, and gooey messes had to be disposed of each spring. Perhaps the least undesirable mixture widely available to the motorist was a mixture of honey and water.

By the 1920s, alcohol in one form or another had become the most satisfactory solution. It was widely sold in bulk, pumped out of barrels into milk bottles or any other convenient container at drugstores, and hardware stores, and finally in garages and filling stations. With good cooling ability and relatively low cost, alcohol soon replaced most of the potpourri of common household additives – despite the now familiar drawbacks of boil-away, odour, toxicity, and flammability. However, because of these features, and because unscrupulous vendors of bulk alcohol occasionally diluted it in the barrel, car owners were still perpetually uncertain as to their specific degree of protection against freezing.

Prestone Makes Its Debut

A big breakthrough came in 1927. That year, the National Carbon Company* obtained a basic principle patent on the use of ethylene glycol as an automotive anti-freeze and introduced a new product called 'Eveready Prestone Antifreeze'. Here, for the first time, was a product pre-packed in cans, with printed charts showing the protection afforded by specific quantities of the product in proportion to water. In addition, it wouldn't boil away or burn and was relatively odourless.

In its first year, Prestone received criticism. Complaints developed about rust-clogging and leakage. So, in 1930, an improved Prestone with chemical rust inhibitors was introduced. Product performance was now sufficiently good that, by 1933, after but two years of field experience, Prestone was advertised as a non-volatile, all-winter anti-freeze and backed up with a guarantee.

But Prestone was still handicapped by price. The original price was five dollars per gallon compared to a price range of from fifty cents to a dollar for alcohol. To overcome this obstacle, Prestone was first sold on consignment. In this way, distributors could be induced to maintain adequate stocks without tying up their money. Still, price remained a barrier in the eyes of the retailer and the consumer. Many retailers attempted to overcome consumer price resistance by pushing Prestone as 'permanent' anti-freeze

* The old National Carbon Company was one of the companies that now make up the Union Carbide Corporation.

that could be used winter after winter without danger of freezing or corrosion of automobile cooling systems.*

The company had already developed flashlight and battery distribution through wholesale drug and hardware channels. These same channels were first used for Prestone. Automotive supply distributors, heretofore unknown to the company, were soon discovered and included during the 1930s and, by 1940, had become the dominant wholesale distribution channel for Prestone.

During the building period, millions of dollars were spent on consumer advertising, and dealers realized good profits on Prestone. An approved retail dealer list was maintained – based on the dealer's ability to service cooling systems. Dealer sales aids and premiums were provided, and the Prestone product story and marketing plans were carried to dealers via large-scale meetings throughout the nation.

As the new brand began to make headway, alcohol producers responded by branding their products, putting them in cans, and advertising them more heavily. While recognizing Prestone's technical superiority, the alcohol promoters tried to capitalize on its vulnerability with respect to price and on rumours circulating about that still hinted at technical defects in Prestone. A number of packaged alcohol products appeared on the market. Some brands of methanol, such as 'Super Pyro' and Du Pont's 'Zerone', also quickly became popular, and some are still on the market today. Nevertheless, Prestone had captured and held at least a sixth of the total anti-freeze market by the late 1930s. To do so, Prestone had to lower its price gradually to a level of $2.65 per gallon by 1939.

---

* Union Carbide says it never promoted Prestone as a 'permanent' anti-freeze. This term apparently developed by spontaneous generation in trade channels. Motorists, however, quickly adopted the term. Prestone promotion referred to 'all-winter' or 'high boiling point' anti-freeze. The phrase 'permanent type' was first used on the can in 1965 after new-car owner manuals began using this terminology in service and maintenance recommendations.

Prestone Is Pressed

Until just before World War II, Prestone stood alone in the ethylene glycol segment of the anti-freeze market. But, by 1940, several oil companies had come out with ethylene anti-freezes and Du Pont introduced an ethylene glycol product under the 'Zerex' name to compete with Prestone.

Du Pont's aim was to give its jobbers, who were carrying the methanol-base Zerone, a full line of anti-freeze products. Zerone was then selling for $1.00 a gallon. To distinguish Zerex as a premium item, and to place it in direct competition with Prestone, Du Pont priced Zerex at $2.65 per gallon.

By 1941 the World War II effort absorbed most glycol production, and comparatively small quantities were available to the public. Prestone was allocated to wholesalers on the basis of previous sales volume, and many wholesalers carried that policy on to the retail level. Some wholesalers, however, did tie-in Prestone with the sale of other products, such as automotive equipment. In addition, numerous commercial operations used considerable quantities of Prestone through government-issued Certificates of Necessity. The net result was that many service station operators and garages were unable to get Prestone in what they considered to be reasonable quantities, and good will was lost by both Union Carbide and its wholesalers.

From the consumer standpoint, conservation of all goods became a patriotic duty. The government, consumer testing and research organizations, and others promoted the saving of all anti-freezes for future winters and published information to help the motorist test and restore the corrosion-resisting properties of his anti-freeze and render it comparatively safe for re-use.

Post-war Gains for Ethylene Glycol

The end of World War II brought with it a tremendous change in the anti-freeze market. Consumer organizations now told consumers they had no need for expensive ethylene glycol anti-freezes such as Prestone and Zerex. They repeatedly publicized the point that alcohol-based anti-freezes gave sufficient engine

17

protection. Still, by 1948 the 'permanent' anti-freezes had captured 25 per cent of the market. In 1950, with ethylene still in short supply, even Du Pont released the results of a seventeen-year-long study stating that 'standard priced anti-freezes (methanols) give more than adequate protection. . . . Higher-priced products (ethylene glycols) are needed only under extreme conditions of cold or at high altitudes.' But, with the help of advertising and with heavy support from service dealers, anti-glycol efforts were killed off. In 1950 sales of glycol anti-freeze added up to about 46 per cent of the total market. The public continued to choose ethylene glycol over other anti-freezes at an astonishing pace. Glycol anti-freezes accounted for 70 per cent of the market in 1955, 80 per cent in 1957, and 90 per cent in 1959.

Considerable increases were also being forecast for some new uses for ethylene glycol in synthetic fibres and other industrial chemical products.

With seemingly favourable demand conditions and supply shortages, a number of companies built glycol plants. By 1951 or 1952 supply and demand were just about in balance.

Excess Capacity

By 1960 there were ten basic producers of ethylene glycol, and supply had raced far ahead of demand. In that year, with an annual output of over 1·8 billion pounds, the industry was able to dispose of only a little more than two-thirds of its total supply. (See Table 1.) As usual, the wave of excess capacity had brought corresponding pressures in its wake.

During the 1950s private-label anti-freezes rapidly proliferated to the point where more than three hundred brands were scrapping for slices of the market – each with its own name, claims, and nomenclature complicating the problem of consumer choice. Chemical companies, even those with their own branded consumer products, were eager to supply oil companies, car manufacturers, and other large marketers in order to mop up excess capacity. Collectively, these private brands soon became Prestone's largest competitor in the important service station segment of the business.

TABLE 1
U.S. ETHYLENE GLYCOL CAPACITY – 1960

Producer	Millions of pounds (estimated)
Union Carbide	755
Dow Chemical	350
Jefferson Chemical	180
Du Pont	150
Houston Chemical	100
Olin Mathieson	100
Wyandotte Chemical	90
Calcasien Chemical	75
General Aniline & Film	35
Allied Chemical	35
Total	1870

END-USE OF ETHYLENE GLYCOL – 1960

	Millions of pounds
Anti-freeze	1000
* Other uses	265
Total	1265

PER CENT OF CAPACITY USED – 1960

$$\frac{1265}{1870} = 68\%$$

UNUSED CAPACITY

$$32\%$$

Source: *Chemical Week*, October 8, 1960, pp. 117–18.

Assured of an adequate supply, oil companies in particular developed aggressive marketing techniques – guarantee plans, price concessions, and increased dealer movement quotas – which squeezed the national brands hard in their then most important class of retail outlets. Typical of the more energetic oil company

* Since 1960, the 'other uses' have grown considerably. But at this time, 1 billion pounds ended up in anti-freeze. Only 0·265 billion pounds went into other uses.

efforts was an ad for one private-label anti-freeze aimed at motorists and stating that its dealers would perform the following services:

1. Check for leaks with special instruments and determine if the cooling system needs cleaning.
2. Drain and flush out the entire cooling system – both radiator and engine block.
3. Inspect the radiator, hoses, clamps, and pressure cap, and check the thermostat, heater control valve, and heater output.
4. Check the fan belt for proper tension and condition.
5. Install sufficient anti-freeze to give engine protection within the temperature range specified by the motorist after being advised by the dealer.
6. Run a final recheck of the engine and cooling system.
7. Issue a guarantee for full radiator protection (no evaporation, cold weather engine protection, no rust or corrosion of metals – including aluminium) providing for free replacement if any loss of anti-freeze occurs before the following April 30.

While it is entirely possible that this oil company's stations indeed performed well on such thoroughgoing customer service, many ethylene glycol anti-freeze producers and marketers were becoming increasingly disturbed that most stations weren't doing the job as well as they should.

A 'do-it-yourself' trend began to develop in the anti-freeze market. Placing much of the blame on the full-service retailer, producers soon began to claim that these dealers were really falling down on the job by passively waiting for procrastinating motorists to appear at the first sign of frost in autumn. By such time, a seasonal sales rush would be in full swing. As a result, service dealers couldn't possibly have the time to provide complete cooling system service. Many a motorist stood by to watch a busy serviceman merely drain his car's radiator, pour in some anti-freeze, and add water – like a housewife making the morning coffee in a rush. Some car owners quickly decided they could do at least as well at less cost by buying their anti-freeze at discount houses and pouring it in themselves. Heavy downward pressures on consumer prices developed and spread.

Automotive wholesalers, closer to the consumer than the manufacturers, sensed the change. They began to let products like Prestone and Zerex – with their relatively high profit margins – seep into discount channels. For some time, Union Carbide and Du Pont resisted this, for they were sometimes severely criticized by service dealers for allowing sales to the 'price-cutters'. Dealers began to react strongly, and the result was further resistance to handling the two most heavily advertised national brands. Manufacturers' price structures were, for a long time, reasonably well maintained. Union Carbide, in particular, now provided both a suggested OTC (over the counter) and a suggested installed price* for its wholesalers and tried to back up these prices under the then existing legal machinery for resale price maintenance. But this very machinery was in a state of near collapse and antifreeze soon became 'the plaything of the scrambled merchandiser'.

In 1950 about 95 per cent of all anti-freeze sales had been made through service outlets. This figure was to shrink to almost half by 1960. Discount stores, supermarkets, and other high-volume, self-service outlets were selling more and more anti-freeze – some of it as 'loss leader' merchandise. All popular anti-freezes, including Prestone and Zerex, were soon widely available – with or without the blessing of their producers – in these types of outlets. Some good private-label ethylene glycol products were selling for $1.39 or less per gallon over the counter by 1960.

Price pressures, private labels, and excess capacity were major factors in the market during the fifties. But there still were more subtle pressures during that decade already adding fuel to a vigorous fire of fear and anxiety affecting many in the industry.

While future non-automotive uses for ethylene glycol held glittering promises over the long term, many producers were pessimistic about short-range prospects in the anti-freeze market. There were valid reasons for at least a little doubt, if not for downright bleak outlooks.

---

* With such pressure, Union Carbide finally was obliged to sell directly to large over-the-counter retailers by 1963 – although the company resisted this move for some time.

21

By the late fifties, foreign cars and domestic 'compact' cars were beginning to cut into the American automobile market – some of them, like the Volkswagen, air-cooled. Industry observers also began to question the efficiency of automotive power plants and Chrysler was then (prematurely) said to be ready to introduce gas-turbine engines in its cars by 1965. While some major producers of ethylene glycol were attaching low probabilities to the eventuality, a few industry observers were then predicting that air-cooled engines (requiring no anti-freeze) would account for a quarter of all new car sales by 1965. Market growth figures for anti-freeze were expressed earlier in terms of market shares between ethylene and other types of anti-freeze – actually, while the total number of cars in use rose from 62 million in 1954 to 67 million in 1957, the yearly consumption of anti-freeze slipped from 110 million to 107 million gallons during the same period. And from 1958 to 1962, the average coolant capacity of water-cooled automobiles decreased 18 per cent – from 18·3 quarts to about 15 – because of the then growing popularity of cars with smaller or non-existent liquid cooling system capacities. Yet, many ethylene glycol manufacturers waited and hoped for a change in an automotive design and fashion cycle which was at low ebb for them – as more cars individually and collectively used up less and less anti-freeze.

Consumers cast another shadow on the doubts of anti-freeze manufacturers. Despite their acceptance of ethylene glycol over alcohol and methanol-based anti-freezes, motorists weren't throwing away their 'used' anti-freeze each spring as the producers wanted them to. According to surveys on consumers' anti-freeze usage released by Union Carbide and Du Pont, many people were re-using their anti-freeze season after season. Du Pont statistics indicated that 62 per cent of U.S. car owners installed fresh anti-freeze each autumn, 27 per cent simply added each autumn to the previous year's mixture, and 11 per cent re-used it without change.

A depression-born price-consciousness, wartime patriotism to make things last longer, the service dealers' earlier profit-motivated usage of the term 'permanently', a 'do-it-yourself' movement, and other factors combined to make anti-freeze re-use an accepted practice by a significant portion of the motoring public.

An 'Educational Campaign'

Consumers had long been warned against the practice of re-using so-called 'permanent' anti-freezes by the National Bureau of Standards, the American Society of Testing Materials, and others. This habit could be penny-wise and pound-foolish, since the corrosion-inhibitors in ethylene glycol anti-freezes had never been completely foolproof. Especially in older cars with worn engines, acidic gases could leak into cooling systems, form corrosive fluids or deposits blocking heat-transfer, and cause severe damage. And these corrosion-inhibitors could, in some cases, break down and become exhausted during the course of a single winter. Motorists had no really suitable means of detecting whether or not the depletion of corrosion-inhibiting reserves had even occurred. It could happen quickly and without a clue, difficult to detect until engine damage had already been suffered. Breakdown of the corrosion-inhibitor could happen even though the solution still offered basic anti-freeze protection (which could be measured with a hydrometer) and heat-transfer properties. Only technically detailed chemical analysis would suffice to test the adequacy of the inhibitors themselves, and this was impractical in the market place. Furthermore, corrosion-inhibitors sold commercially for use in water alone often could not safely be added to ethylene glycol anti-freezes – even where both products came from the same manufacturer – because the chemicals might not be compatible. Therefore, the consumer was told, the safest course of action was to drain the cooling system each spring and put in fresh anti-freeze every autumn.

Although anti-freeze manufacturers had never deliberately recommended the use of their products for more than a season, they realized that the unintended use of the word 'permanent' was hurting them. They tried to undo the damage. To support the stern injunctions against re-use already issued by other groups, the producers themselves undertook a broad educational campaign designed to persuade motorists that the word 'permanent'

C

wasn't to be taken literally. The 'permanent' label, they said, had come about originally merely as a means of distinguishing glycol-base anti-freezes from those with an alcohol or methanol base, which often boiled away or evaporated during a winter. Glycol-base products had come to be called 'permanent' only because they were designed to last for one full *winter* – they were still to be drained and discarded in the spring and replaced each autumn. Union Carbide, Du Pont, and Olin Mathieson (by now producers of 'Permanent Pyro') all embarked upon point-of-purchase pro-motional efforts to prevent the re-use of their respective brands. Oil companies and other private-labellers of anti-freeze also launched activities to break the re-use habit.

These campaigns ran throughout 1958 and 1959 with little or no positive impact. Four out of every ten car owners continued to re-use their anti-freeze from year to year. The campaign proved to be a dud or worse. It did attract some public ridicule and prob-ably confused the consumer. Trade papers lampooned the campaign. 'Do they mean permanent or don't they?' asked one trade magazine. 'While maintaining anti-freeze is not permanent, they have labels that state otherwise.' Within this framework of uncertainties, one consumer-product-rating organization said it knew of a (probably very well-maintained) thousand-car fleet that regularly used one anti-freeze for two winters before draining, with no ill effects. This source also cited a government study indicating no increased engine breakdown in a fleet operated for three years without a change of ethylene glycol anti-freeze. If the motorist suffered from derring-do re-use practices, he either didn't realize it or he didn't care very much.

As it became clear that the industry's educational campaign would fail to halt re-use and thereby keep 40 per cent of the anti-freeze replacement market from drying up, overall anti-freeze market projections pointed to a static or even declining total demand which, in the short run at least, could not be fully com-pensated for by predictable new uses for ethylene glycol.

Here, then, was an industry plagued in 1960 by over-capacity and faced with promising long-term but discouraging short-range demand projections and market conditions.

A BATTLE BREWS

While all producers and marketers of ethylene glycol anti-freeze faced a market-share battle as they entered the sixties, a singular struggle soon developed in which Union Carbide Corporation, Dow Chemical Company, and E. I. du Pont de Nemours & Company were the principal contestants.

Three Titans Square Off

They were three of the top four chemical companies in the United States. Using such conventional measures as annual sales, net income, and total assets, Du Pont was the largest and Dow the smallest of the three. (See Table 2.) Each produced a tremendous array of products, but anti-freeze was not of equal strategic importance to the individual product portfolios of these giants. While the three collectively held more than two-thirds of all U.S. ethylene glycol capacity in 1960, Union Carbide controlled more than twice as much as Dow, while Dow had over twice as much as Du Pont.*

Prestone Is Again Challenged

At earlier points in anti-freeze history, Prestone had first successfully challenged and then resisted counter-attacking alcohol and methanol-base anti-freezes. Union Carbide's Prestone had next been challenged by competitive glycol-base labels and had maintained itself as the leading brand. Prestone's market position continued to offer an inviting target for other companies. Competitors had long hoped for a breakthrough – a significant product improvement that would give motorists a true 'permanent' anti-freeze and would allow them to wrest a few market percentage points away from Prestone and the multitude of other brands on the market.

These hopes appeared as reality in 1960. In January of that year,

---

* As indicated earlier in Table 1, Union Carbide had over 40 per cent of total ethylene glycol production capacity in the United States in 1960. Comparative percentages for Dow and Du Pont were approximately 19 per cent and 8 per cent, respectively.

Dow announced plans to introduce a new long-life coolant under its own brand name – 'Dowgard'. This was for them a revolutionary step. No newcomer to anti-freeze *production*, Dow had been a major supplier of private-label glycols to Shell Oil and others for

TABLE 2
RELATIVE SIZE OF THREE RIVALS: 1959–61

	1961	1960	1959
Union Carbide	$	$	$
Sales	1,563,357,573	1,548,168,000	1,531,343,824
Net income	142,298,406	157,980,000	171,637,065
Total assets	1,734,316,485	1,712,938,000	1,632,250,370
Dow			
Sales	817,514,653	781,433,740	705,442,403
Net income	64,439,878	82,404,342	62,916,016
Total assets	1,039,701,141	901,244,193	859,081,341
Du Pont			
Sales	2,190,960,318	2,142,575,536	2,114,322,970
Net income	418,162,515	381,403,345	418,695,610
Total assets	3,129,884,673	2,948,760,036	2,799,429,634

Source: *Moody's Industrial Manual*, 1962, pp. 1008, 1267, 2604.
Note: Allied Chemical ranked #3 in the chemical industry between #2 Union Carbide and #4 Dow.

years. But now, Dow was taking its first direct step into automotive products marketing at the consumer level, after having already successfully embarked on building a consumer franchise in other markets. (Dow's 'Saran Wrap', for instance, was a national household products brand by 1955 or earlier.)

In April, 'climaxing fifteen years of research and five years of road tests', Du Pont followed suit by announcing its new 'permanent' product, 'Telar'.

That June, Union Carbide decided to make available a new

extended-life product called 'Prestone Long-Life Coolant'. A flood of other 'permanent' brands soon followed these leaders into the market place.

COMPARATIVE STRATEGIES – 1960

What was the nature of the reasoning that underlay these product-improvement manoeuvres? Although there were important strategic and tactical differences among the various battle plans for the new products, as we shall soon see, a few key assumptions seem common to them all.*

It had long been a fact that ethylene glycol was increasing in popularity over methanol-base anti-freezes. It was also a fact that, despite contrary warnings to the consumer, there had been a strong trend towards re-using anti-freeze products designed for single-season protection. From such evidence, it was inferred – explicitly and publicly by Du Pont and more implicitly by others – that there was a 'strong desire' for 'convenience' on the part of a large segment of U.S. car owners – those who wished to be spared from the irksome spring and autumn chores of draining and filling their cars' cooling systems or from feeling guilty and uneasy about neglecting these unpleasant but recommended tasks. For some time, since 1945 in the case of Du Pont, anti-freeze producers had been thinking about aiming specifically at this group of 'discontented' but 'maintenance-conscious' consumers.

* It should be said here that neither Dow nor Du Pont publicly stated that its overriding objective was to increase market share. However, in view of the excess capacity and market conditions then obtaining, it seems reasonable to infer that this was their aim. Other objectives, most of which were publicized, will be described later.

In a letter to me dated November 9, 1967, Dow spokesmen took 'extremely strong issue' with the implication that the basic motivation behind the development of Dowgard was over-supply of ethylene glycol, and said that strong new outlets (i.e. new uses) were developing for ethylene glycol and were evident to the company in 1960. They went on to say that 'the concept of Dowgard came from the intensive research and development effort' of their laboratory and emphasized the point with this summary – 'In other words, the technical development came first, the market considerations came second, and not vice versa.'

What was the key to product-longevity and the other factors that would give assurance of long-lasting engine protection and other benefits to the motoring public? Although marginal product changes might still be made to improve the heat-transfer and anti-freeze properties of the products, the real key to a truly permanent product lay elsewhere. The biggest obstacle to a long-life product had been the industry's lack of success in bringing cooling-system corrosion to a complete halt. The big hope of the industry had long been to overcome that barrier. Although Dow, Du Pont, and the others all adopted the same precept as their point of departure, they attacked the corrosion problem from different angles.

Product Differences

The idea behind Dow's new product, officially named 'Dowgard Full–Fill Coolant', was to focus on the corrosion problem while still stressing the main purposes of a cooling system fluid – to transfer heat from the inside to the outside of an engine and to provide protection against freezing. Conventional attacks on the corrosion problem had always called for chemical inhibitors that coated the inside of an engine to provide a protective shield against ions (electrically charged atoms and molecules which accelerate corrosion) contained in ordinary water. Therefore, reasoned Dow, instead of coating the inside of the engine they should eliminate altogether the problem that called for a coating in the first place. The decision was made to use a chemically pure, de-ionized water as a basic product ingredient.

Dowgard consisted of a mixture of ethylene glycol (52 per cent), de-ionized water, and a rust-inhibitor. To install it properly in an automobile, a serviceman had to drain completely and flush all parts of the cooling system, including the radiator, engine block, and heater, fill the entire cooling system with Dowgard, and seal it. According to Dow, the system could then be safely left for a twelve-month period. No tap water could be added to the cooling system later without danger of contaminating the mixture. Dowgard was said to offer protection in the temperature range of 40 degrees below zero to 240 degrees above. The product was packaged in gallon cans like conventional anti-freezes. The trademark, 'Dowgard', was to become a 'family' brand name for a whole new line of auto accessories, which were to come out after the new coolant had been successfully introduced.

Du Pont pursued a different product concept. Their idea was that a chemically improved corrosion-inhibitor had always been the key to their problem. When they had developed one, they were ready to introduce their new product – 'Telar Never Drain Anti-Freeze & Anti-Rust Coolant'. Telar's basic ingredients were ethylene glycol and an improved inhibitor said to be powerful enough to take care of normal minerals in water and to provide a lasting coating against corrosion good for at least two years, through summer and winter. As an additional feature designed to promote consumer confidence in the long-term reliability of the product, Du Pont added 'Color Check' to the Telar formula. This was an acidity indicator that would enable a motorist to detect whether or not his cooling system was in a safe condition at any given time. This could be done by dipping a stick or a string into the radiator as a part of routine servicing and then observing whether it came out red or yellow. If normally red Telar should ever become corrosively acidic, it would turn yellow in colour. Du Pont's tests had presumably indicated that less than 1 per cent of the cars using Telar had ever experienced a change of colour, so they also offered a guarantee – 'If Telar ever changes colour, Du Pont will replace it free.' Because a cooling system might malfunction through no fault of the coolant (e.g. through a leaky head gasket), Color Check would also warn the motorist about mechanical defects in his car's cooling system before serious damage could result. Finally, if Telar were ever lost through defects in the system, if dilution of strength occurred due to the adding of water for any reason, or if unusually cold weather developed and called for greater protection against engine freeze-ups, it would be an easy matter simply to add a quart or two of Telar to a radiator to bring the degree of concentration of its content up to the desired level. Telar was to be mixed with ordinary tap water as was the case with older glycol products. Du Pont did suggest that the cooling system should be completely

29

drained and flushed before installing Telar. If this were done carefully, and assuming the solution remained red in colour, Telar was supposed to last indefinitely without draining. Two gallons of the product, which was packaged like other anti-freezes, would protect a twenty-quart cooling system down to twelve degrees below zero.

Union Carbide observed these new-product developments with interest but didn't seem greatly disturbed. Regular Prestone was, they felt, securely established with a huge share of the market and a loyal following. Union Carbide viewed neither Dowgard nor Telar as a real revolution in anti-freezes and concluded that they posed no major threat to Prestone. A 'stand pat' position seemed only slightly risky. However, as a purely defensive response, the company announced the introduction of Prestone Long-Life Coolant – a slightly improved version of regular Prestone. This 'permanent-type' product contained ethylene glycol and an improved rust-inhibitor. It had no colour indicator and, unlike Dowgard and Telar, it was 'guaranteed' for just one season. Union Carbide suggested that, as with regular Prestone, the new product should be drained in the spring and replaced each autumn. But most of the firm's chips were still riding on regular Prestone.

Market Orientations

What was the thinking of the three companies on the subjects of marketing objectives, customer targets, and sales forecasts? From the beginning, it appeared, Union Carbide wished to protect or enhance (instead of inhibit) replacement sales, was confident about the market strength of regular Prestone, and saw little sales potential in the new long-life products. Dow and Du Pont saw things differently. Their idea was that if people couldn't be prevented from re-using ethylene glycol anti-freezes then they should be offered a specially designed item made safe for extended use. According to trade sources at the time, their sales forecasts, based upon market research data on anti-freeze re-use practices, estimated that first-year sales of such a product ought to be between 18 and 40 per cent of the 300-million-dollar anti-freeze market. Second-year figures placed the percentage closer to 50 per cent of total sales.

The companies themselves now say they never envisaged a market of quite that magnitude. In November 1967, a Dow spokesman wrote me that, 'Our research showed that 25 per cent of the total market of car owners could be classified as "caretakers" as opposed to the 75 per cent who might be classified as "users". Dow's programme was based on achieving a good portion of the 25 per cent caretaker market, which we identified as willing to pay more for a higher quality product.' Whatever the precise numerical target, Dow and Du Pont felt they were playing for fairly high stakes.

In addition, Dow and Du Pont saw a strategic opportunity to convert a seasonal anti-freeze market into a year-round anti-freeze-plus-coolant market with Dowgard and Telar. By making seasonal draining unnecessary, the new products might lift ethylene glycols from the category of winter emergency goods into the 'staple' commodity class. This would result in savings for the producers by smoothing out peaks and valleys in production, inventory-carrying, and other activities.

Dow, in particular, seemed to perceive some added sub-market opportunities in geographic terms. Dowgard's intrinsic features might give it a unique advantage in local areas where water supplies were hard or corrosive. Dow also saw growth possibilities in the South and Southwest. Here were prospective buyers with no great need for anti-freeze protection but with a presumed interest in anti-corrosion safeguards and the prevention of summer boil-over.

Du Pont felt that there were three types of buyers in the anti-freeze market, differing in their degree of price sensitivity. Each group needed a different product. The most price-conscious buyer could use Zerone, Du Pont's economy-type methanol. Another group of faithful buyers who were satisfied with Zerex would be loyal to this ethylene glycol anti-freeze with proven sales appeal. Finally, Du Pont felt there was a third segment of quality-minded consumers (principally new-car owners and upper income groups) with a strong interest in the convenience of a 'never-drain' product who wanted the best regardless of price. By this time, most new cars were filled with ethylene anti-freezes at the factory. Telar sales, according to Du Pont, wouldn't cut into Zerone or Zerex volume. Telar was to bring in 'plus business'. With a new full-line strategy behind the Telar–Zerex–Zerone family of products, Du Pont felt they could at last 'satisfy the needs and pocketbooks of all car owners'.

Relative Prices

The Dow product was priced at $2.25 per gallon, installed. Thus, a car with a twenty-quart cooling system required $11.25 worth of Dowgard. Telar sold for $5.00 a gallon, installed. Du Pont felt that consumers would pay such a price because the never-drain feature would make the product less expensive than competitive products over the long run and because heavy advertising would effectively communicate the benefits of Telar to car owners. Unlike Dowgard, which came ready-mixed with water, Telar was a concentrate. Two gallons of Telar, mixed with local water, would protect a twenty-quart cooling system to twelve degrees below zero at a cost of $10.00. A gallon and a half gave zero-degree protection to an eighteen-quart system for $7.50. Telar gave the same anti-freeze protection as Prestone Long-Life Coolant. The retail price per gallon charged for Long-Life Prestone varied from area to area, from time to time, and from one type of outlet to another, but it was generally available at prices competitive with Telar, and their printed recommended price schedules were identical. The two products also called for identical installation procedures to achieve satisfactory results.

Thus, for a motorist desiring only anti-freeze protection to −20 degrees F. or above, Dowgard was more expensive than either Telar or Long-Life Prestone. However, it is doubtful that consumers were fully aware of these facts, because of the difficulty of computing true costs.

Promotional Pressures

To appreciate the scale on which the three giants were competing, one need only become familiar with the size of the advertising appropriations of each contender. Du Pont, Dow, and Union Carbide each launched multi-million-dollar campaigns for their respective products, the actual budgets ranging from three to seven million dollars. For each concern, this was the largest advertising budget ever accorded a single consumer product in the firm's entire history.

It has been estimated that Dow spent six million dollars in advertising to introduce Dowgard, although *Advertising Age* magazine reported the first year's campaign costs at just four million. Initially, Dowgard was promoted to the final consumer through the mass media of television, radio, magazines, and newspapers, with copy stressing the full–fill concept and the use of de-ionized water.

Du Pont's advertising budget for Telar was variously estimated at between four and seven million dollars, with the likely first-year appropriation near the low end of that range. With the help of its agency (Batten, Barton, Durstine & Osborn, Inc.), two-colour double-page and triple-page ads were placed in several trade magazines. Consumer magazines, massive television support, newspapers, and radio were all employed, as were 24-sheet outdoor posters designed to 'tell the Telar story in 1800 communities'. This advertising strategy was carefully keyed to the best local anti-freeze markets and designed both to inform the people about Telar's features and persuade them to buy and use the product.

In August 1960 Union Carbide announced that it would launch a three- to four-million-dollar advertising programme to enable Prestone to meet and overcome the challenge of the new long-life coolants. However, it was *regular* Prestone that received this emphasis. Long-Life Prestone was offered without consumer advertising. Union Carbide used TV, radio, and newspapers to concentrate its sales effort on regular Prestone. Once again, this underscored the fact that the new item was introduced only as a modest defensive measure. The basic burden of the hefty advertising programme was that regular Prestone was 'the world's most tested, most trusted, anti-freeze'. To negate the never-drain advertising approach of rival long-life products, Union Carbide

33

advised 1960–1961 motorists to consult their car-owners' manuals – 'Most Detroit car makers say,' their copy read, 'Drain your cooling system and have fresh anti-freeze installed every fall.'

Channels of Distribution

Du Pont, with an established sales force and distributor network already selling Zerex and Zerone, naturally utilized parts of this same organization to sell Telar. But Telar was to be sold only to 'service retailers' such as petrol stations, car dealers, and car repair shops and not to 'cash-and-carry' outlets such as department stores and discount houses at the retail level. Two reasons were cited for this decision. First, only a service outlet could provide the necessary cooling inspection and repair function required at the time of installing Telar. Second, while service dealers had historically been losing sales to non-service outlets, the trend towards decreasing market shares had begun to slow down or even reverse itself by 1960, due in part to changes in manufacturers' price policies which made service dealers more competitive with the carry-out prices of non-servicing discounters. So, Du Pont felt that non-service retailers had no place in the distribution pattern for Telar.

Sales promotion folders and other materials were made available in large quantities to equip sales and distributive personnel at every step in the distributive process with whatever they needed to push Telar on to the next link of the chain. To persuade retail dealers of the profit possibilities in Telar, Du Pont told dealers that its consumer advertising programme would induce consuming motorists to demand Telar over competing products. They would, in short, be 'pre-sold' when they drove up. Dealers were also given a guarantee. They were assured that if the inhibitor in Telar were ever to fail, 'Du Pont will replace at no cost to the customer the amount of Telar initially installed.' To motivate dealers further, fairly high retail margins were granted, with dealers paying only $3.25 for a gallon of Telar to be sold to the consumer for $5.00. To add to the push created by dealer aids and attractive margins, Du Pont also persuaded service dealers that Telar would produce tie-in sales of such products as fan belts and radiator hoses because of the pre-sale inspection and servicing required by Telar.

Dow followed a similar, but somewhat more limited and restricted programme. Although Dow did have a consumer sales organization for Saran Wrap, they had no access to automotive trade channels and had to enter this field from scratch. Dowgard was distributed only through automotive supply jobbers to service stations, car dealers, and repair garages. Because both the Dow and Dowgard names were relatively unknown to service dealers, and because these retailers were afraid to invest in inventories for an unknown brand of product, Dowgard sold on a consignment basis to ensure product availability. A normal retail margin of 20 per cent was extended to the dealers, with Dow emphasizing that this would result in higher-than-normal dollar profits per installation because of Dowgard's relatively high price. The dealer was also supplied with Dowgard promotional materials and point-of-sale displays illustrating the full–fill concept.

Like Du Pont, Union Carbide distributed its new product through an already existing sales force and distributor organization. Although it was sometimes charged that Union Carbide was less restrictive in its retail coverage policy; did not emphasize the installation requirement as strongly as their rivals; and distributed to discount houses and other non-servicing retail institutions, Union Carbide has staunchly denied this.

According to them, Prestone's business had always been based on the service dealer, and the over-the-counter discount selling that was widespread by 1960 was not promoted by Union Carbide. They claim to have deliberately aimed Prestone Long-Life Coolant at the service sealer and that only very small quantities reached the mass retailer during the first year. The new product did not reach such outlets in volume until the product was finally closed out of the line at lower prices.

These, then, were the basic strategic patterns for the opening marketing battle between the three giants. Each had what, to them, seemed like an internally consistent and mutually reinforcing mixture of market, product, price, promotion, and distribution policies all neatly dovetailed together. Each was confident that it would make a significant impact on the anti-freeze market, each had backed up its beliefs with substantial outlays, and each was waiting for gratifying results in terms of sales and profits.

OUTCOMES AND REDIRECTIONS

The anti-freeze market turned out to be much tougher to crack in a big way than anyone, with the probable exception of Union Carbide, had anticipated. While regular Prestone enjoyed the greatest sales volume in its history up to that time during the season of '60–'61, and although Du Pont reported that it had gained market penetration with Telar and predicted growing sales in the future, it was clear very early in the game that the new long-life products would fall far short of expectations unless remarkably effective corrective steps could be taken in time to turn the tide of failure into success.

Early Returns

Sales of these products, originally expected eventually to capture anything from 18 to 50 per cent or more of a 300-million-dollar market, had been grossly overestimated. Based on early sales results, forecasts were quickly and drastically adjusted downward, and sights were narrowed. By the spring of 1961, Dow and Du Pont were now publicly projecting a total market share of 10 to 15 per cent for their new products, and both were doing some soul-searching that would lead to changed marketing plans for the '61–'62 season.

The Plans Are Changed

Aware that something was wrong, but seemingly confident that each still might have a winning new-product concept, both Dow and Du Pont diagnosed their problems and prescribed new pro-grammes to improve prospects for putting their products across. Instead of quitting, the titans appeared to gird themselves for a strong second push through the winter of '61–'62.

Dow and Du Pont both traced many of their problems to consumer confusion and dealer apathy. In addition to Dowgard,

Telar, and Long-Life Prestone, many other 'permanent-type' products had been introduced in the market place, products with names like 'Allstate Multi-Season Permanent Anti-Rust Coolant', 'Wizard Year-Round Anti-freeze and All-Year Coolant', and 'Phillips 66 Cooling System Fluid'. Some contained colour indicators and some did not. Some carried quite clear money-back or replacement guarantees, while others held forth more vague promises of performance and happiness. There were one-year, two-year, and even longer-lived products. Prices ranged widely between brands and even for single brands, depending upon where they were sold. Consumers were understandably confused and apathetic.

And so were the dealers. It had been incorrectly assumed that service dealers, hard hit by anti-freeze discounting, would eagerly promote profitable new premium-priced products. But the producers were confounded when dealers turned out to be just as ignorant of selling points as were ultimate consumers on the buying end. Unexpected dealer apathy soon became acute, then chronic. Dealers either failed to stock the products at all or failed to support and promote them actively. Not fully 'sold' on the concepts behind the new brands, dealers became quietly disdainful of them and sometimes even overtly hostile.

How did the producers respond? Here's what was tried.

Du Pont cut back sharply on its advertising budget and on the intensity of its overall marketing effort. But, within that limitation, trade advertising aimed at the dealer was increased. Consumer advertising emphasized harder selling in fewer media – chiefly magazines, newspapers, and TV. Du Pont experimented and conducted tests to determine the best of several themes, themes such as 'Use the anti-freeze that outlasts your car', 'Avoid the annual rush', and 'Six reasons why Telar is better than the anti-freeze you used last year'. In the autumn of 1961, Du Pont also lowered the retail price of Telar from $5.00 to $3.95 (installed) at petrol stations and distributed it to auto supply stores, which retailed it for as low as $1.49 per gallon over the counter. There were some other plusses going for Telar (for instance, at least one consumer-oriented product-rating service advised its

37

readers that 'Telar seems the choice for the winter of 1961–1962') – but Du Pont's major promotional emphasis was switched back on to its Zerex and Zerone brands.

Dow also retrenched and redirected its marketing efforts. The overall advertising budget was cut and re-allocated on the basis of complex calculations by computers, which took into consideration such input factors as local temperatures, car registration figures, number of dealers, water quality ratings, and income indexes and allocated the total at so many cents per car. Sales output factors were harder to come by. Confessing that they still didn't know exactly where its true market lay, Dow now used varying media in selected markets to try out which segments were best for its product. All national advertising to consumers via mass media was suspended, and the decision was made to concentrate effort at the dealer level. Longer dealer promotion campaigns, emphasizing trade journals and direct mail, were used. Into this new marketing mix, Dow threw a two-year guarantee wherever a dealer installed Dowgard and there was proper inspection, although there had been no basic reformulation of Dowgard itself. Dow also hoped that motor manufacturers might be induced to install Dowgard at the factory in new cars – and by October 1961 was able to announce that American Motors was putting Dowgard in 1962 Ramblers.

Meanwhile, Union Carbide still exhibited a defensively cautious wait-and-see attitude with Long-Life Prestone. Determined to put both Telar and Dowgard down for the count, and unwilling to retrench prematurely, Union Carbide continued to hit away with its largest ad campaign ever for regular Prestone.

Final Results

It soon became apparent that nobody was going to cover expenses on the new products. According to *Printers' Ink* magazine, the final sales forecast had been set at 4 per cent of the market, and even this proved to be optimistic when later set off against the negligible sales eventually racked up. The final tally on the '61–'62 season showed that Dow and Du Pont had captured 1·5 per cent of the market between their two new products.

Before the next season had got under way, it was publicly announced that the production and marketing of Dowgard and Long-Life Prestone were to be suspended. Union Carbide, having successfully bucked the inroads of both Dow and Du Pont in this particular case, seemingly emerged with its regular Prestone as winner and still champion of the American anti-freeze market.

POST-MORTEM AND AFTERMATH

What accounted for the downfall of Dowgard, Telar, and Long-Life Prestone? How serious were these setbacks to the companies concerned? What lessons can be drawn from this bit of marketing history? To begin with, both Dow and Du Pont saw *technical* product performance as a chief key to opening up the anti-freeze market – but this proved to be 'a concept that failed to click'. Why? There *were* signs of market opportunity for products such as theirs. They *could* offer some definite benefits to a portion of the motoring public in the form of greater safety and more convenience. 'The fact is,' said Dow sadly, 'Dowgard was a technical success and a marketing failure.' Not enough consumers were willing to pay enough to convert an apparent technical success into a commercial winner.

Several indicators of consumer price sensitivity were either unknown to or ignored by Dow and underestimated by Du Pont. The re-use practice, the existence of countless low-priced private-label ethylene glycols, the parallel trends towards discount-store selling and do-it-yourself installation of name-brand products, and Prestone's earlier depression experience with price elasticity should all have foretold the fact that motorists might be at least as concerned with economy as with functional product attributes and benefits.

In short, motorists didn't see eye-to-eye with Du Pont, and especially with Dow, on the question of intrinsic product merit *versus* extrinsic concepts of 'value'. Both companies failed to heed the subtle teachings of anti-freeze market history in their understandable and commendable zeal to put over better products. For motorists of almost all classes, there was sufficient price resistance

D   39 and suspicion about new products to make them cling to older concepts of 'permanence' and 'value' in anti-freezes.

As a result, both Dow and Du Pont now admit that they grossly overestimated the potential of the ultimate consumer market.

At the same time, they underestimated problems in the intermediate market – especially at the dealer level.

The resistance of the friendly neighbourhood service operator further crippled the new products. Although it meant sidestepping half of the anti-freeze market, the manufacturers' programmes had initially relied solely on service dealers to sell and install the end product. Most dealers were really neither ignorant nor confused about the claims made for the new products; their apathy eventually stemmed from doubt and disbelief or from a lack of financial motive for pushing the new items.

To the service dealer, Dow and Dowgard were almost unknown names, to which they were indirectly introduced by local automotive supply jobbers sold on consignment – not presently the best basis for creating confidence and co-operation. Although acquainted with Du Pont through long exposure to its Zerone and Zerex brands, dealers expressed scepticism over Du Pont's promise to 'pre-sell' Telar to motorists, who would then 'insist' on the brand at local service stations.

Dealers who, over the years, had seen cooling systems leak, been told repeatedly that corrosion-inhibitors break down, and experienced the difficulty if not the downright impossibility of completely flushing out a cooling system (a total of three to four quarts of liquid was virtually undrainable under field conditions) were not impressed with guarantees or even high unit profit margins attached to prices that consumers would likely resist. Dowgard was the most sensitive of the three products to the cooling system contamination which many dealers thought was too often unavoidable. Dowgard scored low with the dealers on another count – if a motorist sprung a leak or otherwise needed to replace Dowgard, he might go to a dealer not stocking the product or not even having distilled water, so the driver's entire anti-freeze investment could be lost with serious repercussions for the dealer originally recommending it.

All three companies were partly motivated to introduce their new products in the sincere interest of service dealers, who had suffered the inroads of discount competition in the carry-out trade. But dealers were unimpressed with protected high *unit* profit margins for, what seemed to them, good reasons. Many dealers 'live on the replacement business' that these manufacturers were ostensibly willing to kill off with their new entries. Over a period of time, some dealers felt they could make more money on smaller unit margins and more repeat purchases than with high unit margins and no opportunity for a replacement business. Furthermore, by promoting anti-freeze replacement each autumn and spring, dealers had slowly learned that they might be given two chances a year to garner the tie-in business of automobile repairs and the sale of such high-margin parts as fan belts and radiator hoses that semi-annual car inspection and service could stimulate. A truly *permanent* anti-freeze could thus restrict both the replacement and the tie-in business for service dealers. This made them much more loyal to regular items such as Prestone and Zerex than to the new brands.

Recent correspondence with Dow seems to confirm most of these points. As they succinctly put it, 'In broad terms, our post-mortems showed that the better approach may have been to place more emphasis on "pushing" the product through the distribution chain rather than "pulling" it through with consumer advertising. The advent of Telar certainly muddied the water as far as the consumer was concerned.'

Dow and Du Pont had misinterpreted both consumer and dealer needs, wants, and values, produced optimistic sales forecasts as a result, and developed good technical product concepts and equally poor marketing methods. By attempting to convert a seasonal market into a year-round one, they were taking an additional gamble. If the concept of a really permanent anti-freeze had actually taken hold, they might simply have traded market share for seasonal stability and created even more short-run excess capacity for themselves. Maybe they're lucky they failed. In any event, Dow now concedes that the timing was off. Introduced late in the season, these products pressed both consumers and dealers to accept an all-year or longer lasting 'coolant' concept before they were yet ready to change from the simpler idea of a cold-season 'anti-freeze'.

Dow started the fight by developing and introducing the first long-life product. It had plenty at stake, made the biggest gamble, and probably suffered the greatest net loss of the great contenders. Lacking direct experience in the automotive consumer market, it was more 'production oriented' and less 'consumer-marketing oriented' than either Du Pont or Union Carbide as of 1960. While Dow spokesmen have indicated some resentment over this last statement, correspondence with at least one of the company's executives states unequivocally that 'the technical development came first, the market considerations came second and not vice versa'.

Dow never formally conceded that Dowgard was a total failure. As others have often done in comparable circumstances, they stated simply that Dowgard was 'ahead of its time'. And they may yet be proven correct. Dow also insisted that by-product benefits had been gained from their first real adventure in the automotive end-use market. It was claimed that 'Dowgard' had become a recognizable family-brand name that enlarged Dow's corporate image and paved the way for future consumer-market efforts. It was also claimed that the firm had obtained a good distribution system of top jobbers and dealers for future marketing activity in the automotive field. But sceptics questioned whether such dubious gains had been achieved at acceptable costs. The judgement of the sceptics, it seems, has, by and large, since been vindicated. Even before Dowgard, Dow had tried to bring out a conventional semi-permanent anti-freeze to compete with Prestone and Zerex, but it was never pushed very much. Most of its solace has once again been sought in the private-label ethylene glycol anti-freeze business, the siren call of which is always difficult to resist under industry conditions such as those already outlined, and in non-anti-freeze uses for ethylene glycol.

Du Pont's approach to the anti-freeze market was probably a bit sounder that Dow's. Its 'full-line strategy', based on an alleged opportunity for a new product for people relatively

42

insensitive to price, may have been sound in concept. If proved, it would have tapped a new market for ethylene glycol. It simply overestimated its market and failed to produce a product that consumers and dealers were ready to accept as truly revolutionary. The 'quality at any price' segment proved to be absolutely non-existent or at least resistant. Du Pont's emphasis on quality and convenience for the consumer was somewhat misplaced, since that desire on the part of the consumer in fact turned out to be neither strong nor widespread. Only a tiny sliver of the replacement market was sufficiently insensitive to price to adopt Telar. Du Pont found it difficult to get both understandable and believable ad copy and sales appeals to support its brand although, with budgets at least as big as Dow's, Telar had a smaller task to perform than did Dowgard. A long advertising siege was needed to change deeply ingrained habits of motorists and dealers. The multi-million-dollar commitment called for would have resulted in an indefinite and unacceptably long pay-back period for Du Pont, so they de-emphasized the Telar programme.

This case may illustrate some limitations to the pursuit of 'product improvement' as a basic business strategy. The history of anti-freeze shows steady and marked improvement up to Prestone. Then, there developed pretty much of a hiatus. Perhaps the 'super-permanents' took too big a step forward and represented an error in market timing to boot. In any case, it clearly shows that notable companies with notable products can easily produce notable failures in the rough-and-tumble of a competitive market.

But what of Union Carbide and its Prestone? From the very beginning, they had no really basic solution to the industry-wide problems of excess capacity and market turbulence. Their response to a threat was not just an uninformed attitude of 'standing pat' with the brand. They had marshalled thirty-five years of experience in the market, a period during which the 'Prestone' label had reached almost the insistence stage.* Much like Pavlov's dogs,

---

* By some standards, brand awareness and loyalty for anti-freeze are not terribly high. But in the TBA (tyres, batteries, and accessories) business, anti-freeze brand awareness and loyalty have traditionally been much higher than for such products as tyres and batteries.

consumers and dealers had both been conditioned to believe that Prestone was about as permanent as permanence could be. Early dealer and consumer-based use of the word 'permanent' for standard one-season ethylene glycol anti-freezes had at least temporarily and paradoxically redounded to the benefit of Prestone (and to a lesser extent, Zerex), and had thwarted the newer Dowgard and Telar entities. What sponsors of those newer products perceived as market weaknesses or opportunities, Union Carbide then saw as strengths or barriers to entry. Union Carbide knew that consumer and dealer habits would be very hard to change. To the consumer, 'permanents' were 'permanents'. To the dealer, Prestone's claims were modest and believable and its profitability was great enough to overcome the semantic antics of rival claimants to the anti-freeze kingdom's throne. In such a position, Carbide viewed product change as a slender reed on which to base its basic strategy. It decided that the best tack was to defend ruggedly and slowly enhance its market share in a static market. To protect and, if possible, to increase already faltering replacement demand – not to inhibit it still further – was Carbide's goal and the creed underlying its market response. Carbide saw little lasting potential in a truly long-life product and actually recommended (to the dealers' delight and the consumers' satisfaction) the annual replacement of Prestone Long-Life Coolant. To Carbide, the most firmly entrenched of the three in the anti-freeze market, this was probably the soundest solution – at least in the short run.

Prestone, after having overcome the well-established usage of alcohol and methanol anti-freezes and rather successfully meeting challenges from several ethylene glycol products, withstood the 1960–1962 onslaught of the super-products. But its parent had not solved all of its basic problems. Having won a major skirmish, Carbide was still very vulnerable from the long-term point of view. Union Carbide was in an earnings rut that it didn't begin to break well out of until about 1965. A new ad campaign for Prestone was based on the 'Never Pick Up a Stranger' theme, stressing the corrosion protection of regular Prestone and implying that there would always be but two classes of anti-freeze – Prestone and All Others.

Union Carbide's anti-freeze strategy proved soundest in the short run, but offered no long-term solution to the company's basic problems. Dow doubtless failed in the short run and probably placed itself well out of the mid-range or even long-term national-brand anti-freeze and automotive products picture. Du Pont, having failed with Telar in the short run, may still have the soundest long-term perspective on giving the customer what he should have whether he wants it or not. Better assumptions and facts about consumers and dealers, revitalized product concepts, sharpened sales estimates and market forecasts (especially if future automotive needs from which anti-freeze demand is derived can be more precisely pinned down), may yet bring Du Pont and others a victory over Carbide in an on-going 'permanent' ethylene glycol anti-freeze contest.*

* After stagnating somewhat during 'the era of the compact car', the anti-freeze market began to show new signs of growth in the mid-1960s. Specifically, sales grew from 124 million gallons in 1962 to 138 million in 1966.

It should also be pointed out that anti-freeze products were – and still are – a rather small factor in the total sales of each of the great companies mentioned in this chapter. Anti-freezes are but one ingredient in Carbide's, Dow's, and Du Pont's multiple-products picture.

Finally, it should be noted that the technical concepts behind Dowgard and Telar may yet be validated in the market place. Most motor manufacturers are now filling their new cars with extended-life (one, two, or more years) coolant-anti-freezes as original 'equipment', and this is undoubtedly affecting the after-market for coolant-anti-freezes.

CHAPTER III

Epicurean Delights

Gourmets, gourmands, and *bon vivants* must have licked their chops on July 24, 1957. For, on that date, the occasion of an annual stockholders meeting of the General Foods Corporation, the then president, Charles G. Mortimer, officially announced his company's intent to pioneer a new fancy foods line to be called 'Gourmet Foods'.

This line, planned specifically to cater to connoisseurs, was unfortunately destined for a rather short life. Within two and a half years, by February 1960, the entire line was pulled from the market and written off as a failure.

The experience was particularly noteworthy in the world of marketing not only because the food field was and is America's biggest market but because this was the first time in history that a major processor had ventured so far into the luxury food business. To interested observers, this fateful action provoked a number of questions. What did General Foods have in mind in introducing the line in the first place? Was it improper planning and execution of corporate marketing strategy that produced the failure? Were the products themselves at fault? Some understanding of the environmental setting that spawned the original idea again seems essential.

THE FANCY FOODS FIELD

The exotic world of fancy foods – small but growing, and chock-full of both risks and rewards – had long defied precise charting by commercial explorers. Most attempts to delineate the fine foods markets and means to sell to them still end in frustration.

A Question of Semantics

Two people talking about fancy foods will eventually experience a communication problem. What is fancy to one appears ordinary to the other. The shadowy dividing line between plain and fancy foods is largely set by personal background, taste, judgement, and individual powers of gastronomical discrimination. Nobody has yet contrived a universally acceptable definition of the fancy foods field, although many tags are commonly used – specialties, custom goods, imports, nationality foods, ethnic items, gourmet delicacies, and so on.

Most of us might quickly agree that traditional commodities such as ordinary coffee, cereal, bread, potatoes, beans, sugar, and salt are household staples. To extend the list much further, however, is to invite debate. Anyone even remotely familiar with romantic fiction, of course, would probably list champagne, caviar, and pheasant as celebrated and classic aristocratic delicacies. Snails, frogs' legs, lobster bisque, and quails' eggs are also exotic enough to find themselves on almost any epicurean list. But most fancy foods occupy some middle position on a staple-to-spooky spectrum.

Well-known meat condiments, olives, and canned shrimp – all fairly high-turnover items with nearly mass distribution – could be called 'quality staples'. So, perhaps, might any brand of Danish ham. Artichokes, truffles, maybe even certain kinds of mushrooms – products with a limited but loyal following – might be labelled 'specialties'. More esoteric items such as pickled water chestnuts, kangaroo steak, octopus on a skewer, wild boar, shark fin soup, and pickled cockscombs – little-known and little-understood products – seem clearly to be gourmet foods. Novelties, offerings bordering on the bizarre, and foods purposefully served as conversation starters (chocolate-covered ants, honeyed grasshoppers, baby bees in soy sauce) are justifiably referred to in the industry as 'spooky' foods. Harry Lesser, head of Cresca Company, Inc., one of the oldest and largest importers in the fancy foods business, once characterized gourmet items as those 'that add a feeling of pleasure, of well-being, of something more'.

47

Getting down to cases, a public relations consultant for NASFT (National Association for the Specialty Food Trade) has said that 'an olive is not a gourmet food, but a large olive stuffed with an almond is'.

Whatever the definition, and the question of definition is not unimportant, certain elements seem to distinguish the fancy foods, confections, and beverages from more commonplace staple items. Among the chief criteria are these:

1. *Quality* – Fancy foods are usually of higher quality than staples, because of the way they are produced or prepared.

2. *Origin* – A fancy food is often of foreign origin. Two-thirds of all fancy foods are imported, and the word 'import' on food and beverages has a certain appeal not possessed by the Made-in-America label.

3. *Packaging* – Fancy foods usually have fancy, costly, or at least quaint packages.

4. *Uniqueness* – A unique product feature or two are often needed to distinguish between fancy foods and staples.

5. *Status* – Some connotation of elegance, prestige, exclusiveness, or romance which marks the person serving an item as a discriminating host or hostess is another characteristic of fancy foods.

6. *Availability* – Fancy foods are hard to get. A product sold only through exclusive or highly selective distribution arrangements which are not accessible to just anybody without considerable effort or expense is likely to be called a fancy food.

7. *Price* – *Pigeon de bresse*, whole tender thirteen-ounce pigeons at $4.00 each; four ounces of *pâté de foie gras* (goose liver paste) at $5.75; thirty-eight ounces of French apricots in fine champagne cognac retailing for $4.75 – these are fancy enough price tags to justify calling the commodities to which they are attached 'fancy', too.

8. *Impulse Purchasing* – Fancy foods are more likely to be purchased impulsively by the consumer than are staple items.

Presumably, the more of these and similar criteria met by a given food product, the 'fancier' the item is considered to be.

Small Potatoes – But a Growth Industry

If disagreement over definitions has blurred boundary lines for the fancy foods field, it is understandable that statistical data on this market have also been conflicting and unreliable.

The entire gourmet business was, *Newsweek* said in 1958, 'a mere crumb in the U.S. market basket'. Few in the industry felt at the time that fancy foods would ever account for as much as 1 per cent of the vast seventy-five-billion-dollar* American food market. Even fewer dared hope that fancy foods would ever become a billion-dollar industry.

Figures on the actual size of this market have always been the grossest of estimates. High figures on market size are often as much as fifty times greater than conservative guesses, the balloon predictions based often as not on over-enthusiastic trade press reporters' fanciful estimates. Majority opinion, however, seemed to peg total annual fancy foods sales at somewhere between 50 and 250 million dollars at the time of General Food's adventure. This volume was shared by hundreds of companies. Although this was 'small' business by most standards, there was sufficient aggregate potential to attract General Foods, especially since the fancy foods field was growing at a faster pace than staples.

Progressive Grocer, which introduced a regular fancy foods section beginning with its September 1958 issue, quoted NASFT President Harold Roth as stating that sales of specialty foods had increased 250 per cent in the preceding decade. *Business Week* reported that some processors and importers had achieved sales gains of 12 to 20 per cent during the recession year of 1958. Other indicators suggested that the market was indeed growing at an increasingly fast rate every year. Fourteen thousand buyers attended the annual exhibit of the National Fancy Food and Confection Show in 1957 – contrasted with three years earlier when only seven thousand showed up. Applications for membership in NASFT were swelling. Clubs and organizations devoted to the education and satisfaction of gourmet tastes were rapidly spreading. Food editors for the nation's magazines and newspapers reported increasing requests for exotic recipes from all over the country. *Gourmet* magazine increased its circulation 300 per cent between 1953 and 1959 to almost 150,000 and its *Gourmet Cookbook*, first priced at $10.00 and later at $12.50, had

---

* Throughout this book the word billion is used with the American meaning of a thousand million.

sold an astonishing 200,000 copies by September 1958. Specialty food outlets at the retail level doubled in number between 1950 and 1958, from about three thousand to six thousand. One out of every three food stores reportedly stocked some varieties of fancy food in 1958, the year in which Montgomery Ward included eighty-three gourmet items in its Christmas catalogue for the first time. Telefood, Inc., of Chicago, which sold gift packages of delicacies, increased the number of stores handling its products six-fold over a twenty-one-year period.

What were the underlying reasons for the growth of fancy foods? A number of plausible explanations were suggested. The increasing personal disposable income of American consumers, of course, was frequently cited as an important economic factor. The rising cost of staple domestic food items, which had narrowed the price gap between them and fancy foods, was another likely variable. Greater travel, on the part of both tourists and American servicemen stationed overseas, had presumably whetted new tastes and pushed up the volume of gourmet sales. Higher educational levels, together with free publicity and the popularization brought about by increased leisure-time reading of food columns and cookbooks, allegedly developed more sophisticated tastes. Individuals with jaded palates and tired tongues, resulting from a presumed dullness and sameness in many domestic staples and modern 'instant' foods, reportedly sought relief in something 'different'. A new social imperative stressing home entertaining in the decades after World War II was said to have given the industry a fresh boost. And this, according to some observers, had been further accentuated by newly awakened status-seeking ambitions of socially sensitive hostesses. Wider exposure of the general public to fancy foods in the larger number of stores stocking them had stimulated first-trial purchases on impulse.

While many of these somewhat superficial conclusions were doubtlessly valid, they were of little real value in pinpointing the market. Gourmet foods were not exactly new; they had existed long before Johnny-come-lately consumers stepped into the fine foods picture during the fifties. It was not likely that average Joes had suddenly emerged overnight as true food connoisseurs and joined with society dowagers somehow to form a new mass 'class' market. Easy generalizations left many practical questions about fine foods consumers unanswered. Who were they? Where were they? How many of them actually existed? How could they best be served? Questions like these had never been answered satisfactorily enough to permit the painting of an unambiguous portrait of the customer.

Missing: A Consumer Profile

True, some tried to define the market with greater accuracy. *Time* magazine, in September 1958, said that 60 per cent of gourmet sales came from within three hundred miles of Manhattan, with the remainder credited to other large urban areas. But some people objected to this picture on the ground that cities had merely been worked more diligently and that vast untapped potential existed in the hinterlands. Max Reese, of Reese Finer Foods, Inc., in Chicago, stated that, 'The average gourmet buyer is between forty and fifty years old, has an income of $7500 or over, and usually likes to stay home and entertain. But, occupation may be almost anything.' To support this thesis, according to *Business Week*, 'Marshall Field found that its gourmet foods attracted not only the veteran gourmet but the truck driver.' Sara Lee persistently reported that 40 per cent of its customers fell into the $4000 to $7000 income category and that 31 per cent of its dollar volume came from that group. Sey-Co Company pursued a carriage trade approach,* while Louis Barth of Liberty Import Company operated with the conviction that modern buyers were 'the younger generation, the young couples who give cocktail parties and small dinners'. 'It appears . . .' *Business Week* said, 'that the social and cultural factor is more of a common denominator than income.' Another observer seemed to echo that judgement by noting that the gourmet item, which allowed the housewife

---

* 'A few days ago,' the *Wall Street Journal* reported on July 25, 1960, a Sey-Co salesman, 'displaying expensive exotic food in the home of one of Chicago's wealthiest women, was asked the price of a case of imported Danish shrimp. "Madam," replied the salesman airily, "if prices concern you, may I suggest A&P?" ' To such a sales approach, President Rex D. Kane attributed his company's 50 per cent increase in three years.

to be 'different' with little or no effort, was a convenient substitute for culinary creativity in the home. And ethnic consumption patterns, earlier associated with immigrant groups, were also held to be changing – sales of Italian and Chinese foods, for example, came increasingly from non-Italian and non-Chinese consumers.

Thus, there was a variety of contradictory opinions and perspectives on the market held by those people making, importing, and selling fancy foods items. Age, geography, occupation, income, ethnic background, and other demographic and cultural factors were all apparently relevant pieces to the market puzzle, but nobody was very confident about how to put them all together into a meaningful pattern. As *Business Week* noted, 'the gourmet urge has got a bit ahead of the market researchers and trend talliers; and as a result, the profile of the gourmet food consumer is somewhat elusive'.

The Companies Involved and Their Problems

The structure of the fancy foods industry is difficult to characterize adequately in few words. It is made up of a large number of small concerns. That is about all that can safely be said by way of generalization. The producers, importers, and distributors engaged are unusually heterogeneous. There is no typical operator, for each company is markedly unique from every other.

Most of these competitors are located in large urban centres and serve strictly local or regional markets. While there is a superabundance of brand names known locally, there are few national brands in the trade. Some firms are very old* – their names synonymous with experience, tradition, prestige, and quality – while others are new concerns seeking fresh success formulas. Many mail-order specialty houses have existed in the market for years. Some companies specialize completely in fancy foods; others carry them only as an adjunct to staple lines. Numerous ventures have failed; a few have been eminently successful.

---

* S. S. Pierce & Company, a giant in the industry deriving half its volume from fancy foods, has operated successfully for more than a century and a quarter. Charles & Company, New York's pioneer in the gift-package branch of the field, has been in business since 1885.

Some 'big' companies have as much as 4·5 million dollars in annual sales. Reese, of Chicago, was considered a giant in 1958 with a volume of 6·5 million; Cresca did 5 million dollars that year. But these were clearly exceptions. Other companies ranged in size from 2 million dollars to about 30,000 dollars in annual sales volume.

In view of such an atomized industry structure of tiny individualistic concerns, it is not surprising that a 'normal' marketing pattern was simply not to be found. Each operator approached the market uniquely because his personal perception of it was unique. The result was a kaleidoscopic array of marketing patterns. If these variations in marketing tactics were correlates of a fractionated and heterogeneous industry structure, the variety of practices was even further encouraged by a widespread lack of knowledge about consumer markets and competitive activities.

Most operators, especially the old hands in the food specialty trade, imported by feel and played their markets by ear. Marketing research was virtually unheard of, for the modest earnings of most companies did not permit the luxury, and joint industry research with pooled funds had not been attempted presumably because each firm liked to play its own cards close to the chest. Very little hard data on the market was available,* estimates of market potential were seldom reduced to defensible numbers, and no quantification of broad market trends was attempted. Although the firms were small enough to maintain close personal contact with some markets, these markets were never identified with sufficient descriptive or statistical accuracy to permit wholly rational planning. Most companies were long accustomed to flying blind. Personal opinion ruled. Each company had somehow carved its own shelf space in the fancy foods field, and the lack of real knowledge seemed to reinforce a blind faith in the market and perpetuated the *status quo*, for few firms were very willing to gamble by arbitrarily changing approaches that had fortuitously worked well for them over the years.

* Only in 1958 did the census people begin to publish a separate column of statistics for 'canned food specialties' in their *Census of Manufacturers*. The census figures disclose there were ninety-three producers in this sector of the fancy foods field alone in 1957.

Still, there were debates within the industry. There was a vague awareness that the evolving nature of the consumer market was a harbinger of future changes in marketing strategies. Most anxieties centred around distribution – viewed by many as the principal problem facing the industry.

Advertising was rarely debated, since most firms believed themselves to be too small to devote much money or attention to promotion. Product quality wasn't a central issue, for there had always been wide variety in the industry's offerings and probably always would be. And it was an unusual company that thought high prices would scare away customers. An unwritten industry thumb-rule seemed to be, 'When in doubt, price high.' This had been an essentially sound perspective, it appears. High prices, as one theory has it, contributed to the prestige of fancy foods and attracted rather than repelled customers. High prices also allowed the fat mark-ups that made food specialties attractive to retailers. And high prices left even the more inefficient suppliers with margins needed to cover up high costs (often a result of gross inefficiencies in producing, purchasing, and distributing) and supply at least modest profits. Few quarrelled, then, with the basic philosophy of fancy prices for fancy foods.

But distribution problems were definitely appearing on the horizon. The industry couldn't seem to agree whether it should shoot for something closer to mass distribution or continue to preserve its status as a limited specialty field. Conflicting attitudes towards distribution resulted. Some suppliers, feeling that a move towards supermarkets was inevitable, quickly made the necessary transition. But to follow the path to a broader market via supermarket distribution would almost certainly destroy the price structure. Some high-cost suppliers simply couldn't operate in the black with a cut in mark-ups. Others were wary of supermarkets, fearing that they would dim the glamour appeal of gourmet items. And specialty food retailers and department stores openly griped to suppliers about the possible invasion of mass food retailers; some threatened to toss out fancy foods if the chains were permitted to take them on. In 1958 *Business Week* summed up the situation by saying that, 'supermarket distribution might not only upset the price and profit applecart; it could cost the industry its best customers'. To confuse the matter still further, supermarkets that had taken on the foods, attracted by high margins, quickly became disenchanted with the slow turnover and discontinued fancy foods for that reason. Some suppliers saw the supers as an abominable threat; others welcomed supermarts with open-armed enthusiasm. In between were many puzzled and uncertain fence-riders on the distribution issue.

Although a giant question mark hung over distribution, there were also lesser issues of industry-wide importance. The business was highly seasonal, for instance, with a sharp sales peak at Christmas; the field was experiencing increasingly tough competition, both internally and from new 'outside' rivals; and the eccentricities of overseas sources of supply often complicated the management of inventories.

Pesky problems, unsettled issues, limited and unreliable information, an absence of norms, and the smallness and multiplicity of unpredictable and individualistic rivals all served to fill the field with uncertainties. But there was the gambler's attraction to the uncertain predictions – that sales and profits ahead might be irresistible, too.

THE MOTH AND THE FLAME

To operate within the risk-laden, peculiar field demanded no little courage and a great deal of optimism. General Foods was drawn towards this intriguing business. In 1956 GF* made its decision to enter the gourmet foods market.

Credit for the idea was attributed to Harlan Logan, who later became vice-president for research and development at GF. Logan apparently thought that substantial prestige would rub off on the company's mass-produced staple foods by the addition of a greatly esteemed line. The basic conception was very much to the liking of other top executives in the firm, including Charles G.

* To prevent ambiguity, the initials 'GF' in this chapter refer always to the General Foods Corporation, never to the company's Gourmet Foods line.

Mortimer, GF president, who was to state that Gourmet Foods 'will contribute something to the corporate image that we want to build for General Foods in the public mind'. This central idea was elaborated by others as time passed. General Motors, it was said, had its Cadillac; Ford had Thunderbird; Corning had Steuben glass – all products of exceptionally high quality radiating beneficial 'halo' effects upon the reputations of the companies and products associated with them. General Foods might enrich its position as a leader in the staple foods industry if it, too, carried specialty items accepted as the world's finest. This stress upon prestige was to be strongly reflected in every facet of the marketing strategy later concocted for the Gourmet Foods line.

Background Notes on the General Foods Corporation

General Foods, as a single industrial complex, was by any measure far larger than the sum total of all the hundreds of small outfits supplying the gourmet market. GF was a true giant in every sense of the word, though it had grown from modest, homely beginnings.

General Foods was formed as an amalgam of companies carefully pieced together over a period of three or four decades into a pattern of gargantuan proportions. First founded as the Postum Cereal Company in 1922, GF assumed its present name seven years later. After 1929, General Foods rapidly expanded both horizontally and vertically through a combination of internal development and the acquisition of other companies. Eventually, it was to become the largest food processer in the world, and it is still growing. GF would be listed among the very few billion-dollar firms in all of America – 1958 sales were recorded at $1,008,898,000 and volume far surpassed that figure in succeeding years. With each later period showing profits at an all-time high, GF had always been in an enviable financial position. 1958 earnings added up to 48·4 million dollars, and more recent figures were to put that number to shame. Employing upward of twenty thousand workers, the company built a brand-new office complex at White Plains, New York, between 1952 and 1954. Headed by Mr Mortimer, who had gained the presidency after more than twenty-five years with the company, this growth-oriented concern came to be regarded as one with an outstandingly dynamic management team, and investment journals praised the virtues of the high grade shares of stock which reflected that fact. No stranger to international operations, GF chalked up sales in such foreign markets as Canada, England, Ireland, West Germany, South Africa, Latin America, and Japan.

Producing and selling more than 230 different food staples for a world market, GF was determined not to be merely imitative. This mass marketer – experienced in widely advertised, high-volume, low-priced, packaged consumer products – emphasized popularity, convenience, and value. They had not been selling luxury and expensive and exotic food specialties. Only one product category could rightly have been classed as a fancy food at the time of the decision on the Gourmet Foods line – the Good Seasons dry salad mixes, which had been only recently acquired from their developer, Robert Kreis, former chef at Hollywood's Brown Derby restaurant. Ten million dollars or more were earmarked each year for food research and product development. GF was heavily oriented towards new products – new items which persistently paced the company's growth. GF maintained a big test kitchen at White Plains to check out each new product. Of 1959 sales, 13·5 per cent were said to have been derived from products first introduced in the previous decade.

The products of General Foods have been used in most homes from dawn to midnight. They are prominent at breakfast, lunch, and dinner, and during the washing of dishes, pots, and pans after every meal or snack. People knew and bought Yuban, Maxwell House, Postum, Sanka, Birely's, Tang, Kool-Aid, Jell-O, Minute Rice, Log Cabin, Post cereals, Birds Eye frozen foods, La France, Satina, Baker's Chocolate. Coffees, other beverages, cake mixes, syrup, salad dressings, frozen vegetables, fish, meats, cereals, desserts, flour, rice, tapioca, barbecue sauce, laundry and dishwashing aids, gelatin, Swiss chocolate, cocoa products, dog foods – all are in GF's product line. Still, despite its colossal dimensions, relatively few people are familiar with the name of the General Foods Corporation. This state of affairs was deliberate on the part of GF, whose policy until 1955 down-played overall corporate identification in favour of enhancing consumer awareness of individual brands in its advertising and promotional efforts. Swan's Down cake flour, Gaines and Gravy Train dog foods – registered GF brands – were part of the working vocabulary of every housewife and much more familiar than the name of the corporation behind them.

In every division of General Foods there was a heavy emphasis on sales. The company needed mass volume to keep its big plants operating at high efficiency in terms of processes and machine operations, to utilize its tremendous personnel resources to full advantage, to achieve the high turnover of inventories needed to keep working capital in constant productive use, and to protect the future value of its stock through maintaining a sound rate of company growth.

With its orientation towards the mass market and its stress on volume, blue-chip GF had long believed in advertising. The company is usually ranked as the biggest food company in terms of gross advertising expenditures and among the top half-dozen U.S. industrial giants in total national advertising – just behind such concerns as Procter and Gamble and General Motors and often ahead of General Electric, Colgate-Palmolive, Chrysler, RCA, Lever Bros, and Westinghouse. Mr Mortimer saw advertising as essential because, 'You have to sell your product to the people before they get to the store.' To woo the shoppers after they get there, GF also put a great deal of money and effort into packaging and many types of consumer deals and incentives.

The organization of General Foods was highly decentralized. Each product division operated almost as an independent company under the corporate umbrella. Within the divisions, 'product managers' were held responsible for exploiting individual products in the most effective manner. Each brand manager or product group manager worked with his own advertising agency and administered his own advertising budget. The appropriation for overall advertising (which turned out to be eighty-seven million dollars in 1958, or two times net earnings for the corporation) was established by first determining what it would cost to tell the many separate product stories with the frequency and effectiveness needed to create and sustain consumer demand for each brand and by the summing up these figures to arrive at the total advertising budget for the company as a whole.

With the handmaidens of high-volume production and big advertising, GF supermarket and chain-store selling was essential in the mass-marketing picture. Few processers had ever established a trade position in the supermarket field as solidly as had the General Foods Corporation by the time this story took place.

This was the corporate nature of the big moth attracted to the small but flickering flame of fancy foods. Having made the decision to enter the gourmet market, exploration of the field and of the best means for invading it was necessary.

Establishing the Gourmet Foods Division

General Foods chose Joseph B. Starke to head up the new line in mid-1955. General Manager Starke came to GF from Amos Parrish & Co., Inc., a firm of department store consultants, where he had worked for twenty-eight years and was executive vice-president and general manager. From the same firm, Starke brought along John T. Webber as his national sales manager for Gourmet Foods. Ronald Blench was picked to cover the production end; he was working at the time for General Foods, Ltd, of Canada, and had several years of valuable food processing experience in Europe. As cuisine consultant, GF utilized the services of Robert Kreis, the Swiss chef who had originally developed the line of Good Seasons salad dressings.

Starke's team – backed by corporate know-how and resources – was given division status high in the hierarchy, and its offices were located at White Plains. The unit, like most other General Foods divisions, was highly decentralized, and Starke was granted substantial authority and full responsibility for his group. He was formally responsible only to senior vice-president G. O. Bailey for his decisions and deeds, although it was soon clear that Mr Mortimer himself would keep in close touch with Starke at all times.

DEVELOPING A MARKETING STRATEGY FOR GOURMET FOODS

Starke and his staff began with little information on which to base a programme for the new line. Two logical sources of data suggested themselves immediately, and Starke set out to tap both: (1) information on the fancy foods industry itself which might be gathered from people and firms already in the field, and (2) information on markets with characteristics presumed to be similar to the fancy foods market which could be collected from published sources.

Preliminary Fact-gathering and Market Analysis

Starke cited a number of facts which were assumed to document a general trend towards increased consumer spending on high-quality and convenience goods in 1956:

Almost a million Americans were driving Cadillacs, and 293,500 were sold in 1955 and 1956.

11,516 foreign luxury sports cars were sold in the U.S. in 1956 plus 26,000 Thunderbirds and 7500 Corvettes.

Pleasure boating had become a 1·3-billion-dollar business.

Residential swimming pools had increased from 2500 in 1947 to 57,000 in 1956.

Nearly three million American families had incomes over $10,000; 600,000 had incomes over $15,000; 90,000 had incomes over $50,000.

The 'leisure market' was rated at thirty to forty billion dollars a year.

Americans were spending nearly eleven billion dollars each year for pure recreation plus twelve billion dollars additional for vacation travel.

1·5 million Americans planned trips abroad in 1957, not including those going to Mexico and Canada.

In 1956, Americans filled glasses with forty-five million dollars' worth of champagne and bought eight million dollars' worth of caviar.

U.S. camera bugs spent about four hundred million dollars each year for photographic supplies and equipment.

American homes were equipped with 3·6 million air conditioners, thirty-six times the number owned in 1946.
About 12 per cent of all U.S. families had two cars.

With this as a basis, Starke quickly concluded that 'there wasn't much question of market opportunity'. Expanding on this point later, he declared, 'The desire for better quality and finer products has been one of the driving forces of the American economy, and, in early 1956, the time seemed materially right to think about a line of the finest foods in the world.'

Starke spent the last half of 1955 and 1956 travelling some fifty thousand miles in the United States to visit specialty food buyers, merchandising managers in department stores carrying fancy foods, and others with a real or fancied knowledge of the business. To the GF people, the chaotic fancy foods field was full of inconsistencies and inefficiencies, and 'marketing techniques seemed primitive'. They concluded that the field was certainly open to an 'aggressive marketer' who could apply modern and efficient marketing methods.

Although Starke was persuaded that GF had a great opportunity to penetrate a potentially large market, he still didn't know exactly what the potential was nor where it lay. With so few statistics to go on and little research, Starke bravely admitted that his operation was 'an adventure into the unknown'. *Food Engineering* magazine sympathized by noting that GF's usually thorough market research and analysis were practically impossible in the fancy foods field and that General Foods was necessarily 'flying by the seat of its pants'. As Starke was to express it in 1958: 'The few figures we could dig out were fragmentary and confusing. We wanted to know volume figures, for example. How big is the fancy foods business? There were only two logical sources of information. We got to both all right, but they were 4000 per cent apart.'

Market targets for Gourmet Foods were never explicitly formulated. We can infer from the marketing plan subsequently adopted, however, that there was a strong, implicit orientation towards high income customers. The new food line was of high quality, it was priced high, it was distributed initially through carefully selected department and specialty stores, and both advertising and packages were designed to appeal to a discriminating customer group. Corporate prestige resulting from the introduction of the Gourmet Foods line was apparently to be achieved by catering to prestige income classes. Eventually, GF took the, for them, unusual step of plunging without market tests.

With the definite intention of forging ahead, and to define further the scope of his operation, Starke went to Europe to check into fine foods made and sold there and to locate reliable suppliers. He saw his task as one of asking, 'What sells?' He then obtained the indicated items, gathering them together in order of volume importance to European retailers. During these travels, more than a thousand individual samples were sent to GF's test kitchens at White Plains for evaluation and to corporate laboratories for quality analyses. Following a tentative screening of products and sources, Ronald Blench looked into European production and quality-control facilities and tried to find out if raw materials could be assured. Co-packaging arrangements with European producers were discussed. Kreis went to Europe, too, for the purpose of investigating recipes and formulas and to suggest ways of making some of the products better.

Sharpening the Objectives

Meanwhile, GF attempted to tighten its understanding of the objectives to be achieved by the Gourmet Foods line. These were somewhat clarified by Mr Mortimer at the time the new line was announced to the public in the summer of 1957. Prestige was still to be the keynote. The primary aim of the new line was to contribute materially to a favourable corporate image for GF – not only to generate good will among General Foods' customers but to improve GF's image with the general public, the financial community, company employees, and other corporate publics. To establish Gourmet Foods as a prestige line for the General Foods Corporation was thus the first imperative. But it quickly became apparent that GF wasn't willing to pay much if anything to achieve the goal. Whereas Corning was rumoured to be losing money on its Steuben glass and writing off the cost as a promotional expense, GF, after much deliberation, decided to make its new line an operating division rather than charge it off promotionally. Yet, the basic concept was still a promotional one. General Foods would not 'subsidize prestige at the expense of profits' and made but a limited commitment.

Secondary goals were posited to act as constraints on the principal aim of enhancing corporate prestige. Dollarwise, the Gourmet Foods division should stand on its own feet. This was consistent with basic corporate policy that each division should make some contribution, however small, to total earnings – or, as a minimum, to be self-supporting. This virtually guaranteed that the Gourmet Foods division's budget and manpower allocation would be held to modest levels at least at the start.

A third hope, or objective, was that explorations into the new line might uncover new products suitable for later mass production and mass distribution. Gourmet Foods would function as a 'testing ground' for consumer preferences and might identify items for GF's regular product lines handled by other divisions within the company. Furthermore, the prestige of the new division might be used to hold an 'umbrella' over any such new items until they could become established as staple items in a different product line. With these objectives in mind, General Foods was ready to announce exactly what was to be offered to the gourmet market and how this was to be done.

Building the Line

The new products were to be promoted as 'the finest foods from the four corners of the world'. To live up to such advance billing, to ensure results consistent with stated objectives, and to build a systematic product line rather than a mere collection of items, Starke and his group had gradually worked out a set of criteria which each candidate product and the line as a whole would have to meet.

First GF stressed quality. Regardless of price, it would sell only the best. GF regarded high quality as the most fundamental characteristic of gourmet products, and uncompromised adherence to demanding standards of quality was viewed as essential in

63

order to establish Gourmet Foods as the company's prestige line. Thus, Gourmet Foods were to be 'the finest of their kind available'.

Second, and to further ensure prestige, the new line was to consist only of products that would be sold to better department and specialty stores.

Another offshoot of the prestige objective was that the line was to be 'balanced for international flavour'. It would include a liberal number of items never before sold in this country to give the line a novelty appeal and to provide an exclusive selling point and sales advantage over competitors.

The line would include no spooky foods. Somewhat more orthodox items appealing to the true gourmet and having a fairly high frequency of use would be sought to ensure satisfactory turnover and contribute to the profitability objective.

GF wanted a 'complete line'. There would be enough individual items to make up a full, epicurean meal. There would be products that could be served throughout the day (e.g. preserves for breakfast, soups for lunch, items for the cocktail hour, something for dinner). And the line was to be wide and deep enough in variety to be literally an entire fine foods department in itself. This would enable GF to offer a full line to retailers instead of leaving them with numerous suppliers for their fine foods needs.

Another criterion was that the line should offer maximum convenience to the ultimate purchaser. Towards this end, Starke believed the line should consist of 'end products' rather than 'ingredient' items. And no product requiring refrigeration would be admitted to the line to complicate transportation and shelf-life problems.

Taken together, these criteria gave the line its shape. Months of investigation, testing, and preparation produced a line of products that met the standards. When Gourmet Foods were first introduced in 1957, there were over fifty separate items, eighteen new to the U.S. market. Gourmet Foods were presented in eight major categories: biscuits and cookies, preserves, soups, entrées, entrée sauces, desserts and sauces, cocktail snacks and hors d'oeuvres, and coffees and teas. The individual items ranged from fancy staples to esoteric and exotic delicacies: champagne mustard, Okaki tidbits, Numake spread, Sauce Bolognaise, clear onion consommé with sherry, spiced black cherry preserves, Swedish lingonberries, vichyssoise, hearts of palm, canapé cuplets, marinated artichoke shells, Viking brochettes, Bornholm biscuits, green turtle soup, Assam tea, *Sauce aux Fine Herbes*, cherry pickles, and wheat pilaf. While a score of these products were produced in the United States, most came from a dozen foreign countries, including England, Belgium, Denmark, Sweden, France, West Germany, Switzerland, Japan, and Brazil.

Creating the Package

General Foods has always felt that proper package planning is a prime consideration in the commercialization of new products. The design of a GF package is typically a large-scale team effort involving the Research, Production, Traffic, Legal, and Purchasing departments and the General Foods Kitchens, at the corporate staff level, and the sales, merchandising, and advertising sections of the product groups or divisions concerned. At least seven basic elements are always carefully weighed in the design of packages: product characteristics, selection of the most appropriate package material and sources of supply, production aspects, convenience factors, considerations of economy, merchandising angles, and questions of package appearance. The package is an important selling tool at both the trade and consumer levels of the market. Packaging received an extraordinary amount of attention in the case of Gourmet Foods, since the wrapper would be required to sell the subtle concept of quality and bring prestige and status to the company as a whole.

Mrs Josephine Von Miklos, a designer best known for her work in cosmetics, was appointed. According to her philosophy, the first important consideration was the creation of a basic motif that would convey in a dramatic manner three ideas: (1) that these foods were of the very best quality, (2) that they were cosmopolitan in character, and (3) that the products would have permanent appeal and enduring value and not just be riding on the wave of some popular but ephemeral fashion. According to *Sales Management* magazine, Gourmet Foods were meant to be 'international in character and timeless in concepts, luxurious in execution, and just enough off the ground to give an air of lightheartedness'. Whatever that meant, it all had to be captured on the package. It was Mrs Von Miklos' theory that the design should be taken out of the realm of the commercial and be given an appearance that would be appealing on the table or pantry shelf. The label was to convey a feeling of 'character and spontaneity' and to communicate 'dignity and restraint'. She also remarked that 'this is *food*; therefore the package must be clean* and create an appetite for the food inside of it'. To suggest the idea of dining in splendour, she said she would adhere to the basic rule that 'simplicity means elegance'. Finally, the package would prominently display the name of the General Foods Corporation and clearly associate it with the name of Gourmet Foods. These were a lot of requirements to be met in a single design.

As basic colours for the package, she chose pure white with gold and black accents as the combination most expressive of the desired attributes of elegance and luxury. She also developed a fresh logotype consisting of a golden compass; this, of course, was in keeping with the international character of the new line. The words 'General Foods' and 'Gourmet Foods' were arranged in a circle around the four points of this compass, with the common initials 'GF' placed in its centre. The concept of timelessness was worked out by illustrator Lawrence Beall Smith, whose notion of subtle suggestion rather than conventional realism had already produced an entirely new concept in package design. 'Floating' illustrations (product ingredients, tools, or utensils) over floating shadows were used to produce the desired effect. Breakfast coffee, for instance, was suggested by floating illustrations of an old-fashioned coffee grinder in combination with a botanical representation of coffee beans. Copy was kept to a minimum. In addition to mandatory copy (legally imposed information on ingredients, government grade-labelling, etc.), each

---

* It is somewhat ironic that white was later chosen as a 'clean' colour, for shopworn white packages often became so battered as to look much less clean than other colours might have on the final store and pantry shelves.

package expressed only the phrase, 'From the Four Corners of the World' and the name of the product or product combination involved, e.g. 'Gourmet Canapé Magic', 'Gourmet Hostess Party Pack', 'Gourmet Sauce Shelf', or 'Gourmet International Preserve Collection'.

When all of these elements were put together into a box or wrapper for jars and cans, they were supposed to tell the shopper that he or she had purchased something special which 'belongs to another world'. In any event, the result was a sophisticated package, aesthetic but rather severe. Starke said that it 'shrieked elegance'. Containers were also carefully designed to be both functional and ornamental. All labels were manufactured in the United States and sent abroad to food packers or suppliers to assure uniform printing quality and to meet the legal requirements for packaged food products sold in the United States. All imports were packaged in custom-made containers in the land of their origin and to the exacting specification of the General Foods Corporate Research Laboratories. A final packaging decision was to develop packing cases to hold only twelve package units rather than the more customary twenty-four, this being dictated by slower anticipated rates of turnover in retail stores.[6]

Pricing the Line

Most Gourmet Foods were expensive. With the prestige idea in mind, and to cover high costs, GF stuck to its principle of 'quality at any price'. The prices ranged from about 29¢ for party 'dips' to $3.89 for Rock Cornish hen. Soups retailed at from 90¢ to $1.60 a can.

GF also priced high in order to offer the retailer a profit margin that would make the line attractive in the face of anticipated low-to-moderate volume levels. Gourmet Foods provided an average mark-up of 39 per cent, which was slightly higher than the level usually associated with premium-priced specialties and more than double the overall average retail food mark-up.

To preserve profit incentives, which functioned as one of the main selling points for the new line, GF sold under a schedule of 'suggested retail prices'. It was reported that GF at least initially refused to sell its new line to stores that planned to undercut prices and, hence, the structure of retailer profit margins.

Establishing the Distribution System

As we have already observed, the Gourmet Foods line was to be distributed through specialty food shops and department stores. Although the strategy was later modified, the initial aim was to limit distribution strictly to these two types of stores. Of the estimated five or six thousand available outlets, GF planned to sell only the 'best' stores and on an exclusive basis. As a target to shoot at, GF expected to be established in from 1,200 to 1,500 outlets by the end of the first year of operation. A double-edged policy was also set up to require that (1) all retailers would buy the entire line, and that (2) they would set it up as a single unit or section within their stores.

Nieman Marcus in Dallas was the first department store signed up. Other stores to carry Gourmet Foods included Marshall Field in Chicago, Harzfeld in Kansas City, Lord and Taylor in New York, and Rich's in Atlanta. Distribution came more slowly than expected. Gourmet Foods were placed in five hundred stores during 1957. Forty per cent of these were department stores that had never before operated food sections. By August of 1958, one thousand outlets were displaying the Gourmet Foods line, half of them department stores and the rest specialty shops.

The distribution plan was further premised on the belief that the fancy foods field required considerable flexibility of manoeuvre and that 'regular channels were not willing or able to do a satisfactory job' with Gourmet Foods. Since the experience of regular food wholesalers with gourmet items was indeed slight, the plan called for by-passing wholesalers and servicing retail accounts on a direct basis. Because of the relatively small expected volume on the fancy foods, GF further decided that it was not economically feasible to utilize its regular network of distribution centres, which had done so much to expedite the handling of the company's staple items. Six special warehouses were selected to store and handle Gourmet Foods inventories at strategic locations throughout the country – New York, Atlanta, Cincinnati,

68

Chicago, Kansas City, and San Francisco. All imported items were received by GF in New York and reshipped to these distribution points.

It was also felt that the personal attention of a small sales organization was needed to 'teach' retailers how to sell fancy foods. Under the direction of John Webber, National Sales Manager for Gourmet Foods, an eleven-man sales force, trained as purveyors of fine foods, was assembled. These salesmen were located in the six distribution point cities and in Boston, Dallas, and Los Angeles.

This sales and distribution network expedited service to retailers, who were to be billed for their goods at prices quoted FOB the nearest distribution point. Salesmen were in a position to promise retailers a maximum wait of three to five days on deliveries. The salesmen were to assist the outlets with point-of-purchase merchandising and try to ensure that sales-per-square-foot were up to par at each location.

Providing Promotional Support

The media plan was initially limited to magazines, and the first ads appeared in the issues of November 1957. On the schedule were *Esquire, Gourmet, Holiday, House & Garden, the New Yorker, Sports Illustrated, Sunset,* and *Telefood.* For the most part, the initial advertisements were in full colour. They were clearly beamed at the upper income classes on the implicit assumption that these were the people who purchased most fancy foods. GF boasted that it had the country's 'largest gourmet picked audience' in the 9,500,000 readers of the magazines carrying ads for Gourmet Foods.

After the initial push-off, the ad schedule was cut back and concentrated in three magazines – *Gourmet, The New Yorker,* and *Sports Illustrated.* A review of the twelve monthly issues of *Gourmet* magazine in 1958 reveals even further selectivity and concentration. Ads for Gourmet Foods during the first six months were full page and in colour. No advertisements appeared in July or August. Starting in September, the ads were black and white and were one-third of a page. Two such ads appeared in

September, one in October, and two in each of the Christmas-season issues of November and December.

With respect to the creative treatment, GF departed from its usual formula of beautiful mouth-watering close-ups of food ready for serving. Cartoon illustrations were used to tell the product stories, and the copy chatted lengthily in a 'light, humorous, and slightly sophisticated manner' about 'the finest foods from the four corners of the earth'. There were thumbnail sketches of the products and the artifacts associated with them. The ads were not especially eye-catching and, aimed as they were at the food connoisseur, they didn't attempt to educate the less-informed reader. The copy was not always terribly believable and may even have produced negative effects in some cases. For instance, an ad in the April 1958 issue of *Gourmet* showed us a slender man being sent abroad in search of imported foods and later returning fat and jolly. Another ad in *Gourmet*, 'The Magazine of Good Living,' was a one-column, black-and-white ad with a small drawing at the top. Below it were the words:

PARAGONS OF FLAVOUR
BORNHOLM
BISCUITS

Following this heading were sophisticated descriptions of the product and the atmosphere that would be created by the presence of that product:

'We have captured a cocktail biscuit
delicious as a man's dream of heaven.'

'To sniff their aromatic flavour sets
the pulse to scurrying.'

'To crunch these flavoursome seeds,
lolling indolently in their flaky
folds of short rye flour, has caused
elderly ladies to swoon in ecstasy.'

Then, at the bottom of every advertisement, was a personal postscript to the reader from GF:

'P.S. These biscuits are one of over 50 delectable foods, culled from the four corners of the earth. Should your department store or specialty shop not carry them, write us. We will tell you "where" by return mail.

General Foods
Gourmet Foods
White Plains, N.Y.'

Some outside observers said this copy was both too 'cute' and too blunt and that it may have appealed more to conceited gluttons than to true gourmets. Others, obviously the client and the agency to mention but two interested groups, could doubtless debate such a point with some vigour.

The advertising budget for Gourmet Foods seems to have been set with little explicit regard for the objectives sought or the tasks associated with achieving them. The aim most clearly reflected in the expenditure plan was the object of having the new division stand on its own feet. Much less money was actually spent than most people thought to promote the line. Citing figures prepared by the Publishers Information Bureau, *Advertising Age* reported that GF spent a total of $51,308 for magazine advertising of Gourmet Foods during the last half of 1957. Expenditures in 1958, according to PIB data, reached a high of £101,223, while 1959 expenditures totalled but $44,162. Thus, less than $200,000 was dedicated to the advertising support of Gourmet Foods during its full life span.

Faced with limited resources, GF still used selling aids and point-of-sale promotional material, although the sales promotion budget was even smaller than the advertising appropriation. Company salesmen were equipped with easel-type sales presentation kits personalized for each store called upon. For instance, the pitch made to Neiman Marcus was reported to be as follows: 'Neiman Marcus customers appreciate quality . . . quality in home furnishings . . . quality in table settings . . . so why not complete the picture with a top line of foods?' With the help of red-velvet-lined display kits resembling jewellers' cases, salesmen

F   71 emphasized twelve points for the retailer to bear in mind when deciding whether or not to take on the line. Among these points were the advantages of national advertising* and publicity, distinctive packaging, attractive margins, and a balanced line.

Retailers were supplied with their own sales kits and with permanent displays designed by Chaspec, Inc. A special $2\frac{1}{2} \times 5$-foot display unit featured the new GF logotype, or trademark, in full colour and was intended for use in show windows. Nine different newspaper ad mats were supplied in various sizes to encourage local promotional tie-ins with the national campaign. Also included in the promotional kit were 'planograms' for most effectively displaying the new items, maps showing where the foods came from, assorted literature – and, last but far from least, self-addressed mail order blanks. The kit was billed as a 'first' for the fancy foods field.

GF salesmen instructed store personnel in appropriate merchandising techniques, and, during November and December of 1957, the company sent pretty hostesses into major stores throughout the country to introduce and serve Gourmet Foods, to the retailers' clientele. But a large part of the promotional burden still rested on the retailers – many of whom had never before handled fancy foods.

Although General Foods did not offer a co-operative advertising arrangement to its retailers, the Gourmet Foods line received fairly good local advertising support from retailers who devoted a portion of their attractive mark-ups to the task. Free publicity, much of it stimulated by the efforts of retailers, far exceeded the original expectations of all associated with Gourmet Foods. Requests for stories and news items reportedly came to GF 'over the transom, in the windows and up through the floors'. This was a welcome windfall.

In sum, the promotional support programme was limited and

---

* One of GF's principal selling points was the generation of local demand which would result from extensive advertising support of Gourmet Foods. While it was probably true that GF conducted a larger promotional campaign than other suppliers in the industry, some specialty dealers complained later that they had been induced to purchase the line on the promise of more advertising support than they actually received.

selective. The pattern put together by Joseph Starke and his staff was now complete. It merely remained to be seen how well it was to work in the market place.

THE PROGRAMME IN ACTION

The Gourmet Foods line made its debut at the Fancy Foods Exhibit in New York during August 1957. Despite some scepticism and alarm, many competitive suppliers welcomed GF in the belief that its advertising and its opening of new outlets would expand the entire market to the ultimate benefit of everyone in the industry.

The Performance Record

In the judgement of *Sales Management* magazine, Gourmet Foods had 'a successful introduction' and 'got off to a fast start'. The initial impact by November and December seemed good. Sales were reported to be continuously growing as GF pushed out its distribution coverage.

After the first year of operation, Mr Starke made the public statement that 'results in terms of consumer and retailer acceptance of the Gourmet Foods line have been most satisfactory'. Lord & Taylor, according to one paper, was not just pleased but was 'astonished' at the first-year performance of the line. Neiman Marcus and other large department stores reported sales per square foot to be 'well above par'. Meanwhile, turnover in the smaller stores was disappointing. Overall, GF officials expressed confidence in favourable consumption trends for specialty foods.

But, despite the general growth of the fancy foods market, and despite the fact that the General Foods Corporation as a whole was enjoying its most successful year on record, evidence of basic difficulties with Gourmet Foods soon began to crop up. GF was understandably close-mouthed about actual statistics on sales volume, market share, or profits. According to informed trade opinion, however, it was estimated that the annual sales volume for Gourmet Foods was in the neighbourhood of one million dollars, not much for a market reputed to be worth as much as a couple of hundred million dollars annually. *Fortune* magazine quoted Starke as conceding that Gourmet Foods showed no profit through the fiscal year 1958. Persistent remours that prices and quality would be cut were then denied by Starke. He said that he might drop some individual items that hadn't moved well and reported that his seasoned wheat pilaf had sold so well that it might become a new product suitable for mass distribution by GF. But it was soon clear that the Gourmet Foods line was in more trouble than Starke was confessing. The ranking of the original division objectives was apparently shifted somewhat as the profit goal quickly assumed precedence over the prestige aim. And possible harbingers of ultimate failure began to appear in the elastic strategy pursued by General Foods as a consequence.

Shifting Strategy

Joseph Starke was soon openly hinting that some basic policy changes might indeed have to be made. It was readily conceded that the marketing formula for Gourmet Foods was still fluid, and the division began a reformulation very promptly.

The product line itself was modified. Slow-moving or defective products were pruned out like so much dead wood. For instance, those paragons of flavour, Bornholm Biscuits, which had been imported in tins, were discontinued in mid-1958 because they would not retain their freshness in the tin and were often dry and crumbled by the time they were purchased by the consumer. A much-belated move was finally made into the gift-box business. Still, sufficient sales failed to materialize, and President Mortimer, dissatisfied with the product line, announced his desire to make even more fundamental changes. Referring to the Gourmet Foods line, he once remarked, 'At one of these business things I go to, the dowager wife of some fancy businessman sitting next to me said, "Oh, Mr Mortimer, your Gourmet Foods are wonderful! We stock the yacht with them!" And I thought to myself, "Yeah, that's what's wrong with that business – not enough yachts." Thus began some softening of the 'quality at any price' policy as GF sought new items, expanded the line to sixty products, and cut back a bit on prices.

As some prices were cut, the company claimed one of the reasons was because it had learned more about supply sources at cheaper prices. It seems more likely, however, that price reduction was a deliberate strategic move to broaden the market for Gourmet Foods.

Promotional targets were also changed. A shift in emphasis was made from the snobbish connoisseur and the sophisticated woman to the 'gay young socials', and advertising was more specifically aimed at the twenty-five to forty-five age group. But the advertising budget, as we have seen, was quite modest and was even reduced after 1958. Such promotion certainly could not stem any tide of failure.

The most fundamental modifications to the initial marketing strategy were in the field of distribution. GF made a tactical retreat and permitted small specialty and department stores to purchase less than a full line and to display selected items as they pleased. But more important was the realization that, since only 45 per cent of all fancy foods were sold through department and specialty stores, GF had cut itself off from more than half of the market with the single policy decision to market only through those two types of outlets. And the fact that these outlets were sold on a highly selective and exclusive basis had shrunk the total potential market available to GF even further. Thus, it was reasoned that the quickest route to greater volume and eventual profit lay in adding new kinds of outlets to the distribution system.

GF began to view supermarkets with renewed interest, despite the fact that 'supermarket' was a dirty word to many people in the fancy foods industry. *Progressive Grocer* reported the results of a survey made in 1958 which showed that one out of three supermarkets then had a specialty foods section, that 90 per cent of these stores planned to maintain or increase their stocks of fancy foods, and that most of the new supers being built had plans for the inclusion of such items. GF was aware of the increased supermarket interest in gourmet foods and of the opportunity this provided for creating more volume. In any event, the company announced that it would move Gourmet Foods into a limited number of supermarkets as a test. In the autumn of 1959, Gourmet Foods were introduced on a complete-line basis to over one hundred supermarkets in Los Angeles. In the winter of the same year a second test area was established in Boston, again with over a hundred markets carrying the entire line. The results of these tests were to determine the future of Gourmet Foods.

Few real changes were made in the remainder of the marketing programme to meet the special requirements of supermarket selling. Package designs were unchanged and margins of nearly 40 per cent were maintained. Some newspaper ads were used to support the supermarkets during the tests. With the added outlets, the original Gourmet Foods sales organization proved inadequate, and already busy salesmen from the Maxwell House Coffee Division of GF had to assume the sales burden in the test areas. And the test areas themselves were tough markets. Los Angeles was a hotbed for price wars; Boston was the stronghold of venerable S. S. Pierce, a well-entrenched specialty food marketer.

While some importers accused GF of 'dumping' the Gourmet Foods line into the supermarkets, company executives officially stated that GF had been pressured by supermarkets into allowing them to handle the line. Whatever the case, by the close of 1959, Starke was convinced that supermarkets were not going to pull enough additional volume to rescue him from profitlessness. Before this time, *Progressive Grocer* had revealed that the average supermarket (of eight hundred studied) devoted but forty-two linear shelf feet to the display of 142 fancy foods items for a total weekly fancy foods volume of $168 – less than 1 per cent of total store sales. The magazine suggested that many supermarkets carried fancy foods only as a customer convenience to improve their public images as stores that 'have everything'. Turnover was certainly slower than originally hoped.

Total 1959 sales for Gourmet Foods barely exceeded the million-dollar mark again, and all of the strategic changes had failed to produce a profit. So the entire line was dropped.

The axe fell on Gourmet Foods in late February 1960, near the end of GF's fiscal year. Although some retailers protested that the line was being killed off just as it was about to leave the ground, the big food processer lived up to its reputation for crisp decisiveness or, some would say, complete ruthlessness towards any product or line which fails to make the grade. GF, however, still managed to find a few nice words for the deceased.

An Epitaph for Gourmet Foods

In an official announcement declaring his decision to discontinue the Gourmet Foods line, Charles G. Mortimer said, 'The market for these foods simply isn't growing fast enough as yet to provide the turnover and volume necessary for the grocery business, where an endless flow of new products puts a premium on all shelf space.' (This message had been virtually telegraphed in the company's 1958 annual report, which mentioned that 'the constant stream of new products leads to what aptly has been described as a "jungle battle" for shelf space in stores and supermarkets'.) Continuing with the announcement, Mr Mortimer said, 'In the two and a half years we used Gourmet Foods to explore the extent of the epicurean foods market, two of our original three objectives have been achieved. First of all, these high quality foods have contributed materially to a favourable corporate image. Secondly, our experience has suggested one or two items in the line may hold promise of suitability for mass distribution. The third objective – a contribution to earnings – has not been realized because these products at this time do not seem to have sufficient mass appeal to provide a sound basis for building an adequate profitable business – either for our customers or for General Foods.'

There were those who later felt that Mr Mortimer had been too charitable, that Gourmet Foods had really failed to achieve *any* of its three aims to any significant degree. But Mr Mortimer continued in a pardonably benevolent vein, adding that the popularity of premium-quality foods, which had shown gains ever since

World War II, was still growing. In a neat turn of phrase, GF managed – as *Business Week* put it – 'to extract from its failure a pat on the back for its own prescience'. Said Mr Mortimer: 'We continue to believe that an increasing segment of the consuming public will buy premium food products, and we intend to consider that group in our product development planning. As tastes and incomes and our standard of living rise still higher, it may well develop that even the Gourmet Foods experiment was less than a decade ahead of its time.' The line was thus depicted as being, if anything, just a bit too *avant garde*. To this, some trade observers merely said 'Amen'.

Distributors were offered an opportunity to return all unsold stocks of Gourmet Foods to GF. And, for those few determined Gourmet Foods fans who still might want to get the goods, GF said it would 'work out a way to make possible their continued purchase in assortment combinations by mail'.* The company left the faint but still unrealized hope that the line might be back on the scene before many years could pass. The Gourmet Foods demise 'is really a suspension', one observer remarked, perhaps more out of hope than conviction.

One educated guess had it that GF lost three million dollars on its adventure into the fancy foods field. The financial impact of such a failure, of course, was absorbed by the huge company. But this is no way diminishes the point that this was a true misfire. *Business Week* referred to the whole episode as an 'exotic setback' for GF. *Sales Management* and other sources said bluntly that it was a 'failure'.

The Autopsy

What had gone wrong? There was no immediate shortage of opinion in the trade literature, which, with the assured wisdom of hindsight, reported literally hundreds of 'explanations'. It is unnecessary here to catalogue all of the factors allegedly con-

---

* Cynics were quick to say this would last only until GF cleared out its inventories, and they may have been right. By March 1961, the company confirmed the end of all efforts to sell the line by mail.

tributing to the downfall of Gourmet Foods. In essence, there were four interrelated reasons for it.

1. The fancy foods market was sliced much too thinly by General Foods to make it profitable.
2. Basic objectives for the Gourmet Foods line were poorly stated and generally misunderstood within the company.
3. The entire marketing programme was too heavily influenced in both design and execution by the desire for prestige.
4. Considering the nature of its business, General Foods should never have entered the fancy foods field at all and could have avoided the hapless decision in the first place had it formulated and applied appropriate product policies beforehand.

The problem was not that American consumers refused to eat *pâté*; it was that GF didn't know how to sell it to them. There was a market for fancy foods, it was experiencing rapid growth, and it was sufficiently large in the aggregate to attract GF. General Foods simply failed to carve out a big enough piece of it with the strategy it had put together.

In designing its basic approach to the fancy foods market, GF sliced and resliced the market until it had been pared down to a tiny sliver of distinctly limited potential. The market target for Gourmet Foods was perceived and pursued with thoughts more implicit than explicit. But there was nearly unanimous agreement among experts in the field that GF aimed too much at a class market. By orienting itself towards connoisseurs, upper upper-income groups, and women shoppers, Gourmet Foods sealed itself off from the impulsive food buying behaviour of men and from the burgeoning middle-class market which was already providing profits for such companies as Sara Lee and Reese Imports. By initially overlooking the gift-package business, GF also sacrificed a potential motivation for purchase second only to home entertaining in the fine foods business. What market potential remained was then cut in half by GF's decision to limit distribution to department and specialty stores. This residual potential was shrunk further by an exclusive selling policy which was aimed at less than a quarter of these two classes of accounts. By continually peeling off and rejecting layer after layer of potential sales from the market onion, the total ultimately available to GF was so small that not even a large share of it would be likely to produce enough volume to sustain the line. In short, the marketing approach simply aimed at too limited an audience.

Some sought to excuse GF with the reminder that the industry never had been able to agree on market definitions or statistics, that useful data were almost impossible to come by, and that nobody had ever produced an unambiguous portrait of the fancy foods consumer. Less charitable Monday-morning quarterbacks criticized GF's 'adventure into the unknown' and chastised the company for failing to conduct preliminary market research or at least to engage in test marketing before making its plunge. It was perhaps as true, however, that extensive market research was not worth while at the time of this adventure and that GF was justified in preferring to assume an indefinite risk rather than to pay for the definite costs of research. Yet, the fact is that, in the absence of knowledge, prudent marketers have usually felt that it is safer to avoid over-segmentation of markets in the early stages of strategy formulation and execution. *Caveat Segmenter* is a maxim embraced by many marketers of new products until market experience can be accumulated and sights can be safely narrowed.

General Foods began with a highly segmented approach to its market and belatedly tried to expand the target during 1959 to get at a larger potential. But it was too late. By that time the entire marketing pattern had become overspecialized. Not modest changes but sweeping revisions in every dimension of marketing strategy would have been called for. Major modifications to product quality, the composition of the line, packaging, the price structure, advertising, sales promotion, and distribution arrangements would have produced a totally new marketing pattern with little similarity to the original programme and quite out of keeping with original aims.

To trace the origin of the failure another step, let us re-examine those objectives more closely. It will be recalled that there were three: (1) The line was to bring prestige to GF; (2) it was to generate profit or, at least, to break even; and (3) it was to produce new products suitable for mass distribution through other GF divisions.

These goals appear to have been set somewhat arbitrarily, with little or no definite reference to either market conditions or true corporate needs. Right or wrong, they were poorly understood and interpreted within the company, and they are open to criticism on several counts. First of all, they were individually worded so ambiguously as to limit severely their usefulness either as guides to action or as measuring rods for assessing subsequent performance. How was the kind and amount of 'prestige' generated by the line to be measured, for instance? What level of sales volume would have to be generated at what cost and by what date to reach the break-even point?* How many new products for mass distribution would have to be uncovered by the new division to judge its success by the third yardstick? (Probably something more than one or two.) Had answers to such questions been supplied at the beginning, the triple aim would have had greater operational meaning and utility. What is even more important, added definitional clarity might have helped to reconcile inconsistencies *between* these multiple objects which were somewhat in conflict with each other, and there were no built-in safeguards to ensure balanced progress towards their simultaneous achievement. They were never even formally ranked in order of their importance to General Foods. The result was an inevitable tension between the demands of prestige, profits, and products. As we have noted earlier, the prestige objective was accorded the dominant role at the outset. The order of objectives, as we have also seen, was subsequently changed. Shifts in marketing strategy were the natural results of the changes in emphasis among objectives in conflict over time.

* The value of a stated objective is always reduced by the failure to establish the time dimensions attached to it. After the death of the Gourmet Foods line, a former executive of the division bitterly complained that the line had been discontinued too soon. The line, he said, would have realized a profit within five years if left alone. Whether or not this prophecy would have been borne out is irrelevant. What is significant is that this member of middle-management had apparently never been informed that a five-year pay-out period for the line would have been unacceptable to top management.

Even with a changed emphasis on objectives, the earlier dominance of the prestige objective continued to influence most aspects of the marketing programme. The initial product criteria employed to assemble the Gourmet Foods line were largely correlates of the prestige goal. Once defined, they were apparently not changed until it was too late to be effective. As a result, the products always tended to be a bit too exotic. It was the joint influence of the prestige aim and this product policy framework which led to an overly segmented market. By severely delimiting its market target, in turn, GF was running counter to the other objectives of making a profit and finding new mass-market products. And, since the 'marketing mix' (the combined pattern of packaging, pricing, promotion, and distribution variables) employed was the direct operational outgrowth of a narrow market definition, the entire pattern became too exclusive and too 'classy'.

The four principal planks in the strategic platform (the too-dominant prestige objective, the overly exotic product-selection criteria, the overly segmented market, and the too-aristocratic marketing mix were at least mutually reinforcing – even if unprofitable. But inconsistencies and weaknesses later appeared as the shift in the ranking of objectives was undertaken. The exploration into supermarket selling, for instance, was pursued with the same packaging that had been originally created especially for department and specialty stores. The price structure was essentially unchanged – the supermarket shopper was asked to buy a sixty-five cent can of vichyssoise imported from France while good domestic potato soups shelved a few feet away were priced at forty cents or less.

Underlying all other strategic miscarriages in the Gourmet Foods case was the much more basic fact that GF suffered slightly from what Levitt has since termed 'marketing myopia'.[7] The Gourmet Foods case illustrates the consequences of a failure to understand the true nature of a company and to define its basic purpose and essential needs. The Gourmet Foods failure was primarily the result of GF's neglect first to codify and then adhere to product policies which would delimit diversification activity and guide the firm into fields where full advantage could be taken of its unique strengths. In a sense, GF was not capitalizing fully upon its facilities by entering an area where these resources were of no great advantage and its limited experience was a clear deficit.

General Foods was well equipped to operate effectively on a large scale – buying and manufacturing on a mass basis, selling huge quantities of staple convenience goods to a broad market, and doing all this with the help of massive individual-brand advertising and high-velocity distribution. Entry into the fancy foods market resulted in a mismatch of scale. Small concerns in the field had long existed chiefly by nursing a few brands along with loving and personal care rather than by relying on extensive and impersonal promotion. They appealed to specialized needs, not to a mass market, and heavy advertising outlays might well have meant throwing good money after bad. The aggregate market for fancy foods was the sum of numerous small and specialized markets, few of which were easily accessible by GF marketing methods and facilities.

Had some broad-gauge product policy been operational at the time to guide General Foods and applied to the Gourmet Foods case, it might also have reflected the company's strongly de-centralized organization structure and corporate philosophy. Its autonomous divisions were, of necessity perhaps, strongly oriented towards the maximization of short-run profits. Though it may have seemed simple just to tack on a new division to acquire and sell a totally new line, this really wasn't desirable if the major motive had to be measurable profits. If prestige and the projection of a quality image for GF were the desired goals, alternative means for achieving them could well have been considered before creating an entirely new division and a brand-new line. Corporate staff officers, for instance, might have engaged in institutional advertising for the purpose of image-building, although even this would have involved a basic departure from the time-honoured (in GF) preference for pushing individual brands more than promoting the company as a whole as of 1955.

Still more significant is the fact that GF product policy ought

83

to have given due consideration to distribution factors – to General Food's reputation in the grocery trade, to its access into and strategic posture within the supermarket and staple food wholesaling field, to its experienced sales forces, to its unique system of distribution and sales service centres spread across the land. Many observers agreed that distribution of the Gourmet Foods line was faulty. It was faulty because the line just didn't fit GF's customary patterns and because it couldn't draw upon GF's distributive facilities for marketing support. The creation of a new and unfamiliar distribution set-up for Gourmet Foods necessarily raised costs and increased the risks while failing to pull a volume sufficient for profitable performance. General Foods did have experience with overseas suppliers. The company did have skills in packaging and in other areas of importance to fancy foods. It did buy department store experience by recruiting Starke and his team. But this was not enough. Considering the real nature of its business, GF should never have entered the fancy foods field at all and could have avoided the hapless decision in the first place – if it had but earlier formulated and applied product policies and market strategies that duly reflected corporate strengths and weaknesses.

The adventure into Gourmet Foods was a mistake from the outset in light of the fact that GF could not avail itself of its own knowledge, resources, and facilities in marketing the new line. Even non-food items might well have been handled more efficiently by GF than Gourmet Foods – if they had been so selected as to fall within General Foods' normal scope of operation. By definition, one suspects, GF should have restricted itself to the acquisition or processing and marketing of food items closer to the staple than to the spooky end of the food spectrum (e.g. 'fancy staples' rather than 'gourmet items') and to related non-food products that might have moved through mass distribution channels to masses of consumers. The quality-at-any-price philosophy, applied inflexibly until too late in the operation, simply made the marketing of Gourmet Foods impossible in a supermarket environment. By the time the line was finally introduced to supermarkets, many of them were so irked by being bypassed earlier, that they were totally disinterested in whether GF succeeded or failed with Gourmet Foods.

General Foods' officials responsible for new products and other development work now attest that the experience with Gourmet Foods produced certain long-range, non-financial dividends. They report that they continue to draw heavily on this chapter of company history in their present development planning. Mr Starke, too, has moved on to apply his unique and considerable talents in more appropriate marketing environments.

CHAPTER IV

An Instant Dividend

Of all economic groups that 'stumbled instead of soared into the sixties', the major household appliance industry was among the most disappointing. One dealer characterized it as sick in October 1960. Others simply called it demoralized. The appliance field *was* unquestionably in a bad way. On that there can be no quarrel.

An early boom had ended shortly after World War II, periods of depression dotted the industry's economic landscape in the fifties, and appliance sales had dropped so sharply during and after the 1958 recession that, despite a good year in 1959, the industry had never really begun to recover from a downhill slide as the curtain rose on a new decade.

Fiercely competitive, cyclically vulnerable, and chronically depressed, this eight-billion-dollar-a-year giant slumped into the sixties with sluggish sales, excessive inventories, dealer unrest, and unstable prices. Foreign competitors had begun to enter the market vigorously, most notably with radios, profit margins for everyone were razor-thin, and sales volume fluctuated with each shift in the winds of international relations and each new Cold War threat.

Except for a few hot-selling items, the overall market for appliances was generally saturated. Sales came from either the newly married and others starting up households or from people wishing to replace old units. Sales to new homes were almost on a plateau since such purchases varied directly with the then relatively stabilized rate of household formation, and this placed a floor under appliance volume. Any hope to raise the ceiling through additional business had to be sought in the replacement market. A Hotpoint survey showed that 60 per cent of home-laundry purchases, for instance, were replacement sales. Replacement sales, in turn, were more closely tied to the business cycle than were sales to new households. While a newly created family unit might purchase a washer even when economic conditions looked bad, a family already owning one could well decide to weather the storm before replacing equipment otherwise ripe for trading-in. It was the hard fact that major appliances are deferrable purchases, for the most part, that accounted for the high susceptibility of this industry to swings of the economy. As people tightened their purse strings in depression, recession, or other periods of uncertainty, one of the first things closed off was spending for consumer durable goods.

Having survived the recession of 1958, the industry was facing still another after basking in the brief economic sunshine of 1959. As 1960 dawned, appliance manufacturers expected demand to hold steady. But, as the year progressed, a decline developed and shipments of major appliances fell far short of earlier forecasts. General Electric's annual report for 1960 noted that, 'The early months of the year were characterized by high levels of industry-wide production in anticipation of increased demands that did not materialize. The resulting overproduction necessitated inventory clearances with an accompanying softening of prices during the year.' To aggravate a general cost–price squeeze, seasonal gains, which normally appeared in the autumn and early winter months, simply did not come about. In fact, and instead, many producers showed big sales *decreases* during the last half of the year. Most industry observers dismally agreed that 1960 was another recession year for major appliances.

Although appliance manufacturers were in difficulty, the trouble was by no means only at the producers' level. Distribution was often cited as a key problem throughout the industry. Appliance retailers and wholesalers felt the whiplash of underlying economic forces. Producers did not act in ways that were always consistent with dealers' interests. They supplied private-brand merchandise to large mail-order houses like Sears, Roebuck & Company under specification-buying arrangements. Such mass marketers, of course, offered keen competition to national-brand franchised resellers. Excess capacity sometimes also led to distress merchandise being dumped into markets where it was picked up by discount houses and other low-margin, limited-service, low-overhead operators. Department stores also cut prices on appliances during periods of oversupply.

This competition hurt the individual full-service appliance dealers, some of whom worked feverishly to bring lost customers back to the fold. Pressure to regain lost sales further depressed prices and raised trade-in allowances, led to increased selling and promotional costs, and resulted in decreased profits across the board. Panicked marketers occasionally incurred the wrath of those government regulatory agencies that are ever alert for misleading advertising, fictitious pricing, bait-and-switch tactics, and other ethically questionable marketing practices.

All of these forces acted to strain manufacturer–dealer relations, as each party sought its own path to profit and survival. Adequate product servicing had always been a critical industry function. Poor repair service had earlier estranged many a customer. Dealers were sometimes accused by producers of sidestepping or short-cutting crucial service functions to avoid the costs involved in extending them. On the other hand, dealers complained that unjustifiable service delays caused by intrinsic product defects alienated customers when manufacturers or others serviced the units they themselves had sold. Whenever household customer relations became an issue, dealers, distributors, and manufacturers bickered over who was responsible for remedying the situation.

Philco in 1960

By 1960 the Philco Corporation, a well-known name in American business for over seventy years, had become a major producer of electronic products and home appliances employing more than 25,000 persons in the United States alone. It competed in a tough league with such giants as General Motors, General Electric, Westinghouse, and many lesser rivals. Philco was a broadly based producer of a diversified product mix in industrial, government, and consumer goods. Its consumer products – 'Famous for

Quality the World Over' – included TV sets, radios, phonographs, hi-fi equipment, refrigerators, deep-freezes, air conditioners, washers, dryers, and electric ranges. Philco's annual report for 1959 indicated that two-thirds of total company sales came from this consumer products line. About half of all Philco assets were in consumer goods.

TABLE 1

SALES AND EARNINGS – PHILCO CORPORATION

Year	Total revenue	After-tax Earnings	Earnings per share
	$	$	$
1958	351,093,000	2,874,000	0·61
1959	397,792,000	7,176,000	1·67
1960	400,587,000	2,287,000	0·47

Source: Annual Reports of Philco Corporation

In electronics, Philco was trying to be a leader in producing transistors for many applications. The company was an important contractor in varying degrees for military electronic uses, such as radar, missiles, missile guidance and control, advanced weapons, microwave and communications equipment. It had also entered such fields as nuclear research and engineering.

Philco had begun to penetrate the electronic computer field as early as 1955, with the development of TRANSAC (Transistor Automatic Computer). This computer system was reputed to have greatly reduced equipment size in comparison with similar systems available at the time and supposedly resulted in savings in cost, power requirements, and the need for heat dissipation. Philco delivered the world's first commercial, all-transistor, large-scale data-processing system – TRANSAC S2000 – during 1958. Eight such systems were scheduled for delivery in 1959; sixteen were in production in 1960.

At the turn of the decade, Philco sales had been increasing fairly regularly, as shown in Table 1.

Still Philco was ailing. A breakdown of 1960 sales figures

revealed an 11 per cent decline in refrigerator unit volume, a decrease of 14 per cent in home laundry volume, and the third worst year in company for TV sets, sales of which had dipped 9 per cent. Despite high total sales, in short, 1960 was a problem year for Philco. Erratic swings in the profit picture intensified financial problems. While after-tax earnings in 1959 were almost three times the 1958 level, 1960 profits had again slipped to a disappointing 2·3 million dollars on sales of more than 400 million dollars. Cash dividends, paid on Philco stock without interruption for thirty-six years, had been discontinued in 1956. After that, they had been paid only in 1959. Philco's financial condition was also reflected in a drop in the price of its common stock. While the general stock market fell by roughly 12 per cent during 1960, the market value of Philco common was drastically reduced by 43·5 per cent between the end of 1959 and the close of 1960 – from 130·4 million dollars to 73·6 million. The stock-buying public was obviously not infatuated with Philco's earnings prospects.

Philco's profit squeeze was largely due to high start-up costs in its computer division. A great deal of money had been sunk into this effort, and Philco computers were still a long way from bringing in some return on the investment. While the long-term future of computers looked promising to the firm at the end of 1960, no substantial profits were expected for several years. Thus, computers were weakening the short-term earnings position of the company. Philco management apparently felt that government contracts would not increase materially in the short term and decided that consumer appliances would somehow have to take up the slack. As we have seen, it would not be easy to turn the tide with the help of this division, since the entire appliance market was depressed and Philco was on relatively poor financial footing in a troubled industry.

Appliances in 1961

Until mid-1961 the appliance industry remained depressed. Then, during May and June, the slump levelled off. Record-breaking personal disposable income bolstered consumer confidence.

Customer complaints about appliance servicing seemed to wane with improvements in product quality. Housing starts, directly affecting the sale of new appliances, were slowly rising. Increased dealer orders were reported throughout the industry. For the first time in two years, economic observers detected some evidence of a genuine upturn by autumn of 1961, especially in 'white goods' (washing machines, deep-freezes, refrigerators, ranges). Prospects for 'brown goods' (radios, television receivers, sound systems) were still uncertain.

By July, optimism was running decidedly higher than it had ever been in the previous eighteen months. The industry seemed about to turn a corner in the second half of the year. Norge, Kelvinator, and others stepped up promotional spending; most producers speeded up production schedules. By autumn, the business press could report that inventories were at the lowest point in months and that prices were holding fairly steady. But it was still quite unlikely that major increases in demand would come along until there was a healthy jump in household formation, and such a boom was not expected until the 1970s, when post-war babies would be grown up, married, and in the process of becoming householders. The industry was definitely not yet ready to return to its old growth position. And some basic problems still existed. Retail competition, for instance, remained strong and many distributors still felt frustrated. The industry as a whole looked towards year-end with guarded optimism.

As for Philco, its financial condition worsened during 1961. *Financial World* noted that, whereas the price of Philco common stock had climbed from 18 to 21 during the first three months of 1961, Philco had actually gone into the red – and not for the first time, either. Philco's president, Mr James Skinner, Jr, frankly told stockholders, 'Perhaps we have not done as good a job as we should have, but we are trying hard and won't concede that we have taken a nose dive.' Skinner cited as reasons for financial difficulty the 1960 recession, a hard winter with disappointing holiday sales, and the extended costs of computer production. (Supposedly ending in 1960, but revised to a new target date of 1963 or 1964, long-range expenditure planning now called for eventually making computers the firm's major profit centre.) The first quarter of 1961 resulted in a net loss of $1,603,000 for Philco.

By mid-year, Philco had followed other television set manufacturers in announcing that it would market colour TV sets in the autumn of 1961. The company added that TV sets and electronic receiving tube sales were gaining and that this might cover initial losses. However, the *Wall Street Journal* continued to report increasing deficits for Philco during 1961. By August, the loss had increased to $4,372,000. At that time, the corporation announced that unprofitable product lines would be discontinued to forestall further cuts in earnings. Coupled with this announcement were rumours, denied by Philco, that some distributors were shifting to other suppliers. By the end of September, Philco sales volume had reached $304,415,000; yet, the operating deficit then totalled $5,778,000.

Ford Flirts with Philco

Meanwhile, Ford Motor Company had started a flirtation with Philco. The object – matrimony. Though it was not known publicly until September, overtures had been made by Ford towards a possible Ford–Philco merger or acquisition early in 1961. Ford had looked into scores of electronics companies but was particularly interested in entering negotiations to acquire Philco. There were a number of explanations for this, but basically the reasons were rooted in Philco's broad base in the electronics and defence industries as well as consumer appliances. For purely competitive reasons, of course, Ford obviously had some interest in large household appliances. General Motors – Ford's arch-enemy – and American Motors were more diversified than Ford; they were already heavily involved in the appliance business. And Chrysler produced and sold air-conditioning units.

But Ford was chiefly attracted by Philco's defence and space-electronics business. Ford had long been a supplier to the defence market – primarily in the field of conventional weapons such as trucks and tanks. Defence needs, however, had clearly shifted towards nuclear, electronics, and space programmes. True, Ford's

Aeronutronic Division had been specifically created by Ford in 1956 to shift its participation in the defence market towards missiles, but sales and earnings were still unsatisfactory in 1961. (Ford's defence business had declined from fifty-six million dollars in 1959 to forty-two million dollars in 1960, a figure representing less than 1 per cent of total revenue.) Ford clearly needed a more flexible operation for adjusting to the rapidly changing technologies of electronics and nuclear development. Henry Ford II, according to *Barron's*, said the motives behind an acquisition manoeuvre were to broaden Ford's operations, to provide entry into new fields, and make possible a fuller participation in the defence and space effort. Space research, defence electronics, and nuclear production were the reasons stressed. Appliance manufacturing would presumably be but a secondary consideration if Ford were to acquire Philco.

Philco seemed to fill Ford's diversification needs neatly. It showed promise of long-term strength in defence markets. It was a prime contractor for certain missile components, for example, and it had successfully set up and maintained vast space detection and tracking systems for NASA and the North American Defense Command. In both appliances and electronics, actually, Philco held out long-range growth prospects despite pestiferous short-run weaknesses. The *Wall Street Journal* put it rather correctly when it said that it was these very weaknesses that made Philco attractive to Ford.

In evaluating Philco, Ford's people viewed the timing as ripe for acquisition. With low earnings and depressed stock values, Philco would come cheaply. In the eyes of Ford, the basic problems could be remedied. Perhaps all that was needed was time to solve them. But, essentially, Ford thought it could add precisely what Philco seemed to lack – money and management. Ford felt it could supply Philco with top executives, institute cost-saving steps to change some red ink into black, and generally increase operating efficiency through improved organizational procedures and the transplantation of more effective operating policies into Philco soil.

93

Philco's Strategy in 1961

Throughout the first three-quarters of 1961, Philco was steering a difficult and hazardous course between the Scylla of short-run deficits and the Charybdis of long-range disaster. A deal with Ford, of course, could unquestionably strengthen Philco; if everything worked out well, new capital would become available. Philco might then be able to pursue any course of action that Ford could be persuaded to endorse and finance.

But, long before any Ford take-over could be agreed upon, Philco officials were forced to revise their marketing strategies. With or without a Ford–Philco partnership, Philco had to act with dispatch to get itself headed back into the black and build up some working capital. An accumulation of pressures had overwhelmingly tipped the strategic balance away from long-range solutions and towards short-term operations which might produce quick results. Their planning horizons thus shortened, Philco officials cast about for some effective means to attain desired ends.

With high-cost computer development efforts now extended well beyond 1961, with new products (colour TV sets) to bring to market, and with only a few sales categories on the upswing, the critical loss of working capital forced a revision of plans. Philco planned to curtail non-profitable product lines, to cut back on long-range research and development projects which held little promise of a quick investment payback, and to concentrate on getting volume sales in appliances in order to improve the immediate earnings position of the company. The onus fell on its Consumer Products Division. How would this one organizational unit pull Philco's chestnuts from the fire?

Product development was not the answer. Philco appliances were already quite good, and there was little hope of getting quick and decisive results from the product variable alone. Some other element of the marketing mix would have to carry the load. Theoretically, of course, profits might be sought through price increases. But foreign rivals and the sluggish domestic market didn't leave much elbow-room for action in the pricing sphere. Nor could Philco hope to advertise itself out of the rut. There just wasn't enough cash in the coffers to cover heavy promotional out-lays. This seemed to leave but one major component of marketing strategy – distribution.

Philco had long been interested in ways to strengthen its dis-tribution network. (One earlier effort had consisted of offering a ninety-day Television Service Warranty covering both parts and labour. But such action was by no means enough to turn the tide.) As *Electrical Merchandising Week* later pointed out, Philco had slowly been losing market penetration. Distribution had been cited as the number one problem in the division for several years and, while Philco executives may have been strongly motivated to grasp for some panacea, the search for a truly fundamental dis-tribution remedy had thus far been in vain.

To sum up the basic outlines of Philco's strategic posture in the autumn of 1961 – the task was to produce an immediate im-provement in earnings. This job was handed over to the Con-sumer Products Division. There, distribution was seen as the key to profitable appliance marketing, but a really basic solution to distribution problems would probably be needed and time was short. Whether anyone intended to do so or not, the seeds were thus sown for a tremendous distribution gamble.

THE INSTANT DIVIDEND PLAN

In autumn 1961, Philco hit the business world with a block-buster, the so-called 'Instant Dividend Plan'. This programme – generally referred to as 'ID' – was the creation of Richard E. Scott of Sterling, Illinois. According to *Business Week*, Scott sold the plan to Philco for $28,000 plus royalties.

A unique merchandising scheme and simple in basic concept, ID would allow Philco to sell large household appliances through high-volume grocery supermarkets, with a lift built in for ap-pliance retailers, too. The plan would rest ultimately on close co-operation and co-ordination between supermarkets and local Philco dealers. The heart of the plan was that the consumer was to be given, as a bonus for purchasing groceries at a particular supermarket, an opportunity to earn appliances as premium items.

She was simply to save her cash-register tapes, as she might otherwise save trading stamps, and apply them towards monthly instalment payments on selected appliances. The ID plan, occasionally referred to by the more descriptive name of 'cash-register tape plan', would thus reward the housewife with the *dividend* of a major appliance if she concentrated her purchases at a single supermarket participating in the ID programme.

The supermarket shopper was to receive her appliance *instantly*, as soon as she had selected it and been approved by Philco for participation in the plan. In other words, the customer did not have to wait for her prize as was the case in stamp hoarding. She was to get an immediate return from shopping at a particular store. For this reason, the incentive programme came to be dubbed 'The Instant Dividend Plan'. Details of the scheme were more difficult to define and explain.

ID Mechanics

Philco's ID plan worked something like this:* A local franchised Philco appliance dealer tied up with a selected supermarket, presumably with the co-operation of the manufacturer and the Philco distributor in the area. Both the participating Philco dealer and the supermarket had to pass muster with the Philco Finance Corporation, a subsidiary set up some years before by Philco that would now extend its operations to finance and administer the ID programme.

The supermarket was given an exclusive contract on the plan and agreed to provide floor space for displaying major appliances. The Philco dealer then set up a display of the several items to be

* As will be pointed out later, the ID plan was quickly imitated in slightly modified forms. The letters 'ID' came to be applied generically to all these plans, although Philco had copyrighted the name for its exclusive use. The business press sometimes confused the variant schemes and, as a result, the published descriptions of ID details were often inconsistent. In this section, I have relied most heavily on an article by E. B. Weiss in the January 22, 1962, issue of *Advertising Age* and have supplemented Weiss's description with materials selected from various issues of *Electrical Merchandising Week*, *Dun's Review and Modern Industry*, *Sales Management*, and the *Wall Street Journal*. Neither Mr Skinner nor any other person who read my description has found reason to quarrel with it.

offered and staffed the space with a salesman, who would explain the ID plan to supermarket clientele and demonstrate the units.

The supermarket shopper usually selected an appliance directly from this display, although she might also be sent to the dealer's store to see an item shown only in brochures at the supermarket. She signed an agreement to buy it on a no-down-payment in-stalment plan. At this point, the customer was required only to fill out a credit application form, a purchased contract, and other necessary papers. Philco then ran a credit check, demanding the same credit standing as would be required under any other time-payment plan. The customer contracted to pay for her appliance in twelve to thirty-six monthly instalments of ten or fifteen dollars, depending on the price of the item selected. If approved by Philco Finance, she would have her appliance promptly de-livered, installed, and serviced by the local Philco dealer, who also gave her the customary guarantees and warranties.

Once the contract was taken over by Philco Finance, the dealer was immediately paid for his appliance, being compensated very much as in the case where he made a normal credit sale in his own store, with the paper handled by the Philco Finance Corporation.

Upon delivery of the selected appliance, the customer also received a personal, non-transferable card that certified her participation in the ID plan. When this card was presented at the supermarket check-out counter it worked like other credit cards; it was used to impress or stamp data on the cash-register tapes received by the customer when she paid for food and other purchases.

Each month, the authenticated tapes were submitted to the supermarket for credit. (Tapes had to be presented for credit by the customer within sixty – and preferably thirty – days.) The food store granted a maximum credit of $5\frac{1}{2}$ per cent of the total on the tapes submitted. That credit was applied to the agreed-upon price of the appliance.

The tape credit was limited so that part of the appliance had to be paid for with cash. That is, the appliance could not be paid off entirely by tapes alone. There was a monthly limit of $7.50 in

97

tape credit where a customer had agreed to pay $10 monthly for her appliance. A limit of $10 in tape credit was placed on instalment payments of $15, which was the maximum amount that could be paid against the purchase price of the appliance each month. The difference between the tape credit and the monthly instalment figure was paid in cash.

The payment part of the ID plan can best be clarified with a concrete illustration. Suppose Mrs Smith has decided to buy a $200 television set, contracting to pay $10 per month for twenty months. At the end of the first month under the plan, her supermarket purchases add up to $130 (the average food bill for a family of four). At the 5½ per cent rate, she is entitled to a credit of $7.15, and instead of paying the full $10 monthly payment on her TV set she pays only $2.85 in cash. If she continues to buy groceries at the rate of $130 each month, she ends up paying only $57 in cash for her set.

The sale price of the selected appliance was fixed by the Philco dealer. Trade-ins could be accepted. Although some dealers took low mark-ups, the customer normally paid full list price for her appliance. State sales taxes, service and delivery costs, and financing charges were added to the price. The customer paid the normal finance rates for the area in which she lived.

The Appeal of an Instant Dividend

This particular plan of action was chosen by Philco because of its apparently universal appeal. It seemed attractive to everyone concerned. Philco, dealers and distributors, supermarkets, and ultimate consumers all stood to benefit, for ID was many things to many people. As President Skinner later remarked, 'It is interesting to note that everybody that was against it wasn't in it.'

To consumers, ID offered something for nothing or, at least, something at reduced cost. It offered a new alternative way to buy appliances and a chance to secure a rather large amount of credit. While no immediate cash outlay was required, the consumer enjoyed the immediate possession and use of a major appliance merely by changing or reinforcing her buying behaviour somewhat.

To Philco, badly in need of a new approach to the appliance market, ID represented an attractively fast solution to its distribution problems. It gave the consumer a new 'easy to buy' method for acquiring household appliances with supermarkets footing part of the bill. ID might also enliven dealer and distributor interest and strengthen Philco's weakened distribution system, since dealers would have a chance at more high-traffic business exposure than they could otherwise hope to get. New access to previously unexposed potential customers, coupled with more frequent exposure to actual Philco owners shopping in supermarkets, might lead customers into a Philco dealer's showroom. In short, supermarkets would add a new type of retail outlet, deepen Philco's market penetration, and extend distribution out-reach towards the final consumer – all at a time of modest expansion in general industry demand and all without bypassing the traditional retail appliance dealer. Supermarkets would assume part of the burden of appliance marketing and join ranks. Thus, a new distribution channel would be created by the fresh synthesis of both old and new marketing institutions.

To supermarkets – always on the lookout for new ways to increase patronage – ID held out tempting benefits. Some saw ID as a Messianic device for getting more customers to buy more merchandise in at least three distinct ways. It would function first as a traffic-builder; the first local supermarket to hook up with Philco could probably attract some *new customers* from competitive supermarkets and other retailers. Promotion-minded supermarkets saw in ID an alternative to trading stamps and other merchandising gimmicks employed to draw new business away from competitors. Although trading stamps, in particular, had broad consumer appeal because they were redeemable for a wide variety of goods, they were seemingly losing their punch. When every store in an area offered stamps, supermarkets were actually encouraging people to shop around by sponsoring double and multiple stamp offers. Stamps no longer gave a store much of a unique competitive advantage. Thus, supermarkets viewed ID as a new step forward, especially for the store that installed it first in an area and got people signed up. Furthermore, the discount

99

houses were beginning to hurt the supermarkets. Having started out in appliances, discounters were rapidly branching out into new product lines – including foods. ID would give the super-markets a chance to strike back at the discount house and take away some of its trade.

Second, ID might help to increase the size of purchases made by *regular customers* of the food store. Any intelligent housewife would surely realize that the more she spent in a market affiliated with ID, the more credit she would get on her prized appliance. Hopefully, ID would motivate the shopper to buy more products, and some of these items might be of a variety often bought elsewhere, such as toiletries and other non-foods carrying high mark-ups.

Third, ID might help supermarkets stamp out the bugbear of split-shopping, wherein consumers divided their patronage between two or more competing supermarkets. The plan might provide the incentive for consumers to concentrate their pur-chases at just one supermarket. Thus ID could foster one-store loyalty or *captive customers*.

As if anything more were needed to cement a deal, it should be noted that the supermarket and appliance people had more than once joined forces to their mutual welfare long before ID came along. As Mort Farr, chairman of the National Appliance and Radio-TV Dealers Association, was quick to point out, ID was a reverse take-off on older 'deep-freeze plans'. Much earlier in commercial history, supermarket shoppers had bought deep-freezes loaded with food and contracted to have them restocked at predetermined intervals. Under ID, people just bought food, and a portion of their purchases might be applied towards the payment of deep-freezes and other appliances.

Philco, in particular, had established close ties with super-markets under a plan somewhat like ID in the early fifties. During 1950 and 1951, when television had first become an important educational tool, Philco reportedly moved about twenty thousand receiving sets through the Acme markets into local classrooms via cash-register tape credits. However, this gambit, while commercially successful by itself, was chiefly conceived as a public service. Acme apparently never did become interested in extending the method on a regular basis. Be it said, however, that Philco was certainly not anti-supermarket. Past experience with them had been fruitful. Philco, it will be recalled, had decided to move ahead with the marketing of colour TV sets in the autumn of 1961. Philco management, with the history of a happy supermarket partnership behind them, figured that television sets might once again be sold through supermarkets. If successful, such a play might be doubly significant, for colour TV sets were very difficult to sell at the time.

If Philco, its distributors and dealers, the supermarkets, and householders all stood to gain from the Instant Divident Plan, who was to pay the piper? Although the real answer is still cloaked in some secrecy, the cost of the plan would clearly be a function of the number of customers signed up, the average price they agreed to pay for their appliances, and the amount of premium credit they earned on supermarket purchases. The $5\frac{1}{2}$ per cent rebate to the consumer was to be split between Philco and participating supermarkets on some kind of sliding scale. If a customer were to spend $50 or less in a supermarket each month, Philco would pick up the bill. If, however, the housewife's monthly food bills were to reach $120 or more, the supermarket would pay 3 per cent and Philco $2\frac{1}{2}$ per cent.

ID IN OPERATION

The ID plan seemed to be a short-cut solution to problems facing both Philco and the supermarkets. At the outset, each party thought the scheme was enough of a bargain to warrant moving ahead with it.

Launching the Plan

Philco kicked off with its new plan in the autumn of 1961 and managed to get it established with amazing swiftness. Although initially rebuffed by the American Stores Company, Philco started a dry run in the Midwest, in the B&A Markets of Midland, Michigan. This pilot attempt to put the plan over in September

1961 was not widely publicized. Supposedly successful, however, it encouraged Philco to push on and open a bigger show with ID.

By late October, Philco was negotiating with Thorofare Markets, a Pittsburgh-based chain (1960 sales 123 million dollars) of stores in Pennsylvania, West Virginia, and Ohio. On November 7, ID officially bowed in Thorofare's Pittsburgh unit, reputed to be the most promotion-minded store in the city. Thorofare was said to have experienced a hearty consumer response. In any event, Louis B. Smith, Jr, president of the chain, was soon sufficiently satisfied to announce the expansion of ID to cover all of his stores.

Philco pushed the plan vigorously that autumn and rounded up a number of other supermarket chains, or parts of them, in different sections of the country. By mid-November, they had lined up Hinky-Dinky Stores of Omaha, which agreed to use the plan in four of its units in Lincoln and Columbus, Nebraska. Big 'C' installed ID in seven of its supermarkets in Oregon and Washington. Colonial Stores, with 450 units mostly in the South, made plans to tie in with Philco, initially authorizing ID displays in eight stores. By late November, Food Fair, another of the nation's largest food chains with 450 stores, announced that it expected to institute the plan in its Eastern and Southern divisions. Food Fair first experimented with ID in Lansdale, a suburb of Philadelphia. This area was of special interest to Philco, for although a principal company plant was located there, the company had experienced difficulties in gaining a market toehold around Lansdale. Thus, by swinging the Food Fair deal, Philco hoped to penetrate its own home market with real power for the first time. Food Fair also announced that it planned to expand ID to other areas of the country at a later date. During this same period, Jewel Tea agreed to test it in San Francisco, and Stop & Shop, Inc., of Boston, said it would try the new plan in some of its 130 units operating in New England. By early December, Eberhard Supermarkets had introduced ID to nineteen stores in Grand Rapids and Owosso, Michigan, and Star Supermarkets had launched the programme in forty-one stores in up-state New York.

In the course of a few weeks, ID became a large-scale operation covering over two hundred food stores. From a modest beginning, ID had become a household term in many markets in just about a month.

Immediate Results

Early reports on the results of ID were largely enthusiastic. Sales under the plan had often sky-rocketed, and some observers hailed the programme as a truly creative and revolutionary development in food and appliance distribution. For the most part, those directly participating in the plan were a very happy family. ID appeared to be doing precisely what it was supposed to do for everyone concerned.

Consumers seemed pleased with ID, for early participation was even greater than the planners had originally expected. Philco dealers associated with ID were overjoyed with the shot in the arm it gave them, and the trade press carried quotes from several exuberant dealers. In late November, a salesman for a Philco dealership linked to Thorofare said that business under the plan was 'fantastic'. While declining to cite hard figures, he claimed that, 'We have sold more appliances in the last three weeks than we've sold all year. Business is so good we bought a new truck to make deliveries.' It was rumoured that over 3,300 appliances moved through Thorofare Markets in Pittsburgh in the first six weeks with ID. In Coalesville, Pennsylvania, a dealer who previously had complained about discounters in his market had this to say: 'In the first two weeks I did some six month's volume. I'm selling ten times as many appliances as before, mostly in the upper price ranges, and all at list price.'

Supermarkets tied in with ID also appeared to enjoy all the benefits originally predicted – new customers, larger purchases, less split-shopping. Some of the first supermarkets to report on the plan cited remarkable success stories. In Pittsburgh, shoppers reportedly stocked their pantries full of groceries, asked neighbours to buy food and other items for them, and used other methods to accumulate appliance credits. Many new supermarkets were negotiating with Philco for ID privileges. Thus, the atmosphere during the first few weeks of ID's operation was decidely rosy.

Imitation by Competitors

If imitation and adaptation are the sincerest forms of flattery, Philco's new merchandising concept was soon to be shown in even more favourable light. Few supermarkets were totally disinterested in ID, and many were afraid of underestimating its power. As news of ID's success spread like wildfire through the food and appliance industry, supermarkets quickly linked arms with rival appliance dealers and offered similar plans.

Loblaw's, a forty-three-store Pittsburgh supermarket chain, offered an AB (Appliance Bonus) Plan featuring Norge and Sylvania appliances. In fact, AB actually beat ID to the punch in Pittsburgh. While Philco had quietly tried its plan for some time, ID was not officially introduced to the public until November 7 in the Pittsburgh area. Mr Melvin S. Landow had smelled what was cooking, visited an ID test store, and heard the ringing of bells. 'To me,' he said later, 'a connection between food and appliances in the supermarket is a perfect marriage.' Landow concocted the AB plan in a hurry and installed it at Loblaw's on November 5 – two days before ID became official. Loblaw later called its AB plan a 'complete success', claimed to have moved 'trainloads of merchandise' with it, and suggested that the plan might well 'set a new selling pattern for supermarkets'.

Right on the heels of Loblaw and Thorofare, Giant Eagle Markets began to offer a GB (Giant Bonus) Plan in its thirty-two stores after joining forces with Emerson and Kelvinator dealers in Pittsburgh. But Giant Eagle was less enthusiastic. 'We're not happy about getting into this,' a store official was quoted as saying, 'but it was necessary. Several instances have come to our attention where we have lost regular customers who are leaving Giant Eagle to sign up at a competitor who is offering the plan.' In a very short time, three of Pittsburgh's five major chains were 'wading waist-high in appliance tapes'. Every appliance distributor in Pittsburgh and Philadelphia was reportedly approached by at least one local supermarket to discuss ID-type programmes.

Elsewhere in the nation, interest in ID was also reported. The nationwide A&P stores, which already offered tape deals on specialty items such as watches, considered expanding the plan to include major appliances. But most variations on the plan were strictly local in nature. For instance, Walt's Super Markets – a chain with eight stores in Indianapolis – teamed up with an Admiral dealer in that city. Philco was the only major appliance manufacturer to support ID on anything like a national basis, and Pittsburgh – incubator of variations on the ID theme – proved to be the chief battleground for the plans.

ID KICKS OFF A MERCHANDISING WAR

By early December 1961, supermarket tape plans were growing like a bunch of fantastically healthy babies. But *Electrical Merchandising Week* remarked that 'to some observers the infant looks more like a monster'. From the outset, many had questioned whether ID was really an ingenious merchandising scheme destined for widespread and lasting success. Some onlookers, not swayed by the initial progress of ID, were passive. Others openly ridiculed the plan and sarcastically dubbed it a 'gimmick' and 'a flash in the pan'. Still others bitterly denounced ID as something that would bring certain disaster to everyone touched by it, one fellow commenting crisply that 'ID' stood for 'Instant Death' or 'Insane Delusion'. Soon the fur began to fly. Not since the discount house had delivered its near-mortal blow to resale price maintenance had there been such heated controversy in the world of appliance marketing.

Supermarket Counteraction

The tape-plan concept was anathema to many non-participating supermarket operators. Some were envious because they were too late to get on the bandwaggon themselves. Some were appalled at the idea of 'captive customers' being tied to a single store for years by the plan. Other holdouts were irritated by the grumbling of regular customers requesting ID. Some were just vaguely fearful of the encroaching success of participating markets. Using such ammunition as outdoor signs, newspaper ads, store windows, and word-of-mouth, they declared open warfare on ID in Pittsburgh.

Typical of the enemy camp was Verscharen Markets, a major independent food store. Verscharen needled Thorofare and ID with in-store placards reading 'Thorofare – Too Big to be So Small'. Verscharen also placed cartoon-type newspaper ads featuring a caricatured coal miner chanting the words, 'I owe my soul to the company store . . . with stamps, gimmicks, and tapes.' Another independent, Haines Supermarket, posted a huge outdoor sign warning shoppers that, 'The high-price stores are offering less desirable appliances at ridiculous prices and you're paying for them. For example, a portable TV that lists for $159 and can be bought for $125 is listed at twenty-seven payments of $10 per month, or $270.' Kroger units in Pittsburgh, losing regular customers to tape-plan markets, retaliated by doubling the number of trading stamps offered during the heavy Thanksgiving shopping period. Some stores responded with special sales and unusually attractive price-off promotions. Others took the tack of simply promoting the absence of a tape plan as a shopper advantage, hinting that food prices were raised to cover the costs of the appliance programme in stores connected with it.

In the face of such adverse publicity, which had the effect confusing the ordinary shopper, tape-plan markets experienced some misgivings and began to perceive new drawbacks in the programme. Freshly lost new customers, the partial loss of merchandising control resulting from having another merchant operating in effect on supermarket premises, the slowing up of checkout procedures by ID clients, and the frustration experienced when shoppers unjustly blamed the supermarket for faulty appliance performance and servicing which was really the responsibility of the manufacturer and his dealers all injected sour notes into the score. Some supermarkets felt that bulky appliances gobbled up too much of their precious floor space, which might better be allocated to other products and services. As imitators came out with their own versions of ID, exclusivity was lost. Further doubts about the efficacy of the plan developed as some feared the same kind of stalemate that had developed in trading stamps. Those tied up with it simply couldn't give it up unless everyone else followed suit; yet, the plan produced a heavy built-in overhead burden. And outside observers seriously questioned whether traditionally low-margin supermarkets could long afford to share in the giving of discounts on appliances.

Despite such doubts, however, tape-plan marts initially weathered the storm of protest and publicly defended the plans while inwardly adopting a stance of watchful waiting. If supermarkets were the first to feel some pinch from ID, appliance dealers were not far behind.

Furore Among Appliance Dealers

'How can it miss? It helps the dealer and the consumer!' 'It has put the small dealer in a panic!' Such contradictory statements appeared early in the game as ID battle lines began to form. We have noted that some dealers were zealous adherents and champions of ID, believing it to be a sure-fire way to move big-ticket goods *en masse*. But there was a deep schism among appliance dealers similar to that which developed in the supermarket industry. While some dealers enjoyed a sales boom, others were fretting.

Philco dealers were frustrated for a number of reasons. The plan itself was inherently discriminatory; it was clear from the beginning that some dealers would be left out simply because the number and locations of participating supermarkets did not precisely match dealer coverage patterns. Philco tried to meet this problem by having several dealers participate in a given supermarket on a rotating basis. But the solution was sticky in actual practice. One dealer could set up a sale only to lose it the next day to another dealer whose turn it happened to be to work the supermarket at that time. Some dealer resentment and alienation was an inevitable result, as individual outlets felt they had come out on the short end of the deal.

Other Philco dealers feared that ID was the beginning of the end for franchised appliance merchants. They suspected that once ID had become firmly established Philco would begin to sell directly to the supermarkets – bypassing dealers and distributors altogether and leaving them out in the cold. Thus, the plan, designed to bolster distribution, could weaken dealer loyalty and threaten traditional manufacturer–dealer relations. Although Philco tried to assuage these fears with assurances that dealers would forever make up the primary membership of the distribution system and that ID represented but 'an extension of the dealer's showroom into the supermarket', some dealers continued to perceive ID as a threat to their very existence and fought a bitter campaign against the programme or shifted to new suppliers.

In essence, the dealer reaction was rooted in uncertainty. Nobody knew what sales volume would ultimately be traced to ID, what the level and incidence of the full cost burden would eventually become, how long the plan would last, or what the net impact would be on established trade channels. Uncertainty and confusion bred fear in some dealers, whose natural response was to retreat from ID and to wish for the plan's destruction.

Competitive appliance dealers also reacted negatively. One Pittsburgh dealer posted a card in his shop window reading, 'Don't let yourself fall victim to a food market appliance purchase scheme. Buy your appliance at a lower price HERE; compare first. Retain your freedom of shopping choice. Demand a discount on your food purchase without buying an appliance. Beware of being overpurchased on future FOOD PRICES.' General Electric dealers in Pittsburgh ran newspaper ads stating that, 'Nobody, but nobody gives away anything for nothing. Yes, $4,732 in groceries, all from one store, will buy a low-priced television, and it should. But you can own this most reliable GE television receiver for $159.95 and you can save money on food bargains at any store you choose.' A Westinghouse distributor, while not referring directly to ID, bought a full-page newspaper ad calling attention to easy credit terms and low prices at Westinghouse dealerships. Furthermore, many dealers complained that the selling of appliances in self-service outlets would downgrade and destroy the creative and aggressive personal demonstration and salesmanship deemed essential to appliance marketing.

The organized resistance of several trade groups pressed the battle. Dealer-oriented trade publications came out strongly against ID. For instance, Mr Nathan Boolhack took up the cudgel editorially in the December 1961 issue of *Electronic and Appliance Specialist*. Referring to ID as a 'new competitive threat' and a 'crackpot scheme', Boolhack charged any manufacturer supporting tape plans with 'selling his birthright for a mess of groceries and destroying his legitimate dealer structure at the same time'. Taking a position unqualifiedly against the plans, he summarized by stating that, 'Under the plan, a family would have to eat itself into the grave in order to "earn" a major appliance. It just doesn't make sense. This is an ill-conceived scheme which can wreck havoc with an industry which is already subject to more than its share of slings and arrows.' In Chicago, the *Buyer's Guide to Nationally Advertised Home Furnishings* threatened to exclude Philco from its spring and summer catalogue, published for some 150 retailers in the area. In early December, Mr Laurence Wray, editor of *Electrical Merchandising Week*, referred to tape plans as a 'phenomenon of the post-war retailing revolution', predicted that they would 'spread like a prairie fire across the nation by the time the snows begin to melt and the baseball training camps are open for business', speculated on the answers to a variety of 'disturbing questions' relating to ID, and ended his editorial with these peevish words: 'We never got into soup or salami, soap flakes or cigarettes, tooth powder or Pablum, pickles or peanuts. Why this once-proud industry feels that it must engage in sales-slip shenanigans, or become bloodied with ketchup, is a little incomprehensible.' Meanwhile, in his weekly crystal-ball column in *Advertising Age*, E. B. Weiss envisaged an early and justifiable death for the ID plan and its close relatives.

NARDA – the National Appliance and Radio-TV Dealers Association – hastily passed a resolution condemning the tape deals. NARDA officials quickly jumped to the conclusion that dealers were in jeopardy and that consumers were being hood-winked by the programmes. 'We call it a crime,' said Jules Steinberg, executive vice-president of the group, in late Novem-ber. Victor P. Joerndt, then president of the six-thousand-member association (and himself an appliance dealer in Kenosha,

Wisconsin), expressed revulsion at ID. 'As any housewife knows,' declared Joerndt, 'judicious shopping of various supermarkets – buying one special here and another there – can result in savings of more than \$2.00 on the household's weekly food budget.' These savings could be added up and spent in any way the consumer so chose. Joerndt continued: 'I believe that once these facts are known to the public, food tape plans will fall of their own weight. It is the duty of every appliance dealer to see to it that this job of education is accomplished swiftly.' He advocated newspaper ads and talks before local women's groups as means for stamping out ID.

But some NARDA members continued to be intrigued by the possibilities of the plan, and the association's dogmatic position began to soften. NARDA called a committee meeting in December to consider the subject more objectively, stating carefully that the group (a) did not have a complete understanding of the workings of the tape plans, (b) did not see any legal loopholes in them, and (c) had heard of no producers with a definite disinterest in starting such programmes. However, it felt that the plans were essentially a promotional gimmick that could be met by other dealer promotions. By January 1962, when NARDA held its convention in Chicago, the association was following a middle-of-the-road approach. Some dealers seemed to be saying, 'Why fight them when you can join in and make money?' A few dealers came to the convention with blood in their eyes. The bulk of NARDA's membership reportedly came just to listen to the extremists. As the smoke began to clear, NARDA further hedged its original position. A new policy was adopted. Henceforth, the association would act as 'a clearing-house for all the pros and cons'. Sam Boyd, newly elected NARDA president said, 'There is no censure or criticism of the tape plan from NARDA. We'll watch it very closely. We see some dangers.' Mort Farr, chairman of the NARDA board, prophesied that 'there will be an initial impact that will diminish. I don't think the plan will have a life of over six months'. A week after the Chicago convention, the ambivalent association leadership had almost completely reversed its original stand. NARDA was reported conferring with Philco officials and ready to endorse ID if Philco would change certain features that were unacceptable to NARDA, such as the basis for selecting participating dealers.

A strong note of opposition to tape plans was sounded at a mass meeting in Pittsburgh sponsored by the 187-member Electronic Service Dealers Association of Western Pennsylvania. Joseph Doyle, the group's secretary, warned of dealer disaster, consumer discrimination, and the possible illegality of such programmes. The group urged dealers to fight against the plans, distributed seventy-five thousand handbills to supermarket shoppers denouncing ID, drew up a petition asking the Federal Trade Commission to look into the situation, and threatened Ford Motor Company that they would buy no Ford automotive equipment until Philco had scrapped ID in the Pittsburgh area. (Ford had acquired Philco in early December.)

The Reaction of Appliance Manufacturers

ID also caused a stir among the producers. First to tee off publicly against tape plans was Mr S. R. Herkes, marketing vice-president for consumer products at Motorola. Herkes asserted that the appliance industry had been 'brainwashed' into seeking easy short-cut solutions to fundamental marketing problems. He blasted ID plans as degrading and claimed that the programmes were 'a deliberate violation of the trust or franchise which should exist' between manufacturers and their dealers.

Another sharp critic was R. C. Connell, sales vice-president for the Eureka Williams Company. At a press conference Connell attacked the ID concept. 'No manufacturer, except as a last desperate gamble or as an act of self-defence, or one who cared nothing of his company name or future, would take such a foolish step. Of course he can do a large business volume for a short while. But other food chains and other equally desperate manufacturers won't let him cut them up for long. In short, he is having a full-course dinner before taking a morning-after walk to extinction.' Concluding, like many others, that the results of these plans would undermine the industry's whole retailing structure, he made it clear that his firm would not adopt an ID plan.

Meanwhile, most of the appliance behemoths – GE, Hotpoint, Westinghouse, GM – were mutely avoiding the scrap and refraining from public comment on ID. Between the silent giants and the vociferous attackers of ID on the manufacturing side of the fence stood two other camps. Companies like Kelvinator, Sylvania, and Norge walked a tightrope; while publicly opposing factory-sponsored tape plans, they permitted dealers to act on their own and form tape arrangements at the local level. RCA, Maytag, and others issued official statements which were almost non-committal, except for mild overtones of disapproval at the mention of ID. It was quickly apparent that no manufacturer other than Philco was willing to go very far with the tape-plan concept – not, at least, until Philco could prove that it was something more than a short-term gimmick. The chief concern of the manufacturing group, of course, was the fear of disrupting already troubled dealer networks.

Mixed Emotions of Other Observers

Department stores, discount houses, and other kinds of retailers that handled appliances were typically dead set against ID. Yet, as late as mid-January 1962, *Sales Management* magazine said that 'Philco's shrewd merchandising manoeuvre is being watched by many marketers, even envied by some. Philco has outsmarted the appliance giants by coming up with a revolutionary scheme, maybe a brilliant one.'

The Consumers' Concern

Undoubtedly, both Philco and the supermarkets created some customer ill will through credit refusals, the dunning of laggard instalment debtors, and inevitably the repossession of some appliances. This ill will added to the adverse publicity already rained upon ID from other quarters. Individuals sometimes felt inconvenienced by the restricted choices of appliance brands and supermarkets under the plan, and they became restive about being unable to take advantage of store sales, loss leaders, and other consumer attractions offered by non-participating supermarkets without sacrificing tape credits.

The mechanical aspects of tape plans were also bothersome. The programmes were complicated and difficult for many consumers to understand. When people became ill, died, or moved from a neighbourhood, questions arose whether the plans would be suspended or transferred to other persons and other stores. Some housewives asked for impossible exceptions to the rules of the game, e.g. by requesting appliance credit on tapes more than sixty days old. Many such problems had apparently not been anticipated and provided for by the initiators of these plans.

A fundamental question: Was ID a good deal for the final consumer? The best answer seems to be 'Yes and No'. Not all consumers could benefit equally from ID. As *Progressive Grocer* put it, *if* Mrs Housewife had a big family and a big food bill, *if* she liked to shop at the particular appliance-tape store, *if* she had confidence that she would be satisfied with her appliance and the mechanical aspects of the plan – then ID offered definite consumer merit. The plans, in effect, penalized the small family, the housewife preferring to pay cash for her appliances, or the shopper with a houseful of new equipment. And ID offered no new incentive to those shoppers who concentrated their grocery purchases at one supermarket before the plan came along. It was predicted that easily acquired customers would be fickle and quickly shy away from ID as soon as the novelty effect started to evaporate.

The market appeal of ID was substantially more narrow than originally expected. Philco did realize that its plan benefited the large family more than the small and levelled with supermarkets on this basis. But, caught in the crossfire of charge and counter-charge, individuals often could not tell whether they were being helped or harmed by the plans. Emotion-laden and often misleading statements about ID confused the general public. In the interest of consumer protection and education, watchdog groups stepped into the picture.

A Look-see by BBB

'In my twelve years with the Bureau, I have never experienced such a public reaction to any merchandising or marketing programme as the appliance-tape plans. We received hundreds of calls and letters from the public wanting to know what we thought of it,' commented J. K. Orr, Assistant General Manager of Pittsburgh's Better Business Bureau in early 1962.

TABLE 2
COMPARATIVE PRICES ON PHILCO APPLIANCES

Appliance	ID price	List price	Actual retail cash price
	$	$	$
Portable TV			
Model 3222SA	270	212.59	169
Dryer			
Model DE 624	290	244.80	169
Refrigerator			
Model 14RD16	540	397.06	299
Washer			
Model W-22	360	264.70	239
Refrigerator-freezer			
Model 13RD21	420	328.13	299.95

Source: *Electrical Merchandising Week*, December 11, 1961, p. 3.

The BBB was mainly interested in the charge that ID resulted in unusually inflated prices for appliances. This organization undertook extensive comparison shopping to see whether the customer was getting a bargain or not. Some preliminary findings on Philco products by the Bureau are shown in Table 2.

The BBB reported that in many cases tape-plan appliances were being offered in supermarkets 'at prices substantially higher than regular retail going prices for identical items'. Businessmen opposed to ID used such statements as propaganda ammunition to fight the plan.

Actually, however, the new statistics themselves unintentionally tended to mislead the public. The Pittsburgh Bureau made more detailed comparisons, such as the analysis in Table 3, of prices paid for a 19-inch portable TV set.

Any direct comparison of prices seemed to put the ID plan in an unfavourable light. Consider, however, a housewife who spent $120 each month in a food store and received a credit of $6.60 towards her TV set. She paid but $3.40 monthly in cash. Totalled over the twenty-six months of her contract she actually paid out

---

TABLE 3
COMPARATIVE PRICES FOR 19-INCH TELEVISION RECEIVER

Tape-purchase plan	*Direct purchase*
$206.34 – List price	$161.00 – Selling price
53.66 – Financing charge	6.44 – 4% State Sales tax
$260.00 – Total contract balance	$167.44 – Sales price w/tax
8.25 – 4% State sales tax	21.74 – Financing charge
$268.25 – Total	$189.18 – Total contract balance

Source: *Progressive Grocer*, March 1962, p. 71.

---

only $88.40 – far below the dealer asking price and well under the price that even discount houses received. Clearly, such a customer would benefit from ID. Recognizing, nevertheless, that not all shoppers would benefit to this extent, the BBB officially suggested that 'prospective participants should carefully investigate the plans and decide for themselves whether participation . . . is in their own best interest'. Bureaus in such cities as Grand Rapids, Michigan, took similar positions. The BBB statements were front page items in the local papers, and *Advertising Age* carried an article entitled 'Pittsburgh BBB Warns of Supermarket Appliance Buying'. Such publicity was apparently interpreted improperly by casual readers as a condemnation of the plan, and it served to undermine public confidence in ID.

Lawsuits Over ID

To add to an already imposing list of headaches, Philco was sued in a Los Angeles court by Sol Hirschhorn, secretary of the Credit

Merchants Association of Southern California. Hirschhorn's suit, seeking $250,000 in damages, charged that Philco's ID plan was based on an idea that Hirschhorn had submitted at Philco's request in 1955. (Hirschhorn claimed to have copyrighted a plan with similar features in 1952 involving the merchandising of food freezers to retail food stores.) Philco, in turn, filed piracy suits against imitators of the copyrighted Philco plan. One of these defendants came right back with a countersuit for one and a half million dollars, charging Philco with violation of the anti-trust laws and conspiring to fix prices. These legal entanglements were not only costly and frustrating, but their publicity also tended – rightly or wrongly – to give Philco and its ID plan another black eye.

The FTC Investigates

At the end of 1961, the Federal Trade Commission initiated a multipronged probe of cash-register tape deals, teaming up with experts on anti-trust and deceptive practices. To determine whether the public was in any way deceived by ID, they planned to look into descriptive and promotional materials to see if consumer savings were exaggerated, if credit terms were revealed clearly and fully, and if fictitious pricing – such as the deceptive use of list prices at the retail level – had been practised. Possible violations of the Robinson–Patman Act (illegal discrimination between competing retailers in pricing, advertising allowances, or service arrangements) were also sought. In addition, exclusive dealing practices were to be scrutinized to determine whether illegal restraints of trade covered by the Clayton anti-trust act might result from the plan. Extremely broad in scope, this investigation got off to a slow start and dragged on for some time. It, too, put a dent in ID.

ID – Panacea? Palliative? or Poison?

ID truly kicked off a merchandising war, the swiftness, intensity, and scope of which is rarely seen in the business world. Interest in it was wide – surely wider than Philco had foreseen. Supermarkets, discounters, department stores, appliance dealers and distributors, trade associations, newspapers and business publications, the general public, many manufacturers of appliances and other products, Better Business Bureaus, government regulatory agencies, and the courts – they all had a stake in the plan.

As is true in propaganda wars, the rapidity, complexity, and contradictoriness of the claims and responses bred a mixture of emotions – including panic, fear, anger, hatred, tolerance, hope, and bandwagon effects. This ferment brought uncertainty and confusion in its wake. From the outset, it was clear that there was nothing magical about ID – the plan had weaknesses as well as strengths – but the true pros and cons were rarely if ever properly perceived by any one person or group that, at the time, felt its interests to be at issue.

This reaction to ID was totally mixed in character. Believers thought it would prove a panacea at best and a palliative at worst. Scoffers saw it as a palliative at best and a poison at worst. On balance, the reaction was apparently negative. Publicity seemed heavily weighted against Philco and the tape plans when one considered the diversity of forces arrayed against them.

ID AFTER THE STORM

During the controversy over ID, Philco had little to say publicly about the plan except to indicate that it was here to stay. In early December, at the height of the hurricane, *Advertising Age* reported that 'Philco officials could not be reached for comment'. They apparently had premarital nervousness, for negotiations had by this time brought Ford and Philco nearer to a union. Since many acquisitions are followed by personnel changes and new policy decisions, it is not unreasonable to suppose that Philco executives were walking on eggs. Questions uppermost in the minds of executives in Philco's Consumer Products Division were: (1) What's in store for *us*? (2) What will happen to the *division*? and (3) What's the future of *ID*? To most, the third issue was likely viewed as the least important at the time.

It was known that Ford viewed Philco management as deficient. Thus, Philco people doubtlessly felt some pressure to prove their mettle in order to avoid getting caught in an organizational shake-up. Philco profits had been drifting deeper into the red all year long and by early December, four of the six Philco divisions were operating at a loss – and the Consumer Products Division was one of them. Industry gossip, then denied by Philco, held that Ford was giving Philco a deadline to make appliances profitable. For purely personal reasons, if not for the purpose of upping Philco's sale value to Ford, there was pressure to get the division closer to black ink. Financially weak, Philco couldn't have long resisted some alliance with Ford even if it had wanted to – in spite of the fact that the appliance industry as a whole was now predicting a 5 per cent sales increase in 1962 over 1961.

Furthermore, it was known that Ford had made strenuous efforts in its own company to strengthen and improve the automotive dealer set-up. This raised the question of Ford's attitude towards ID, and the charge that the plan tended to undermine dealer loyalty. Thus, personal insecurity, the fear that Ford might close out the biggest piece of the company, and uncertainty about ID's future under Ford might understandably have made Philco officials silent on ID. Although mum, they felt conflicting pressures – first a desire to push forward quickly and vigorously with ID in the hope that it *might* pull both individual and corporate chestnuts from the fire; and second, a don't-rock-the-boat fear of sticking their necks out too early and too far. In any event, the gag was quickly removed.

After winning stockholder approval, Ford acquired Philco as a wholly owned subsidiary paying just under 100 million dollars in common stock for the firm – less than Philco's book value. The official date for the take-over: December 11, 1961. A press conference was called to announce the purchase.

Charles E. Beck – formerly director of the Ford business planning office, the man personally responsible for leading Ford to Philco – was quickly appointed as president and chief executive officer of Philco to succeed outgoing president, James Skinner Beck, Jr. quickly came to the point. Ford, he said, planned to push appliances. 'Approximately half of Philco's assets are in the consumer products area. You can be sure we intend to make good use of them while making Philco more of a force in the industry.' Beck also publicly approved and endorsed ID and denied that it had hurt Philco dealers. 'We think it is an excellent merchandising plan,' said Beck. These soothing words were soon reaffirmed by Irving A. Duffy, Ford's vice-president and their first Philco chairman, who declared that Ford would back Philco's Consumer Products Division *and* the ID plan to the hilt.

Henry E. Bowes, destined to be Philco vice-president and general manager of the Consumer Products Division, expanded on these remarks. A few quotes catch the flavour of his press statement:

> We firmly believe that ID sales benefit customers, Philco dealers and distributors, Philco itself, and our whole industry.

> From our test results, we . . . believe that our . . . programme may revitalize appliance and electronic goods sales in the U.S.

> Where we have had ID programmes in effect for several weeks . . . we are told that all dealers – whether they are participating actively or not – are increasing their business on our lines.

> We are behind our dealers and distributors 100 per cent and, now that we can finally talk about the plan officially, we are going into the market places with detailed explanations of it. Until our merger . . . was finalized, we could say nothing. Dealers should have no cause for alarm with the plan – it will be of tremendous value to them when it comes to their area.

Mr Bowes could not understand why some Philco competitors considered the plan unfair, since every pre-existing level of the appliance industry handled each piece of merchandise as it had always done under other distribution methods. He stated that he had received no complaints from Philco dealers and knew of none from distributors (upon which, *Advertising Age* commented that, 'This does not jibe with other reports'). Although he didn't know of any ruffled feathers, Bowes attempted to smooth them by saying that Philco had no intention of selling direct to supermarkets and sidestepping distributors and dealers. Supermarkets, he said, simply didn't want such headaches as delivery

I

and service, and they couldn't profit from performing these functions as efficient full-service dealers might. He summed up this point with the somewhat curious suggestion that ID was instigated not to get supermarkets into the appliance business but to sell more Philco products and strengthen regular dealers and distributors. While admitting that the stand of NARDA and other groups would have some effect upon ID, Bowes stated that the plan had exceeded all expectations of the company. By the summer of 1962, Bowes predicted, ID would be in full swing.

Expansion of ID

With the apparent blessing of Ford, and with the lush Christmas buying season just around the bend, Philco continued to sign up additional supermarkets for its dealers under the ID plan. Two California appliance trade associations came out for the plan: in Indiana and elsewhere, distributors of other appliance brands hastened to work out comparable schemes. Meanwhile, back in Pittsburgh, Thorofare Markets publicly welcomed the BBB investigations of ID and re-endorsed the Philco–Thorofare adventure with this statement: 'We can assure you that Thorofare's participation was not a frivolous decision and was undertaken only after reliable assurances of legality and good business ethics.' Later, *Progressive Grocer* said: 'Indications are that the plan used by Thorofare has generally been found mechanically sound and is favoured by the suburban locations in which the chain operates.'

Ford capital supported the new Philco thrust, especially with advertising and sales promotion. Copy played up the marriage of Ford and Philco, and both corporate insignia began to appear side by side in ads. The theme of the 1962 trade campaign for Philco was 'Ford Means Business'. It reviewed division accomplishments subsequent to Ford's acquisition and told what the new team effort would mean in terms of dealer profits. 'Operation Impact' was announced – this was to be a multi-million-dollar advertising campaign laying heavy emphasis on consumer electronic and appliance products. Philco dealers, reportedly impressed, seemed to show new interest in the Philco line.

Encouraged by new support and fresh successes, Philco under Ford toured the country lining up additional participants for ID. Like the pioneers of old, Philco eventually eyed the West. From Oregon, D. B. Ryan – state manager for ID – reported in early February: 'We've had so many calls from different sources that manpower has kept us from expanding. We just haven't had the manpower to expand as fast as we could.' From Idaho came word that ID had bogged down only because of lack of goods. On February 7, 1962, *Home Furnishings Daily* quoted Mr C. K. Hakimian (then recently chosen General Sales and Marketing Manager of Philco's Consumer Products Division) as saying: 'ID as an effort to promote more business activity for retailers, distributors, and supermarkets has been extremely good.'

Before long, ID was to have been introduced to about three hundred supermarkets in some twenty cities all over America. But, even before that coverage was achieved, it was clear that the bloom was off the rose.

The Flower Fades

By Christmas of 1961, trade reports from Pittsburgh had told of faltering purchases under tape plans. The programmes began to fold about as suddenly as they had blossomed. On January 10, 1962, *Business Week* quoted Sol Godlen (manager of retail marketing for the Whirlpool Corporation) to the effect that, 'It's dying a ghostly death in Pittsburgh.'

In that city, some of ID's imitators had already begun to beat a hasty retreat. First to quit was Giant Eagle's 'Giant Bonus' tie-in with Emerson and Kelvinator. Giant Eagle simply said, 'We goofed. We jumped into the Giant Bonus Plan because we thought there was an overwhelming customer demand for an appliance tape plan. We were wrong. Demand has been so low that we decided to drop the plan.' Three weeks later, Loblaw's announced it would kill its AB plan, effective February 5. Thorofare continued to stay with Philco. (When Thorofare introduced ID in November, the first payments for participating customers were not due until January 30, 1962. This fact, together with the approaching holiday season, helped induce Thorofare to hang on with ID.) Food Fair, previously testing Philco's plan in ten stores, stopped participating in early February of 1962.

What was happening outside of Pittsburgh? The manager of B&A Markets said that ID had added only three customers in his Michigan stores since he joined the plan. Jewel Tea, after studying the plan, rejected it because of the unknowns involved. Ninety western Pennsylvania dealers reportedly sent a letter of protest to Philco. Star Supermarkets, an early ID signee based in Rochester, N.Y., cancelled out. In the announcement ending its ID plan, Star said, 'It appears that we have gotten the maximum promotional value from the programme during the two-month period we have used it. Its appeal to new customers is diminishing and we will put our efforts into new programmes.' On February 21, four months after starting with ID, Stop and Shop, Incorporated, ended the plan in the eight stores trying it. And what went wrong at Stop and Shop? 'We don't know,' said Don Gannon, retailing vice-president of S&S. 'I never saw a promotion that ran so smoothly. Philco gave us all kinds of co-operation.' Gannon stated that there was no opposition to the plan from non-participating dealers and no complaints from non-participating shoppers who might have felt deprived of the $5\frac{1}{2}$ per cent credit on grocery purchases. High rates of credit rejections, reportedly a factor in the Giant Eagle plan, were not considered to be an important factor. 'The volume just wasn't there,' said Gannon. 'People weren't sufficiently enthused to tell their neighbours about it. It was just another promotion.'

A similar story soon appeared elsewhere. In Oregon, said *Home Furnishings Daily*, 'Philco and its distributors are happy, dealers are unhappy, and supermarkets are cautiously noncommittal over the Philco ID plan. . . . [The] consensus of dealer remarks was that the plan had gotten off to an excellent start but had slowed to a trickle.' A week later, the same source reported that Eagle Foods of Clifton, Iowa, had cancelled their participation in the tape plan.

The general reason cited for supermarket disenchantment was insufficient volume to justify the expenses involved. Non-participating markets that had previously reported sales slumps as ID entered their areas now indicated that customers were returning after having shopped at ID stores and that business was near normal.

The February 26 issue of *Electrical Merchandising Week* said that Philco was still 'testing' the effect of ID plans. 'We know it's good for us and for the consumer who buys a lot of food,' a Philco spokesman had said, 'but we're not sure it's good for the supermarket.' Philco, he continued, was running a market survey to see whether the plan had resulted in net gains for participating supermarkets. In the meantime, Philco was not pushing for further expansion. Referring to Star's dropping of ID, he said, 'We don't think they really know if the plan has been beneficial or not. We're trying to find the answer for them.' As soon as the results of the survey could be made available, the new Philco management would decide whether or not the plan had long-term merits.

ID Is Dead

Then, all of a sudden, ID was no more. Before the February page could be torn from the 1962 calendar, Philco's new management tossed another bombshell into the business world with an unheralded announcement by Charles Hakimian that ID was to be killed. Here is his press statement, as reported in *Advertising Age*:

'When Philco became a wholly-owned subsidiary of Ford ... management immediately began a review of the Instant Dividend Plan, on which tests had been started last fall, to determine as thoroughly as possible whether this plan did, in fact, serve the interests of Philco customers, dealers and supermarkets. It also authorized extensive market research among consumers to determine the plan's effect on their purchases.

'The surveys have not proved to Philco's satisfaction that the present and future increased sales volume, over a long period, would be profitable enough to dealers and supermarkets to support continued promotion of the plan, despite the satisfaction of customers who made ID purchases in test areas.

'Several supermarket chains, checking the results of the plan independently, are reaching the same conclusion.

'Therefore, Philco is notifying all who are participating in the Instant Dividend Plan tests that, subject to existing agreements, which are being terminated as quickly as possible, the plan is being withdrawn.

'Every customer who made a Philco purchase under the terms of the Instant Dividend Plan will be able to complete that purchase on its original terms; that is, his cash register tapes will continue to be honoured by the supermarkets until his purchase has been fully paid.'

The new Philco was bashful about revealing the actual number of appliance units sold under the plan, but the press soon threw some new light on a foggy situation. Although the plan apparently didn't lose money for Philco, it wasn't working quite as well as expected. While Philco dealers in Pittsburgh had got new business in a hurry, it had just as quickly tapered off. Participating supermarkets got fewer new customers than they had hoped for. Surveys showed that the cost of operations and the time required to administer the plan would be too great to make the plan profitable over the long haul. Interestingly enough, it was not until ID was almost finished that Philco began to refer publicly to the plan as an 'experiment.' Hakimian said that the words 'test' and 'experiment' had been forgotten at Philco.

Back in late November of 1961, a Philco executive candidly had admitted, 'We don't know if it [ID] will last ten months or ten years.' Both figures were optimistic. Less than four months after the official debut of ID in the Thorofare Markets, and less than three months after both Ford and Philco officials had jointly hailed ID publicly as a great success and a daring merchandising undertaking, it was shown to be flawed. Before the first of March in 1962, ID – one of the most controversial and short-lived large-scale operations in marketing history – was dead.

POST-MORTEM

During most of the brief life of its tape plan, Philco never seemed quite sure whether ID was to function as a modest tactic or a grand strategy. Those critics who had called ID a potentially profitable short-time gimmick but a dubious long-term concept seemed to have been most accurate.

A Boy-sized Plan for a Man-sized Job
While ID was initially adopted as a short-term manoeuvre to
deliver its sponsor from an increasingly desperate cash position,
Philco soon came to expect – and sometimes to claim – much too
much from the ID operation. 'Philco's claimed saviour for a
troubled industry' proved to be no cure-all because it had few
built-in strengths to ensure long life, and many complex weaknesses.

Although a winsome notion, the idea of selling large appliances
through supermarkets was unrealistic for the long term. As a lasting element in the distribution set-up, the supermarket was just
not a logical outlet for large household appliances – not, at least,
at the stage of evolution in which most supermarkets found themselves in the early sixties. The rationale behind this judgement is
rooted in the fact that food and other products handled by the
typical supermarket were and still are intrinsically different – in
both physical attributes and marketing requirements – from large
household appliances. The standard supermarket merchandise
assortment consisted of widely advertised, rapid-turnover, low-
bulk,* staple items, convenience goods, and impulsively bought †
specialties which were saleable by self-service and impersonal
merchandising methods to a decision-making or family-purchas-
ing clientele consisting largely of women. By contrast, large
household appliances were typically bulky items requiring
personal sales techniques. Customers usually purchased them only
after a reasonably studied comparison of price, quality, style,
special features, and so on. The final choice tended to be a family
affair, with both husband and wife participating in the buying
decision. Furthermore, large appliances, plan or no plan, turn
over slowly. One industry expert, for instance, estimated that
refrigerators were replaced about once in every twelve to seven-

* Because of high occupancy costs, many supermarkets calculated expenses
and returns on the basis of inches and feet of store space consumed by any
unit of product. Supermarket operators have often been called 'space sellers',
'landlords', or 'rentiers'.

† One well-publicized survey indicated that as much as 70 per cent of all
supermarket purchases resulted from buying decisions made *after* the shopper
entered the store.

teen years. In short, certain basic characteristics of supermarket products and large household appliances were so contradictory that the probability of making them compatible shelf-mates was remote.*

While ID clearly had limited potential, Philco – before and after Ford – either misjudged or failed to consider its narrow and short-lived market appeal.† *Progressive Grocer* referred to ID as 'a variation on more or less standard-type plans long familiar to supermarket operations'. Many supermarkets viewed ID purely as a 'hypo' to stimulate sales, since earlier joint ventures between food stores and appliance people had always resolved themselves into short-run tactics. Supermarkets never did want more than 15 to 25 per cent of their customers hooked up with ID or its variants at any one time for fear the plans would become too costly. This put a lid on expansion and a limit to the life expectancy of the plans. It is hard to conceive of a hardheaded supermarket executive viewing ID as anything more than a unique and temporary promotional stimulant. Competitively, it must have been fore-seeable that it would be only a matter of time before rivals of both Philco and the supermarkets offered comparable plans on a wide-spread basis to neutralize their effects. Thus, there was almost no hope of gaining a permanent and strategically unique advantage with tape plans.

* *Small* appliances, such as toasters, grills, portable irons, and hair dryers, might well have been a different matter. In the peculiar jargon of the appliance industry, such products have long been referred to as 'impulse items' – graduating from a previous status as shopping goods or specialties. While several nationwide chains had rejected the Instant Dividend Plan and the entire concept of selling *large* household appliances in supermarkets. A&P and others were reported to be more seriously studying the feasibility o taking on small appliances with merchandising characteristics more in common with traditional supermarket offerings.

† Ex-Philco president Skinner essentially agrees with this point. In one letter, he has said, 'The programme seems to have been oversold due to initial successes far out of proportion to its potential. We approached super-markets with an estimate of one or two contracts per store per day. We hoped to sign five to ten thousand stores. One or two sales per day would have created a huge business. How long it would last was anybody's guess, but we figured six months per store as a minimum. The actual time period was to be determined through experience.'

Quick successes can mislead. Quick success in the early stages may have given Philco officials a false impression of ID's basic strength, led them to lose sight of the short-range character of the plan, and induced them incorrectly and implicitly to attribute long-term powers to ID.

The timing was right. If ID couldn't succeed in the final quarter of 1961, it probably never would. A fourth period up-turn lifted 1961 sales 3 to 6 per cent over 1960 levels for the entire appliance industry. Almost everybody recorded sales gains during the Thanksgiving and Christmas holidays. Philco sales increases, largely a result of generally improved business conditions, may have distorted an interpretation of causal influences and led to an optimistic illusion of strength in ID.

Early successes also led Philco to forget the word 'test'. A plan rapidly extended to three hundred supermarkets in twenty scattered cities could scarcely be termed an experiment. It may be of some significance to note that it was only *after* the fate of ID had been sealed that company officials began widely referring to ID as a test. It seems clear that Philco moved too far too soon. Instead of *testing*, it *plunged* headlong into ID – for reasons already mentioned. Philco probably expanded too quickly, and unattended details demonstrated a persistent capacity for not working themselves out. Formal research on ID was never attempted. Before and after Ford's take-over, Philco operated more on the basis of executive impressions than on rigorous planning and research. And Philco exuberance seemed to slight the critical function of prompt information feedback, which might have alerted them sooner to the fact that ID was destined for an early demise.

Publicity unquestionably hurt Philco and ID. The plan mortgaged a certain amount of consumer and dealer good will in the expectation of gains that never completely materialized. From a public relations standpoint, ID left lasting effects that Philco couldn't easily write off. Although neither the intensity and scope of the reaction to ID could have been completely foreseen, the fact that there would be *some* resistance to, and emulation of, the plan could have been anticipated at the start. It has always been something of an axiom in marketing that substantial changes in complex distribution patterns are met by strong resistance to change. And it is usually better to head off ill feelings before the fact than attempt to restore lost good will* and alienated associates after a deed is done. In this case, decision-makers and executors apparently forgot to project the full consequences of their programmes and to check out the implicit assumptions on which they were premised. ID was a risky and delicate step. It may not be unduly unkind to suggest that, in view of its previous distribution problems, Philco should have consulted its dealers before adopting the plan. That Philco learned a potentially costly lesson can be inferred from Mr Hakimian's obituary for ID, which stressed that the company would not go along with any future programmes unless they were 'mutually beneficial to all parties concerned'. This obviously meant dealers and distributors in particular.

However, these remarks should not be construed as support for a hypothesis that ID died solely from externally inflicted wounds. Adverse publicity was not *the* cause of death, although it was at least an important ancillary factor. ID was destined for a rather short life even without the public reaction it occasioned. The industry response merely upped the odds against success, rendered ID somewhat less potent than it might otherwise have been, and served to hasten the demise of the plan.

ID died of natural causes – from limitations inherent in the plan itself and the way it was carried out. Viewed as a long-run strategy, ID was clearly a failure. From the short-range tactical perspective, it could charitably be judged as a success. Hakimian was quoted as saying that 'the plus and minus of the programme have cancelled each other out'. Even if this were to be granted,

---

* Unfortunately, the asset value of good will has typically been ignored or understated by most managers. This is partly due to conventional accounting treatments of the asset in financial statements, which often value it at a dollar – or nothing at all. Yet, the Supreme Court of the United States has defined good will as the predisposition of a pleased customer to return to a place where he has been well treated. Obviously, this 'predisposition' – sometimes referred to as a 'customer franchise' – is an incalculably valuable business asset in need of continuous maintenance.

Philco was right back where it was before ID. Having risked much, it had gained really nothing.

Although there were no concrete standards by which ID could be assessed, and although the costs and benefits connected with the plan are still not precisely measurable, it is not uncharitable to conclude that ID failed because it just could not fairly be expected to confront squarely or overcome all of the deeply imbedded problems facing Philco and the appliance industry. This is in no sense an indictment of the programme itself, backed by Ford both before and after its acquisition of Philco.

A Postscript: Philco Under Ford

Ford's hopes for Philco rested on two factors – Ford's management and money.

Charles Beck, Ford's first Philco headman, was quick to comment that, 'Whenever you get to a spot where you run a company to conserve cash, it's not a question of whether you're going to fail, but how soon.' Ford was quick to learn that even it couldn't turn Philco around on a dime – much less a lot of dollars. Ford was forced to cut costs in the early stages of its attempted rebirth of Philco.

Ford first cut out some sixty former Philco executives and reduced the total number of company employees from about twenty-seven thousand to near twenty-two thousand. Ford did promote some of Philco's middle-management people but brought in many of its own executives, some of whom were also replaced again in rather short order. Says Mr Skinner today, 'It's a shame that there was no continuity of management, for at least part of the problems of early 1962 were created by personnel changes.'

ID failed in part because too much was asked of it and because it may have been jilted at the time of its greatest need. At any rate, neither ID nor Ford's money and management were sufficient to turn what is now called Philco–Ford into the black.

Time and tender loving care, universal prescriptions for almost any disorder, would be needed to nurse Philco back to health. Under the aegis of Ford, Philco–Ford is slowly learning to stand, however wobbly, on its own feet.[8]

CHAPTER V

The Fourth 'R': Regional Lessons

Every human drama needs a setting, a beginning, and some characters. This one opens in New York City in 1933. It seals with the brewing industry and with the makers of a well-known beer in particular. Whether teetotaller or imbiber, it is virtually impossible for anyone living or working in New York today not to have heard of Rheingold.

FROM REPEAL TO WORLD WAR II

The year 1933 marked the repeal of the Eighteenth Amendment to the Constitution of the United States of America. This brought to an end a futile thirteen-year-long 'noble experiment' to persuade Americans not to engage in the manufacture, importation, transport, sale, or consumption of alcoholic beverages from moonshine to malt brews.

The Brewing Industry After Repeal

Although there was an occasional slip between the law and the lip, brewers were out of business by federal decree from 1920 to 1933. It is understandable that the re-legalization of beer caught some brewers less well prepared to open shop than others.

In the New York market, the Jacob Ruppert Brewing Company quickly found itself in a rather fine position. During Prohibition, Ruppert had continued to use its kettles to produce 'near-beer'. While the production of near-beer was generally unprofitable, it had served to preserve its makers as 'going concerns' – maintaining their organizations, names, and old-world traditions of quality production. Shortly after Repeal, Ruppert was very nearly the biggest brewer in the country.

Founded in New York in 1842, and having also produced near-beer during the Prohibition period, the F. & M. Schaefer Brewing Company was also quickly able to produce a good light lager beer and to launch an advertising campaign with the claim that 'Our Hand Has Never Lost Its Skill'. Schaefer turned out some 300,000 barrels of beer in 1933 and expanded every year for several years thereafter. Adhering to a conservative* but stable pattern, Schaefer volume was to reach 1,300,000 barrels in 1940 – which placed them in fourth position in the entire nation behind Anheuser-Busch, Pabst, and Schlitz, all of which were then out-of-town 'shipping' brands. In surpassing Ruppert to become New York's leading product, Schaefer attributed its success to low-pressure selling combined with persistent advertising of a single product sold at one price within one market – a concentrated seventy-five-mile radius around the city of New York. The firm's 'success formula' was based on the three 'C's' of concentration, consistency, and constructiveness.[9]

Meanwhile, Liebmann Breweries and its Rheingold brand came out of the Prohibition Era in worse condition. But, by 1936, outside financial interests had acquired half-ownership of the Company, insisted on boosting quality, and brought in a new brewmaster. From Munich, Dr Herman Schüelein, the son of a great Bavarian brewmaster, and himself perhaps Germany's leading brewer until Hitler came to power, joined the organization. He later became Chairman of the Board and chief executive. Although he spoke no English when he arrived in America, Schüelein soon learned enough of the language to gain a good sense of direction for improving the production and marketing of Rheingold. He insisted on using the finest barley, hops, and water. Beyond ingredients, he was the first brewer in America to use a precision charcoal-filtering process to make a lighter, clearer, paler beer without superimposing undesirable tastes on the new

* Schaefer was to be the last New York brewer, for example, to make the move from bottles to cans.

product.* At first, Dr Schüelein made both a regular beer and a 'premium' lager that came to be called 'Rheingold Extra Dry'. Though high-priced, the latter began to sell. As volume grew, 'Extra Dry' Rheingold was dropped from a premium-priced to a popular-priced beer, and volume began to increase even faster. Still, Rheingold had a long way to go in its market to catch up with such New York labels as Schaefer and Ruppert.

The company now had a superior product at popular prices, and other brewers soon tried to emulate Schüelein's process. To counter such tactics, the firm began to advertise more heavily. Between Schüelein, the Liebmanns, and the ad agency, the 'My Beer is Rheingold, The Dry Beer', the 'Beer as Beer Should Taste' and the 'Often Imitated But Never Equalled' themes were developed to back-up intrinsic product merits. Rheingold slowly grew. By 1939, Jinx Falkenburg became the first of many 'Miss Rheingolds' to form a pretty focal point for the product's advertising programme.

On the eve of World War II, Rheingold had solved its basic product quality and advertising-support problems, and the brand was selling at an annual rate of just under 800,000 barrels – enough to make Liebmann Breweries rank ninth in the nation, although still spread thinly along the Atlantic coast from New England to Florida.

Rheingold's early sales organization was less than the best but was gradually improved. As the brand was strengthening during the thirties, so were pressures leading up to World War II.

World War II

With the advent of Pearl Harbor, most brewers throughout the country soon became more preoccupied with supply than with demand considerations.

Many readers can still recall the wartime rationing of such products as petrol, meat, sugar, and shoes. Government supply restrictions were particularly difficult for breweries. By the early part of 1942, the War Production Board denied the use of cans for

---

* If too much charcoal were used, for instance, beer would take on new properties and lose its character.

beer. Brewers switched back to bottles. Then, a few months later, the WPB substantially reduced the amount of steel and tin available for bottle caps. Rationing extended to malt and then even to the cork linings of bottle crowns.

Yet, Rheingold used the situation to advantage. While other brewers emphasized the quart bottle to conserve materials, this concern pressed for greater use of twelve-ounce bottles 'to satisfy more people while the industry was undergoing supply problems'. By adroit manoeuvring, all within the letter and spirit of the law, it managed to procure enough cork, malt, and other items to stay in business. As aware of consumer demand and competitive activity as of governmental restriction, the company was probably the first in New York City to notice, for instance, that a major competitor happened to produce a few batches of bad beer and took steps to maintain product quality. For the duration of the war, Rheingold hung on with determination, achieved sales gains, and struggled towards product leadership in New York.

BREWING AFTER THE WAR

With the end of World War II and its supply restrictions, brewers looked forward to the future. The future arrived but it was enough to drive men – brewers – to drink.

The Beer Market Goes Flat

While pent-up consumer demand for wartime-scarce items exploded into rapidly growing early post-war sales for most goods and services, the effect was not enjoyed by American brewers. As total population grew, beer sales associated with it were almost evenly matched by a depressing *decline* in *per capita* consumption. About half of the adult populace drank beer, and a mere 10 to 15 per cent of beer drinkers accounted for two-thirds of total consumption. With market potential concentrated in so few consumers, any deep change in the composition or habits of this group was bound to affect the fortunes of all who depended on it for survival or profit.

At the time, three aspects of the malt beverage market were held to be of critical importance. The first had to do with the age distribution of the population as a whole, for the major market for beer lay in the twenty-one to forty age bracket. This segment contained both a higher percentage of beer drinkers and a larger number of *heavy* beer consumers than any other age group. The ratio of beer drinkers to non-drinkers decreased sharply at ages over forty, and the average number of glasses or bottles quaffed per drinking man also slid as he aged. Because of such factors as the low birth rate of the thirties, the loss of servicemen during the war, and the increased life expectancy brought about by advances in medicine, the fastest-growing general market sector were the 'under ten' and the 'over fifty' age groups. The age class that normally accounted for the bulk of beer sales was shrinking in relative size.

A second explanation generally used to account for declining *per capita* consumption was rooted in the tremendous redistribution and up-levelling of personal income that had taken place. For years, industry observers had asserted that changes in beer demand were inversely correlated with changes in the average level of personal disposable income. In other words, the more money a man made, the less likely he was to spend it on beer. If the hypothesis held true, the new income patterns then emerging would affect beer consumption even more adversely.

The third variable in the beer sales forecasting model then in common use was the volume of beer 'substitutes' (e.g. soft drinks, wines, whisky) sold and consumed. After the war, the demand for such substitutes had risen, and their gains were felt to account in part for sales losses suffered by the brewers.

Whether these explanations for sluggish beer demand were all valid or not,* the actual fact was that beer sales had reached a plateau, with yearly fluctuations around static long-run industry

* In recent years, the income hypothesis seems to have been disproved, with most experts now saying that the consumption of beer does not vary from one income class to another and a few saying that beer is positively, not negatively, correlated with changes in income. The effect of the sale of beer substitutes had also come to be regarded as having little or no predictive value for beer sales forecasting. The age factor *is* still viewed as one critical element.

demand trends further adding to short-term competitive pressures among the brewers.

Dynamics in a Static Market

While aggregate demand levelled off, changing consumer preferences and habits injected new dynamics into an otherwise slow-moving market. Brewers were hard-pressed to keep up with and respond to these changes. Consumers, for instance, began to change the sites of their watering spots. They moved away from taverns and restaurants and into their own homes. And the drift from 'on-premise' to 'off-premise' or 'take-home' sale was accompanied by drastic changes in other beer marketing practices.

Shifts towards home consumption understandably made packaging an increasingly important competitive function. As the importance of bulk, or draught, beer began to be de-emphasized and then to decline, many new types of bottles, cans, cartons, carriers, and containers came into widespread use. Innovations in packaging were a condition of survival.

With package changes came new names. Several new brands were placed on the market, and brewers laid heavier emphasis on new labels to lure consumers into switching brands and to provide a basis for fresh promotional tactics. The 'quality labels' got special attention and emphasis. With several hundred domestic brands to choose from, consumers had sometimes become confused and restless. They did switch brands often, but they sometimes grumbled about the taste of unfamiliar products they now bought, for American brewers were almost universally making light, bland beers rather than the fuller-bodied, Old World brews that had been popular prior to Repeal. As a result, it became difficult or downright impossible for many drinkers to distinguish clearly one brand from another (even though fights could still result between brand loyalists who claimed the ability to determine important product differences).

Distribution altered as a consequence of burgeoning take-home purchases. Supermarkets, packaged-liquor stores, and other off-premise beer outlets soon began to account for larger beer sales

K

than did restaurants and taverns in many metropolitan markets. Now the housewife emerged as a powerful buying influence, although the man of the house still claimed that he specified the brand of beer she should pick off the shelf. Yet, the woman did function as a purchasing agent for her family. As such, she was sometimes induced to change her mind about beer brands once she was inside a supermarket and was exposed to temporary price inducements, shelf positioning, and point-of-purchase promotion of individual items. Such tactical instruments had quickly come to be of increasing competitive significance to the brewing industry.

National-brand brewers, with larger budgets, developed marketing advantages over small local brewmasters. While local and regional brands typically had some price advantage over brands shipped in from distant sources, partly because transportation and physical-distribution costs were important for a product of relatively low value in relation to weight and bulk, this was seldom enough to compensate for the overwhelming strengths that the national and larger regional brewers possessed in other areas of marketing, such as packaging and promotion.

With stabilizing demand, and with both marketing and production costs rising across the board, virtually every company in the industry felt a squeeze on profits. Although average annual earnings after taxes had reached an all-time high of 7·7 per cent on sales in 1946, this figure plummeted to 2·8 per cent on 1954 sales – a full percentage point below the U.S. figure for average business corporations of all types.

A Game of Musical Chairs

With sagging profits, rivals in this officially legal but heavily regulated and punitively taxed industry entered a period of intense competition for bigger shares of a seemingly stagnant total market. The post-war era in brewing was, as *Business Week* then put it, 'a day of skirmishes, shoving, and fast footwork'. Each brewery worried about its rank in the industry. While Budweiser and Schlitz began a slugfest for a king-of-the-hill spot, other brewers battled for lesser peaks.

Merger with or acquisition of competitive brewers was often

chosen as the shortest and fastest route to increased share of market. This is reflected in government statistics which showed a steady decrease in the number of independent brewers operating in the United States. In 1934 we had 756 brewers. By 1947 the number was 485. A 1949 count showed 440. Although actual numbers could not have been accurately foreseen in the early postwar years, a clear trend was evident – a trend that would show less than 300 brewing companies in 1955, 230 in 1957, and less than 200 by the end of 1965. In the early fifties, the top four American brewers had cornered some 24 per cent of the beer market.

As nationwide beer marketers grew bigger, via both internal growth and merger-acquisition, regional and local concerns tried to strike back.

THE RHEINGOLD RECORD: 1933–1953

Liebmann Breweries, Inc., came through World War II, and into the fifties in amazingly good shape for a regional brewer. With the exception of two years, 1938 and 1946, the Rheingold brand reached new sales records every year for the first two decades after Repeal. By 1953, the company was running three plants with over four thousand employees at 80 to 90 per cent of capacity, an enviable annual level by industry standards.

The 1953 sales of Rheingold passed the three-million-barrel mark. After a twenty-year drive from almost nothing to first place in a part of the East, the Rheingold brand held more than a 30 per cent share of the New York City market and a very solid core of loyalty extending in at least a fifty-mile arc around the city. On a national basis, the firm was always listed among the top ten brewers and held at least sixth position in the ranking as of 1953.

Dr Schüelein had functioned with eminent success as chairman of the Board and chief executive. In 1950, Mr Philip Liebmann had become the firm's fourth-generation president at the age of thirty-five. He was described by *Business Week* at the time as 'young, big, massive, enthusiastic, shaggy, booming voiced friendly, tenacious in making a point . . .'.

A Success Formula

The astonishing sales success of Rheingold was attributed to several factors.

Both Dr Schüelein and Mr Liebmann credited most of the success to the product itself. They insisted that there were important differences among beers and that the product had to be made with loving care. As Phil Liebmann put it, 'It isn't manufactured. . . . You *grow* beer. . . . Your product is desperately important. . . . In beer, people recognize quality. Any fool can get people to try a product, but keeping them depends on your quality. . . . We have a quality beer and that's the image we want to put in people's minds. . . . It's got to be genuine – nothing but the best.[10] If the sales record was a reliable indicator, New Yorkers seemed to agree that Rheingold was a superior product.

But Schüelein and Liebmann were also quick to point out that there was more than taste involved in selling beer. The product had to be backed by good advertising. Dr Schüelein had been personally responsible for developing many effective promotional ideas for the brand. And Phil Liebmann had been a 'bug' on advertising since his student days at the Wharton School. As a result, Rheingold was the most heavily advertised beer in New York. Great reliance was placed on print media, for New York – with its many train, bus, and subway strap-hangers – had always been 'a print media market'. For years, Rheingold had been the largest single-product advertiser in the city's seven newspapers. It was the largest suburban train car-card advertiser in the metropolitan area. It had the largest display promotion programme in the city, and this was tied-in directly to support general print media advertising. An outdoor poster advertiser for twelve months each year, Rheingold also employed an intensive schedule of radio spot commercials and shows and sponsored both filmed and live shows on television.

To many New Yorkers, the most familiar advertising was the 'Miss Rheingold' campaign. Miss Rheingold was one of the best-known personalities ever created by modern advertising, and knowledgeable people agreed that she had been an important part of the recipe that had lifted Rheingold to the top perch in its market. Every year New Yorkers were bombarded in many media, and at the final points where beer was bought or consumed, with the patriotic message that they ought to get out and vote in the nation's 'second biggest election' – the contest that determined which of many lucky maidens was to reign for a dozen months as local queen. During its royal heyday, the annual Miss Rheingold contest drew as many as twenty million votes, which, if one ignored the stuffing of ballot boxes, did make the queen's election second only to the quadrennial presidential election measured by the number of votes cast. Each year since 1939, the brewery had distributed, collected, and counted ballots cast in voting boxes scattered through metropolitan bars and taverns. It is difficult for those not having some personal acquaintance with this race to appreciate fully the scale and intensity with which it was carried out. The pretty winner of this election became the focal point for about 30 per cent of Rheingold's entire year-long advertising campaign. The programme's original appeal, its year-after-year continuity and repetition, and the publicity and public relations link-ups undoubtedly added materially to Rheingold's steel-like grip on the New York market. Miss Rheingold lent her delicate hand to all of her sponsor's personal selling, advertising, and merchandising efforts, and it is impossible to measure the numbers of dollars she really accounted for – in either marketing costs or sales results. It may suffice to say that it is reported to have cost the company in excess of fifty thousand dollars each year just to count the ballots for her election. At its peak, something like a quarter-million dollars per year is said to have been spent on the Miss Rheingold campaign. That some men apparently had abiding faith in the gambit's effectiveness is shown in the fact that the programme was repeated annually for well over two decades – a steady stream of what one trade source described as 'Anglo-Saxon-style' beauties wearing panchromatic confectionery smiles in millions of ads and thousands of public appearances for the wider promotion of 'Rheingold Extra Dry'. (For the record, many were not really Anglo-Saxon.)

But Rheingold seemingly sat on a three-legged stool. One leg was that of product quality. A second was the promotional effort built around powerful advertising that included a fresh Miss Rheingold each year. The third leg of the stool was called 'distribution'.

Here, the brewery had further strength. Rheingold was distributed from the company's own branches directly to retail stores, bars, and taverns by a wholly owned delivery system. The firm maintained close control over market coverage, delivery schedules, customer service, and distribution costs right up to the point of sale in retail accounts. This helped to assure the company's ability to price its product competitively with other local and regional brews and a nickel or so per bottle under the premium-priced national labels.

It was a seemingly strong stool on which the Rheingold giant sat. With a clearly dominant position in the New York market, an excellent product, big and fine advertising and promotion programmes, and a controlled distribution system covering almost 100 per cent of the available outlets, who could ask for more? Many members of management in Liebmann Breweries did.

Success Brings New Problems

By 1953, the aggregate market for beer appeared to be levelling off at a volume of ten million barrels per year. With a 30 per cent share of market, depending on one's concept of its geographic boundaries, New York City was already pretty well saturated with Rheingold. There was little hope for added sales volume through improved distribution. Aggressively strong rivals, Ballantine and Schaefer in particular, were constantly and eagerly on the alert for ways to wrest customers from Rheingold – they relished nothing more than to slice into Rheingold's position in their market. And by 1953, Rheingold plants were operating at 88·57 per cent of capacity annually – sometimes even rationing beer during peak periods.

Corporate executives deliberated individually and collectively to solve the now more pressing problems of how to survive, prosper, and grow.

Search for Solutions

Although it wasn't formally recorded as such, a two-pronged strategy seemed to emerge. The first was to assume a defensive posture in and around the New York market to protect hard-won gains and to correct for small slippages wherever they might occur – some executives, for instance, were concerned when they saw decreases in the large-volume Harlem segment of their New York business and weakness in New Jersey and Connecticut.

As for the second prong, it was perhaps natural for this brewer to search for new territory to conquer. Discussion and debates centred most heavily around the issue of just which of several markets that might have more favourable demand, distribution, and competitive features than New York did should be selected as the object of offensive commercial warfare.

Los Angeles, the second-largest metropolitan market in America, ultimately seemed an obvious candidate for close examination. It was, moreover, one of the few remaining metro markets still recording steady growth in the consumption of malt beverages. In the first ten years after World War II, L.A. beer sales were to rise from 1·8 per cent of the industry total to 3·3 per cent. The state of California would come to consume 7·8 per cent of all U.S. beer during the same time span. There was little or no excess capacity in the area. The market was serviced by a number of relatively well entrenched but small local brewers with brand names like Acme, Lucky Lager, and Regal Amber.

With such characteristics, Los Angeles and other Western markets quickly attracted the attention of brewers across the nation. Several national and semi-national brewers soon decided to invade those markets and give the local boys a run for their money. Falstaff, then a semi-national brewer with about a third of the national market covered, bought up a plant at San Jose, California, in 1952. But most brewers were more interested in the bonanza lying further to the south – the gold mine seemingly waiting for all at Los Angeles. Rumours of a full-scale invasion of this market by out-of-state operators filled the air. They soon came true. Pabst, for example, set up a fifteen-million-dollar brewing facility in the L.A. area in 1952. Within roughly a year, Budweiser and Schlitz had each built a twenty-million-dollar plant in the area. All of these concerns had set up distribution through beer wholesalers and were producing in quantity by 1953 and 1954. With these outfits seemingly ready to rack up sizable sales gains, and with Los Angeles shaping up quickly as the big beer battlefield of the mid-fifties, many other brewers – including Rheingold's – moves towards a decision whether they should join the fray.

A Schism Develops

Some saw great commercial possibilities if they could get into Los Angeles quickly before even more competitors entered the Western picture. 'Go West, Young Man, Go West!' That advice must have seemed as fresh to some Rheingold executives in 1953 as it had been when Horace Greeley first uttered it a century earlier.

Some, of course, were steadfastly against the L.A. move, and this made for conflict. It was argued that the name 'Rheingold' was completely unknown on the West Coast, that its management knew virtually nothing about California markets, and that there was not sufficient time to permit adequate product and market testing or to conduct other types of marketing research. Some felt that it was both a safer and more profitable alternative to penetrate more deeply into the fringe markets surrounding the core in New York.

The split-up board of directors of Liebmann Breweries, Inc., decided to attack the West.

Rheingold Hits Los Angeles

Late in 1953 the company bought two breweries from Acme, one located in Los Angeles and one in San Francisco. At a cost of six million dollars, it thus obtained production capacity of about a million and a half barrels per year on the West Coast. With two plants at its disposal, the firm quickly concocted a 'two-beer strategy'. The Rheingold label was to be brewed in Los Angeles. It was to be marketed northward as far as Paso Robles and southward to San Diego and the Mexican border. A second product, bearing the name of 'California Gold Label', was to be produced in San Francisco for eventual distribution in northern California, the Pacific Northwest, and other Western market areas.

Initial marketing effort was to be concentrated on attacking the Los Angeles market by using essentially the same success formula that had worked so well for Rheingold in New York and by striking in blitzkrieg fashion with lightning-like speed and force. The entire promotion campaign was worked out in just twenty-nine days and launched with great confidence in April of 1954. As *Business Week* put it, 'When Rheingold hit the West Coast, it did so with a foamy splash that saturated the advertising media.' The beer was billed as the nectar of the gods, and 'the West Coast knew that Rheingold had come to town'.

However entry into the market was characterized, early operations indicated that Rheingold might well succeed in its bid for a lucrative piece of the Los Angeles market. Sales in the first few months ran high. Quite soon, however, volume began to taper off at a rapid rate until the product held but a small residual share of the market. Rheingold was finally ranked tenth in sales among California brewers with a physical volume that had slid to less than 150,000 barrels per year by 1957. Failing to achieve sales and market-share goals, and forced to flee California because it was losing too much money, Rheingold sold its Los Angeles plant to Hamm's in the summer of 1957. It later got rid of the San Francisco brewery. A major strategy had misfired. Like the sun, Rheingold had risen in the East and sunk in the West. 'It was,' said Mr Liebmann ruefully, 'a regional lesson for us.'

EAST IS EAST AND WEST IS WEST

There are and always will be significant regional differences between markets that require different marketing strategies – even when the same product is offered to two markets. Marketing, like politics, is inherently local in nature. Each local or regional market often has its own unique needs, characteristics, institutions, and problems and, therefore, typically requires a specially designed approach. This was the principal strategic lesson learned the hard way by this company. But let's take a close look to see what other concrete regional lessons can be learned from this misfire.

Market Misjudgement

The firm really knew little about the Los Angeles market. Its people relied on subjective judgement and poor research and, by failing to realize fully that Los Angeles and New York were radically different, badly misjudged the L.A. market. It is possible here only to speculate on the nature of that misjudgement.

Psychological and cultural differences between the two markets added to Rheingold's problems. As an outsider and a New Yorker to boot, Rheingold came to L.A. loudly tooting its own horn. 'We resented it,' more than one Los Angeleno told reporters. Whether born there or not, and most were not, Californians had developed a fierce pride in the West, a strong antipathy towards Easterners, and a greater valuation on new rather than old and traditional things. At the time, the biggest seller among Los Angeles beers was 'Lucky Lager', whose slogan reminded both original and transplanted residents that – 'It's Lucky When You Live in California'. Rheingold's approach, using the image of the hustling and sophisticated New Yorker in the shirt-sleeved and (perhaps) more leisurely Los Angeles market may have been off-target. Although the tack failed in L.A., 'it might have worked in San Francisco'.

Advertising: Villainous or Victorious?

This company made an unsuccessful attempt to advertise Rheingold out of the rut into which it had fallen, but opinion at the time was diverse as to the actual effectiveness of Rheingold advertising in the West.

As but one example, it was said that the Miss Rheingold part of the programme didn't really impress the folks in Los Angeles to any appreciable degree. As a city already up to its ears in beauty queens and identified as the 'mecca of the aspiring motion picture star', a feminine glamour back-up for a beer called 'Rheingold' may just not have carried much sex appeal in L.A. More than a few ads in this campaign conveyed a distinctly Eastern flavour. In contrast, ads for Lucky Lager beer showed skiers at Squaw Valley, gave Californians at least something to identify with, and probably provided better communications with intended audiences.

There were also questions directed towards Rheingold's media selection. In the East, its main experience had been with print media. But, as anybody who travelled in the West could verify, Los Angelenos were more manacled to steering wheel and patio than Easterners. This made L.A. much more of a 'broadcast' and outdoor media market than New York City. But, local broadcast media were overcommitted with competitive commercials. Radio stations had already refused more beer ads because their 'spots' were too closely bunched together on the schedules. Even outdoor advertisers were turning down advertisements for beer because they already had too many of them scattered along California roads and felt that more might offend public opinion. Perhaps Rheingold's media-mix could have been better matched with the market.

A Too Dry Beer?

When Rheingold took over Acme's brewery in Los Angeles, it promptly transferred all of the brewing knowhow behind it to achieve the same quality of product in L.A. as was brewed in New York. Except for the water used, the basic recipe was unchanged. But, unfortunately, the beer New Yorkers appeared to relish so much didn't seem to appeal to the people of Los Angeles. It had long been claimed that Rheingold was custom-brewed for the New York market, where constant watch had been kept over the years for subtle changes in taste preferences. Los Angeles imbibers had simply never tasted the kind of extra-dry beer that this producer made. Could a beer presumably 'fitted' to New York tastes succeed in Los Angeles?

From a strictly technical point of view, of course, there were clearly differences of importance in beer formulations and beer tastes. Different brewers used different sources of water and

145

barley malt and various kinds of hops. Some employed 'adjuncts', such as rice and corn, to achieve product distinctiveness. Some used foam-stabilizing injections to modify the 'heads' on their beers. Protein derivatives sometimes controlled bubble size. The result was a range of variation in beer taste and consistency that experts, at least, could easily detect. But it was seriously doubted by many that an average, blindfolded consumer could really differentiate between most domestic brands of beer. Any assumed 'awareness' of differences in beer taste was likely to be attributed as much to the 'brand images' that had been created through promotional activities and habitual consumption patterns as to truly intrinsic and ordinarily detectable differences in the real qualities of various beer brands.

Whether it was some missing ingredient in product quality or a lack of pertinence in advertising approach that failed to carry the day for Rheingold remains something of a moot point. There are two schools of thought on the matter.

The argument in defence of the advertising programme holds that, despite some admitted oversights and deficiencies in the promotional effort, Rheingold advertising actually did achieve everything that could possibly have been expected of it. As early sales results demonstrated, the people of Los Angeles did respond to advertising to the extent of at least testing the product to find out how good it really was. If advertising's purpose was merely to induce first product *trials*, then this function seems to have been adequately fulfilled. And, if it follows that the goodness of the product itself had to *retain* these customers, the product seemingly failed to fill its role. Thus, it is argued by some that this was more of a product failure than an advertising failure.

Another camp takes a diametrically opposed position. It begins its argument with the proposition that a customer's satisfaction with beer is largely a question of mind over matter. This school holds that Rheingold's advertising simply didn't create enough psychological satisfaction among the people to make them want to repeat their purchases. The build-up was too big, and customer expectations were raised to unrealistic heights by Rheingold's promotional self-praise. No product of the type could possibly have lived up to such billing, and consumers were inevitably disappointed. Also, late-comer Rheingold had to break historical buying habits and destroy whatever 'consumer franchises' had been established through years of previous competitive advertising activity. And the product couldn't do all this with ballyhoo alone, it is charged.

That Rheingold couldn't hold on to early customers won over by initial advertising was perhaps equally attributable to the product itself and the advertising support behind it. With neither a demonstrably different and superior product to produce true *gustatory* satisfaction nor a really believable and persuasive advertising programme to create *psychological* satisfaction with the brand, Rheingold couldn't hope to cling to the niche initially carved out in the Western market place. In any event, the product-plus-advertising combination that had clicked in New York went over with a loud thud in Los Angeles.

Distribution Dilemmas

Rheingold's management also discovered that a new regional market could present unique distribution and servicing problems. In New York, Rheingold was sold direct to retailers This technique was considered by many to be the next best thing to owning retail outlets themselves – the way all beer used to be sold before Repeal outlawed that kind of beer marketing. So, when Rheingold went West, it took its own method of distribution along with it. Through bypassing wholesalers, of course, the firm tied up much of its money, both in terms of initial capital investment and later operating expenses. But several other factors were to be even more influential in inhibiting the effective use of a direct distribution system for beer in the Los Angeles market.

Rheingold ran head-on into local customs, traditions, and practices that often virtually forced brewers to sell via wholesalers. The attempt to buck such pressures was another factor contributing to Rheingold's failure in L.A. There was strong resistance and opposition put up by local distributors against Rheingold's methods. Well entrenched in the market, wielding considerable influence with local brewers and retail customers, and more closely knit than beer wholesalers in many other market regions, these distributors had already waged many successful campaigns in an effort to prevent or hinder the side-stepping of their members by retail buyers and brewers.* They succeeded in making Rheingold's selling job more difficult than it might otherwise have been.

In the salesroom of one prominent local brewer was a large sign reading, 'Stop Rheingold!' All sorts of unkind rumours were flying about, including one to the effect that drinking Rheingold would make one impotent. While these rumours were never tracked down to their sources, they were believed to have been started by 'the trade'.

Another force operating against this brand was the vast geographical sprawl of the Los Angeles market, for the ratio of distribution costs to sales revenues under direct distribution methods often rises rapidly as a market's density decreases. The larger area to be covered also resulted in some loss of distributive control, and Rheingold experienced some difficulty in keeping its accounts supplied with adequate stocks of beer at certain times.

With a distinctly different pattern of resale institutions in Los

* One long-drawn-out battle lost by the distributors after a hard fight was centred around an attempt by Safeway Stores to cut out the wholesaler. For years, Safeway (owners and operators of about five hundred supermarkets in California) purchased all of its beer through a wholly owned wholesaling subsidiary, Beverage Distributors, Inc. When a state examiner recommended revocation of the BDI licence on the grounds that it was a Safeway captive and not a bona fide wholesale distributor, Safeway sold the organization to the employees who were running it. BDI then lined up other supermarket chains as additional customers and offered a 3 per cent discount off the invoice for paying cash within ten days plus a special allowance for warehouse pick-ups to all of its customers. Competing wholesalers were quoting delivered prices without cash discounts. To stop this practice, two breweries refused to sell any beer to Safeway. Thereupon, Safeway and BDI, acting as co-plaintiffs, countered with an anti-trust suit against them. The brewers, supported in their struggle by California beer distributors, lost the case. In California, beer shipments could now go directly from the brewery to chain warehouses and by-pass regular wholesalers, and the brewers were legally enjoined from boycotting the chains. Despite the precedent set by this case, however, local brewers and distributors were still in a position to exert subtle pressures against Rheingold's distribution methods if they chose to do so.

Angeles through which to reach the ultimate consumer market, Rheingold faced still further problems not encountered in New York. New York City had about three times as many retail beer outlets as there were in Los Angeles. And New York had many small outlets, including tiny corner delicatessens and neighbour-hood taverns. In Los Angeles, where a much larger percentage of beer was sold for household use, supermarkets were the most important outlets. With much larger and fewer retail buyers, and with different types of retailers dominating the L.A. market, Rheingold had to shift its emphasis away from the familiar sales techniques that had worked in New York towards methods and customers with which it was quite unfamiliar.

For example, Los Angeles supermarkets required different kinds of point-of-sale promotional treatment than Rheingold had been accustomed to supplying in New York. And L.A.'s bigger stores purchased in larger units, requiring fewer sales calls and delivery stops than did New York retailers. With less frequent selling contact between Rheingold and its retail accounts, some of the advantages of direct distribution were thus lost. And, with their large purchases, in terms of both individual order size and annual volume per store, California retailers also demanded large profit margins. If they weren't supplied with them, they simply wouldn't push a product or display it in advantageous locations. To complicate matters more at the same time, Western brewers were hoping all along that Eastern beers would do what they had done elsewhere – keep prices above those local labels and fight among themselves with purely promotional ammunition. Although Pabst did lower its prices by about 6 per cent to retailers while holding its consumer prices above Western brands, Rhein-gold and most of the other Eastern invaders either priced above the market to the consumer or shaved margins provided to retailers.

Rheingold also had difficulties in on-premise retail accounts. To cite but one example, the company had decided not to make draught beer in Los Angeles and had sold its empty kegs to Lucky Lager. This hurt the brand by making enemies of some saloon-keepers who were left without draught to sell to their patrons.

All of these factors combined to produce Rheingold's failure in Los Angeles and to force the firm to sell the plant to Hamm's, who had somewhat better luck in the West.

THE HAMM'S MODUS OPERANDI

Starting from its base at St Paul, Minnesota, Hamm's had begun a programme of geographical expansion aimed at achieving nationwide distribution by the target year of 1970. It slowly built its market through a sequential chain of strategies, successively attacking such markets as Chicago, Texas, and San Francisco. A basic principle seemed to be that they would get a firm hold on one market before invading the next.

Hamm's apparently recognized one thing Rheingold did not – that brand loyalties for beer varied in strength from one market to another and were not entirely a result of intrinsic product qualities. Tactics for entering a new market called for slowly incorporating a product into established regional cultural and distribution patterns. If lasting public acceptance were to be gained for a new label, buyers and consumers would have to be gradually exposed to it with consummate skill. To be more concrete, let us see how Hamm's operated in San Francisco after buying the Rainier brewery there in 1953.[11]

After purchasing its brewery, Hamm's immediately began spreading public relations material to the effect that it was going to operate a model plant, the West Coast having been specifically chosen as the perfect place for a 'model brewery'. Hamm's recruited a Western manager and a sales force which promptly contacted distributors and retailers on the Coast for the purpose of building up a fund of information on the market. Their advertising agency opened an office in San Francisco to begin 'preconditioning' ads aimed at both the trade and the public. Early research revealed that it would be wise to change their slogan from 'Hamm's – *from* the Land of Sky Blue Waters' to 'Hamm's – Refreshing *as* the Land of Sky Blue Waters'. Next, salesmen received special training for West Coast selling. Opening day was planned in great detail, with every salesman directed to be at a certain place at a certain time when D-day was signalled. Teaser ads saying that 'Hamm's is coming soon' had gone up two weeks before opening day, and Hamm's used a test community (Redding, California) to iron out many bugs in its plans before hitting with full force. The company's distribution methods, which made heavy use of existing wholesalers in the area, were particularly effective for breaking into a new region. Hamm's shopped around and lined up a lot of small distributors ('the boys who are hungry') and built a team of exclusive representatives out of them. This won important friends for Hamm's and gained them access to retailers via already-established channels. Advertising copy was deliberately created so as to be flexible enough for use in media ranging from radio to in-store posters. Hamm's took out some final insurance by making sure that its advertising sponsored some type of civic activity in order to win the further favour of local people. (In Chicago, Hamm's had earlier gone so far as to sponsor *both* local baseball clubs.)

Like Rheingold, Hamm's was the largest-selling beer in a major metropolitan market (Chicago) before moving to the West. Like Rheingold, Hamm's had a quality beer and used one brewing formula for all markets. And, like Rheingold, Hamm's had won many awards for the excellence of its advertising. But there the similarity ended.

Hamm's did have some strengths which Rheingold lacked. It was experienced in working through beer wholesalers. And Hamm's felt it was not a total stranger to California when it moved in; thousands of Hamm's Midwest customers had migrated to the West Coast in prior years to form the nucleus of a ready-made market there. With relatively less of an out-migration of New Yorkers to the West, Rheingold was more of an outsider when it appeared on the scene.

When Hamm's took over Rheingold's L.A. plant in 1957, the company applied the lessons it had learned in San Francisco and elsewhere. It spurned the transplantation of entire 'success formulas' from one market to another. Realizing that the Los Angeles market build-up would take time, Hamm's avoided the risky 'blitzkrieg' approach to it. Using the same caution that had characterized its San Francisco campaign, Hamm's system-atically and carefully approached the Los Angeles beer market and prepared for its invasion with something close to battle-plan precision. This tactical difference in *method* probably contributed as much to Hamm's initial success as to Rheingold's ultimate defeat in Los Angeles. Hamm's did experience more difficulty in L.A. than it had in San Francisco and attributed part of it to a combination of the old Acme name and the Rheingold record that preceded them in that market.

This strategic and tactical comparison of the Rheingold and Hamm's programmes on the West Coast is not intended to imply that Hamm's had all the answers. Hamm's has since learned some regional lessons of its own by experiencing difficult situations in L.A., as well as in such markets as Baltimore and Detroit. Many a brewer has, in fact, received similar regional instruction.

The point is *not* that most outside national and semi-national brewers achieved success in the West, while Rheingold was the battlefield's only prominent casualty. Overall, outsiders initially held less than a third of the California market by 1957. The difference between success and failure in this case can be measured almost entirely in terms of the degree of market knowledge pos-sessed by each competitor and the ways in which they utilized that information to tailor products and programmes to the specific needs of the local market place. There is a moral here that has been learned and relearned by numerous domestic and inter-national marketers of many kinds of goods and services. Hamm's certainly didn't become a national brand by 1970. With the excep-tion of a few brands – Coors and Olympia in particular – most out-of-staters took their lumps out West.

RHEINGOLD SINCE 1957

There can be no doubt that the Los Angeles venture caused the company to lose several notches in national rankings. Total yearly sales for the brand slipped by one third of a million barrels between 1955 and 1961, at which time volume was fluctuating around an annual level of 2·9 million barrels. While part of this slippage was due to a generally sluggish market for all brands in Greater New York, Rheingold also lost market share. Rheingold seems to have held on to first position in New York City proper, but it yielded leadership to Schaefer in some contiguous areas surrounding the five boroughs of the city.

By 1960 Rheingold's executives were showing outward signs of genuine concern over sales in the East and were beginning to institute dramatic changes. During 1961, it was clear that the company was concentrating mainly on advertising as its road to salvation. As both Miller's and Coor's began to push towards passing Rheingold nationally, Rheingold shifted 1·2 million dollars of its advertising budget into sponsorship of the New York Mets baseball team.

Meanwhile, outside financial interests were well aware that Rheingold's market was changing and that further steps had to be taken to rejuvenate the brand. In late 1962, Schaefer had begun an unabashed promotional pitch, based on solid research, to specific ethnic groups and to the heavy beer drinker – with 'the one beer to have when you're having more than one' theme. In 1962 and 1963, the industry as a whole was beginning to show new signs of life. Stories of a growing rift between Rheingold's executives began to circulate, and it was rumoured that Miss Rheingold might be dethroned. During this period, Rheingold had shifted dollars from print to broadcast (radio, TV) media and had come out with a couple of notable packaging innovations – including the unique, wide-necked 'Chug-a-Mug' bottle. But, these gains seemed small when set off against growing problems for the product in New York. Brands like Budweiser, Schlitz, and Pabst were moving into the market and flexing their muscles. Schaefer continued to grow while Ballantine was about to fall on evil days. Union pressures mounted. Soaring real-estate costs inhibited further expansion of the capacity of local breweries. In the autumn of 1963, after sixty days of negotiation, a proposed acquisition of Liebmann by Falstaff fell through. Change was in the air.

In May of 1964, Liebmann Breweries, Inc., was sold to the Pub United Corporation (formerly Pepsi-Cola United Bottlers). According to the *Wall Street Journal*, the price was twenty-six million dollars in stock. The Liebmann name was changed to the Rheingold Corporation in 1965.

By 1967, implying that only a real pro could make it in New York, Rheingold's theme had changed to 'Either You Have It or You Don't'.

Today, the organization has survived many changes in agencies, promotional approaches, and managements. It is a restless brand in a tough segment of a turbulent industry.[12] If its current leaders have anything to say about it, the Rheingold brand will not only survive – it will grow, prosper, and profit from lessons learned over the course of a long and exciting history.

CHAPTER VI

GEE: Misfire or Strategic Coup?

The story now about to unfold is as much the story of an industry's marketing problems as the others were of individual company episodes.

Observers of business and economics have long struggled to understand the intriguing complexities of petrol marketing. Such marketing programmes are heavily influenced by technical aspects of exploration, production, and refining inside individual concerns and by fierce rivalry between them. On top of this, the oil business is technologically linked to numerous other complex industries yielding or requiring efficient sources of energy. That the demand for petrol is largely derived from the demand for motor vehicles provides a convenient point of departure for studying yet another chapter in the history of American marketing.

ON ENGINES AND APPETITES

With minor exceptions, U.S. cars have always been built with internal combustion petrol engines. In the beginning, those engines were far from efficient but, as drivers and designers came to view the car as a really permanent replacement for the horse, both dreamed of power plants with increasingly effective operating characteristics.

One key to improved automotive performance lay in the boosting of compression ratios,* for the harder one could squeeze the

* Compression ratio is the numerical expression of the relationship between the gas volume in a cylinder at the start of a piston stroke and the volume at the end of the stroke.

air–fuel mixture before igniting it in a car's combustion chamber, the more powerful the vehicle could be. By the late 1920s, compression ratios were commonly about 4:1 – a level that had furrowed a few brows among the fraternity of automotive engineers.

A Battle to Beat 'Knock'

Early compression ratios jumped at a faster rate than improvements in petrol quality. The result was a kind of engine indigestion called 'knock' – exemplified by an annoying, high-pitched, metallic rapping or pinging sound whenever the engine was strained. Knocking was, and still is, more than acoustically irritating. It represents fuel wastage, a loss of power and performance, and a potential source of serious engine damage.

Interest in anti-knock research grew. It was soon realized that knock was a result of a mismarriage between engine design and available fuel so that fuel was not burning as it should. Even before 1920, Boss Kettering and his staff at General Motors saw that a ceiling would soon be placed on compression ratios and car performance unless better fuels could be found or developed.

Towards a Better Diet for Cars

In general, the higher the compression ratio of an automotive engine the greater is its 'octane' need to prevent a kind of gastro-intestinal burping. Motor petrols are rated according to a measure called 'octane number' – a figure used to express the degree of anti-knock properties of any liquid motor fuel. Although many ways have been developed to measure and to express octane numbers, the petrol industry has most often used a standardized testing method resulting in a RON, which stands for 'Research-Method Octane Number'. A 70 RON petrol, for instance, would not knock as easily as one rated at 60.

While knocking could be limited by improved designs for the combustion chambers of engine cylinders to some extent, early designers felt that the anti-knock battle could be won over the long run only by developing new and better fuels.

TEL for Indigestion

Early anti-knock research, spearheaded by Kettering, resulted in a long succession of frustrations and failings. But, persistent effort finally paid off. It was found that a petrol RON could be boosted significantly by adding a chemical called tetraethyl lead (TEL) to the fuel. Fuels beefed-up with TEL were first marketed in the early 1920s under the name of 'Ethyl' petrol.

While an important discovery, TEL didn't solve the entire problem. It increased lead deposits in engines, caused some damage to spark plugs and valves, had corrosive effects, and was extremely toxic.

'Scavengers', chiefly compounds of bromine and chlorine, were mixed in to mitigate the undesirable side effects of TEL. Although TEL, it was claimed, could theoretically boost RONs up to fifteen numbers, a legal limit of 3 cc's per gallon of petrol was placed on the TEL additive. (The high toxicity of petrol 'leaded' with TEL adds to air pollution and continues to be a social as well as an economic problem.) This forced researchers to look to other alternatives for knock-free motor fuels.

Improving Petroleum Refining

Automotive engineers had been in the vanguard of fuel improvement efforts. But, as kerosene and other petroleum products decreased in importance, and as automotive fuels came to assume greater importance in the product mixes of more and more oil companies, petroleum refiners themselves began to pay greater attention to the production of motor fuels. In part, this effort took the form of exploring and developing better types of crude oil. Perhaps more significantly, refinery technology was modified to improve the molecular structure and chemical stability of petrol, to boost its volatility, to promote more uniform burnability, to increase energy content, and to cut down on harmful by-products of imperfect combustion. Technological changes on the refining end began to result in purer fuels that either reduced the need for TEL or yielded higher RONs at constant TEL levels.

By 1930, the major refiners could produce petrol tailored to seasons and climatic zones, although those fuels were of rather low RON by today's standards. World War II finally forced the widespread development of catalytic cracking and even more advanced process improvements that made 100 octane aviation gas possible – though still less than economical for wartime and postwar motorists.

Creeping Octanes

Through the thirties and forties, automobile compression ratios – and related horsepower ratings – crept slowly upward. Refiners of petrol alternately followed or led octane requirements by small RON margins. As late as 1950, there was but a slight spread between the compression ratios of the least and the most powerful cars on the American road. Horsepower ranged between the fairly stable figures of 100 and 115 for many years prior to 1950. Therefore, there was an octane number range of just two or three numbers between the average petrol produced and the highest and lowest available or required RONs.

The Two-grade Petrol System

By the debut of the fifties, it had become traditional for major oil companies to refine and market two grades of petrol. The first, usually called 'regular' petrol was intended for six-cylinder cars and others with low compression ratios. The other, 'premium' petrol, was aimed at eight-cylinder, high-powered vehicles.* With two quality grades, each of which was periodically boosted in RON as Detroit slowly upped the dietary requirements of its cars, the oil companies were able virtually to satisfy, and some-time over-satisfy, all cars on the road. Regular accounted for some 72 per cent of total auto fuel sold about 1950; premiums and sub-regulars accounted for the remaining 28 per cent.

---

* Some two-graders produced a 'regular' plus a 'premium' fuel; others offered 'regular' and 'sub-regular' petrol. At least one refiner of significance still produced but one grade of motor fuel.

SEEDS OF FERMENT: 1950–1954

Circa 1950 or 1951, after the unsettling recession of 1949, petrol RONs seemed poised as if on the end of a balanced seesaw. Average RON might move either up or down. Majority opinion held that octane ratings would move up. Although Ford and others were paying some attention to a budding small-car market, all intelligence at the time indicated that volume production of such vehicles was not commercially feasible.

Up to 1950, crude-oil supply had been generally in balance with the demand for final petroleum by-products – including petrol. While some people dated 1948 as a turning point, whereafter the industry would have to contend with oversupply and erratic demand, the oil companies were in fact levelling off pretty well as the decade of the fifties commenced. And yet, although World War II and the Korean conflict had brought about capacity increases in both crude-oil production and high-octane refining facilities, subtle demand forces began to press against the RONs then being produced.

By 1950–1951, the compression ratios of our most powerful cars crawled past the 7:1 mark, and octane ratings of premium fuels began to inch past 90. In 1950, one member of the American Petroleum Institute publicly expressed concern that petrols were nearing the end of the road. Without major investment in new technologies, a RON of about 95 would be tops. To go beyond that number would involve tremendous refining costs and call for further increases in consumer prices on motor fuel. At the same time, a GM chemist urged oil outfits to make the higher-octane investment, saying that some top cars would soon be needing a RON of 95 to 100. To aid sagging sales, Chrysler gave its biggest engine a healthy horsepower jump in 1951. Throughout the 1952 model-year, Detroit continued to press the oil companies for better petrol.

By 1953 there was open unrest among oil companies. The *average* car now had about 133 horsepower and – more significantly – the 'octane spread' (difference between the octane requirements of the least and most powerful cars on the road) had increased to some seventeen numbers. This made it increasingly difficult for oilmen to bridge the gap with but two grades of petrol to offer the motoring public.

At the time there was at least one notable exception to the traditional two-grade petrol system. The Sun Oil Company relied on a single grade of fuel said to be intermediate in quality between most regulars and premiums and selling at prices competitive with regular. This product, called 'Blue Sunoco', was designed to satisfy the anti-knock needs of 90 per cent of all cars on the road. The goal, historically, had been relatively easy to achieve by making small year-to-year changes in Sun's octane pool. By 1953 Sun was worried. The 10 per cent of cars unsatisfied by Blue Sunoco were increasingly in the newer, high-compression models. Sun was missing out on sales to new-car buyers and foregoing a major opportunity for building brand loyalty. And forecasts pointed to fewer old cars, rising average compression ratios, and an increase in octane spread. By sticking to its one-grade policy, Sun would be obliged to elevate continually and rapidly the octane rating of its entire petrol output, a position which could quickly become untenable because of basic refinery economics. While Sun was privately worrying, the two-graders publicly developed some schizoid tendencies. The industry was showing signs of splitting into rival camps.

Additives vs. Octanes

In mid-May of 1953, Shell Oil fired the opening shot in what was to become a major struggle in the petrol industry with the announcement that it was putting a new additive called 'TCP' (for tricresyl phosphate) into its premium fuel. It was claimed that Shell premium with TCP would give up to 15 per cent more power, increase spark-plug life by 150 per cent, boost mileage, and otherwise result in better engine performance without harming a car in any way. Shell also announced that its new fuel would require a consumer price increase of only one-half cent per gallon, a cost to the motorist that they felt would be more than offset by benefits gained. Under vigorous promotional support, sales of the new product zoomed beyond anyone's expectation.

The sale of the premium reportedly rose from 20 to 45 per cent of total Shell petrol sales in selected areas. This success story caused considerable excitement, and a host of new disciples and advocates of 'the additive approach' to better fuels made an appearance. On the heels of TCP came a variety of new additives with labels such as 'ETC', 'AD', and 'TTP'.

By mid-November, Shell and its followers were being challenged by critics who insisted that anti-knock properties could only be improved by boosting octane numbers in the refining and blending processes, not by using non-TEL additives.

The emergent leader of the basically anti-additive group was Esso.* Esso proclaimed, 'Let's forget the rest of the alphabet and look at the ABC's of premium petrol.' It backed up words with action by hiking the RON of its premium to 95, the highest octane fuel ever marketed to the public by Esso up to that point in time. Cities Service (now CITGO) and others began to express thoughts similar to Esso's as divergent strategic patterns began to form.

A Power Race Begins

By 1954, engine horsepower ranged from 150 to 225. No new cars were introduced with a compression ratio of less than 7:1. Almost a fifth of all new cars came out with ratios of between 8:1 and 9:1, and the overall average compression ratio eased past the 7·4 to 1 mark.

As for fuels, regular petrol now averaged about 86 RON; premiums went to 94 or more. Although but a small percentage of all cars on the road technically needed premium fuel, many motorists were buying it. Customers had become quality conscious, even though few could actually judge petrol quality.

* The 'Esso' brand of products is currently marketed by the Humble Oil & Refining Company, a wholly owned domestic affiliate of the Standard Oil Company (New Jersey). America's biggest oil company, and second in size only to General Motors among all industrial firms, Humble was formed in 1959 as a successor to five of Jersey Standard's former domestic affiliates – the old Humble Oil Refining Company, Esso Standard Oil Company, the Carter Oil Company, Oklahoma Oil Company, and Pate Oil Company. Humble currently markets the Esso, Enco, and Humble brands in forty-six states and the District of Columbia.

Thirty per cent of all petrol sales now went to premiums as motorists showed their willingness to pay more for power and performance both in the prices laid out on their cars and on their fuels. Esso and Cities Service had sustained price increases of a penny a gallon on new premiums; Shell and Standard of Indiana a half-penny. Higher price differentials between regular and premium motor fuels were beginning to stick as they never had before.

New car designs posed many problems, and some oil companies occupied themselves with meeting new needs in the TBA (tyres, batteries, and accessories) field, but most were especially concerned with further improvements in motor fuel – via either the additive or octane route. As octanes reached the low 90s, the 'additive vs. octane battle' began to solidify, since catalytic cracking processes could not economically go much beyond that point. Many oil companies had been and still were making huge investments in refining processes just to reach or slightly surpass the 90 mark, and a new ceiling on RONs would soon be met by those not taking the costly additional step beyond catalytic cracking to catalytic reforming and other refinery process improvements.

There were, of course, many cross-currents of opinion and comment among oil industry observers and forecasters. Ford had by now formally designated people to work on plans for smaller cars. Some were intrigued by this fact and all of its portents, but most automotive and petroleum people behaved as though they would rather ignore eventualities along that line. By May 1954, the business press could almost simultaneously report that Shell was increasing market share considerably with TCP and that the auto industry would be calling for fuels of up to 105 octane in a few short years. Shell and Esso remained as the leading advocates of two schools of strategic thought as the battle of additives and octanes continued to wax hot far into the year of 1954.

By early to mid-spring, the advocates of higher octane seemed to be tipping the balance. Esso upped the octane on regular gas, claiming it would now meet all the standards of typical premium fuels offered by many others. Texaco, straddling the additive and octane fence, came out with 'Top Octane Sky Chief Supercharged with Petrox'. Socony Mobil did about the same, claiming a fuel with 25 per cent more power than ordinary premiums and increases in petrol mileage of 23 per cent. None of these moves, of course, caused dismay in Detroit. Auto makers gained new flexibility for playing with compression ratios as a result of fuel improvements, and they copped a promotional plus by being able to advertise that many of their cars would now perform perfectly well on regular, albeit even better on premium, petrol.

By August 1954, the *Oil & Gas Journal* was predicting that premiums of 100 octane would be on the market within three to four years. In September, *National Petroleum News* quoted a Humble technician's prediction that top premium motor fuels would hit 110 octane by 1960.

When 1955-model cars were introduced in the autumn of 1954, all manufacturers announced power increases. Forty-four per cent of new cars carried recommendations for premium fuel – up from 31 per cent the year before. Cadillac reached an all-time power peak with the 1955 Eldorado boasting 270 horsepower. Both horsepower and octanes reached higher levels than ever before.

To sum up, 1954 was a year of continued warfare between advocates of additives and more octane. As late as December 4, *Business Week* magazine cautioned that there would come a time, perhaps by 1960, when the octane surge would slow to a trot as Detroit ceased to find further commercial advantages in pushing power and performance ever upward. Yet, although few Detroiters would admit to such a thing, the words 'power race' were beginning to appear with increasing frequency in the nation's press.

BUILDING TOWARDS A CLIMAX: 1955

While Shell and others continued to push additives, fierce competition created strong incentives for the introduction of new technology. By February 1955, business papers were saying, 'Those that can are talking octanes.'

In early 1955, the average compression ratio was nudging 8:1. Five per cent of all cars on the road now needed premium fuel, and 47 per cent of the 1955 models required it. There were over fifty million cars in use, and the total market for motor fuel was estimated to be about twelve billion dollars per year. Within that truly enormous market, at least three rivals were active in the premium grade race, and several others waited in the wings to threaten further rivalry.

On January 5, 1955, a new 'Esso Extra' petrol was introduced and billed as 'the highest octane gasoline ever offered . . . higher by far than any other gasoline'. On January 25, 'Cities Service New 5-D Premium' was put on the market with the ringing claim that, 'Nobody – literally nobody – tops it in octane.' On January 31, advertisements appeared with copy that said, 'No gasoline – No, not a single one – has higher octane than "New 1955 Gulf No-Nox".' Apparently comparable in many respects, these fuels were rated at around 96·5 octane, although it was claimed that Esso Extra reached a high of 98 RON in some markets during 1955.

The New 1956 Car Models

By autumn, Detroit left little doubt that the industry was engaged in an all-out power race. The new models had more zip, could pass other cars in shorter distances with greater safety, had more pick-up and hill-climbing ability, and offered greater riding comfort than any commercial vehicle ever before made. The new cars were wider and longer. They carried more power-eating gadgetry (automatic transmissions, power brakes and steering, air conditioning, etc.) To provide power for all this, compression ratios were again stepped up. Numerous new cars with higher horsepower were introduced. The average compression ratio took its biggest jump in history – a sharply dramatic change from around 8:1 to 8·5:1 in the course of a single year. Automotive experts were predicting 300 horsepower cars for the following years and were confidently forecasting future compression ratios as high as 14:1. The auto industry was unexpectedly stunned by a record-breaking sales year that substantially exceeded seven million units in 1955. Some Detroiters were jubilantly predicting an eight-million auto year not far ahead.

Many of these developments caught some oilmen by surprise. A 95 octane fuel was needed at an 8·5:1 compression ratio, while a 10:1 ratio called for 100 RON. At this time, the average available premium was about 95 octane; none were above 98. (The average regular fuel was perhaps 88 or 89 RON at this time.) Under conditions where the average new car needed the average premium fuel, it was clear that many new cars weren't being satisfied with available diets.

Even Esso began to get complaints about knocking from new-car buyers. According to Esso, which had actually expected a slight *decrease* in compression ratios and octane requirements for 1956 before contrary facts began to come in, 22 per cent of the new cars and 5 per cent of the total auto population would not be satisfied at then-current octane levels.* Esso promptly re-examined its projections, forecasted that 40 per cent of all 1957 models and 9 per cent of all cars on the road in 1957 would not be petrol-satisfied, predicted a future continuation of upward trends in compression ratios and octane needs, concluded that they had been much too conservative, and decided they would have to push for an earlier introduction of 100 RON fuel than had been previously planned.

Spread-eagle

If we conjure up the image of a hapless fisherman unloading at the dock, one foot dockside and the other on a rowboat drifting away, we get a pretty fair picture of the position in which many petrol marketers were finding themselves. With only two grades of fuel

---

* Some oilmen disagreed with Esso. In 1955, several claimed that 98 to 99 per cent of all 1956 models could then be accommodated with existing fuels. In part, this was due to differences of opinion over the exact relationship between compression ratios and octane requirements. The relationship, which does not appear to be linear, is very complicated and impossible to establish to the mutual satisfaction of all industry technicians. It should also be noted that the industry exhibited vast differences among individual sales forecasts and between estimates of most likely future compression ratios during this period.

to offer, oilmen found it difficult to bridge adequately a rapidly widening gap between the highest and lowest octane needs of American cars. Octane spread was beginning to cramp both technological and marketing muscles. In 1955 the auto population had a life expectancy of well over ten years, and the average actual age of all cars was about six years. Every car had its individual petrol requirements, but to satisfy it at any given service station there were never more than two items on the menu. The traditional two-grade system was under some strain.

Looking for Leadership

Because no two petrol companies were in quite the same strategic situation nor viewed the future in a comparable light, there was an understandable lack of unanimity over whither the industry was tending. It was operating at near capacity and trying to increase high-octane yields from available technology. Beyond that point, heavy refinery investments would be required and, once built, such facilities could be relatively inflexible.

Surface disorder reigned in the petrol market place. Between 1947 and 1955, petrol demand had grown more than 6 per cent per year. Most industry growth had been in premium-grade auto motor fuels. As octane numbers rose arithmetically, refining costs increased geometrically. To complicate matters further, still higher octanes could swing the entire petroleum market out of balance – as crude oils were refined to higher and higher octane numbers at the top, the bottom left more and more heavy oils and residuals that would have to be sold off, for instance, as winter heating fuels in apartments and homes. All along the by-product line there was a cost–price squeeze on petroleum products.

As 1955 drew to a close, it seemed that almost everyone in the petroleum industry would have to do something. But what? And when? Timing was tremendously important, not only from the demand side but also from the technological and capital-budgeting sides of the coin. How high would octanes go? By what methods should new fuels be produced? Would Detroit back off from the power race or push on with it? Although nobody seemed to have

166

the whole answer to his future, most oil companies waited with private forecasts and unresolved questions – waited for some kind of industry leadership pattern to emerge.

HIGH DRAMA IN 1956

Some producers couldn't wait. Problems and opportunities were just too great. It wasn't long before pioneers appeared.

Sunoco's Blender

The Sun Oil Company, no giant and selling just one grade of petrol, but with projections of increased octane requirements, had begun in 'utmost secrecy' as early as 1953 to find solutions to its problems. On February 23, 1956, the cloak of secrecy was removed. That day, Sun announced plans for a 'five-grade experiment' in seventeen of its stations in Orlando, Florida, and surrounding markets.

A unique concept, first proposed by Sunoco's chairman of the board,* suggested that Sun should seriously consider a 'Custom Blending System' whereby Blue Sunoco might be mixed at the pump with a super-powerful 'octane concentrate' to deliver just what the customer wanted. An Operations Research task force was given the job of exploring the engineering aspects of this and other alternatives for top-management consideration. Its first step was to examine the feasibility of the concentrate. The second was to find out whether a good blending pump was also possible within cost constraints. Computer-based simulation techniques applied to refinery operations yielded a suitable concentrate capable of producing any number of separate octane-levels

---

* As with most innovations, the true source is difficult to find. Here I have followed James S. Cross, 'Operations Research in Solving a Marketing Problem', *Journal of Marketing*, January 1961, pp. 30–34, in which Cross credits his employer. But note that George Prince, President of Synectics, Inc., a consulting firm, stated in the November 10, 1966, issue of *Sales Management*, p. 66, that, 'Veeder Route, which makes counters, told us that their business with the petrol pump manufacturers had levelled off and asked us if we could stimulate it. As a result of those sessions, we invented the idea of "dial your own octane", which Sunoco is now using.'

of motor fuel. Two years of research produced a serviceable blending pump that could vend five or more different octane blends. While requiring an investment in refining and in new pumps that was huge for such a small firm (small in industry terms), the concentrate and blender offered substantial flexibility at the point of sale. According to Sun, the new system could dispense RONs of from 94 to more than 100 – probably the first such octane level offered on the consumer market. It was for the purpose of field-testing this new system that Sun made its public announcement in February of 1956.

Sunoco forced the hand of industry giants many times its size in the bold poker stakes of the oil game.

Esso's Super-premium

On May 1, 1956, the public relations department of Esso Standard Oil Company issued a press release announcing that company's departure from two-grade marketing. To its regular 'Esso' and premium 'Esso Extra' would be added a new super-premium petrol of better than 100 octane, called 'Golden Esso Extra'. The press reaction was swift, extensive, and favourable. By the next day, virtually every newspaper of importance across the face of the United States, from the *Christian Science Monitor* to the *Jewish Advocate*, brought the news to the attention of the public.

On May 5, Golden Esso Extra – soon dubbed 'GEE' by lovers of acronyms – began to go on sale at the first of seven training stations in six cities. With laboratory and road testing behind it, Esso was now to test customer reactions to its new product. And what 'tests' they were. Typical of them all, which ran from early May to late June, was the one run in Baltimore. Here is that story as told in the *Esso News* from the Baltimore refinery.

Television, radio, the press, word of mouth, and every major medium of communication were brought into play to bring the news of the new product before the public at 10 a.m. on May 1. At that time, Esso President Stanley C. Hope and sales division managers simultaneously announced to the press and wire services that Esso was introducing its new three-grade system. Charles A. Newland, manager of the Delaware–Maryland–D.C.

168

sales division, brought the story to a gathering of business editors and reporters at the Southern Hotel in Baltimore. The Associated Press and both major local dailies covered the conference, and the Baltimore *Morning Sun* carried a story of the news break on its back page – top play for that paper. Meanwhile, radio and TV announcers were busy with the same story, and Esso's own reporters reserved time to announce the big news. In on the ground floor in bringing GEE to market, Esso's company-owned station at York Road and Bellona Avenue came into the act. Mr Newland's company car was the first in the area to be topped-off there with Golden Esso Extra. The first paying customer, also an Esso employee, was a Mr Jim Hurd, whose new Oldsmobile took on more than fourteen gallons of the stuff. According to Esso, 'It needs it,' and, 'Jim says he can already notice improved performance.' By the end of a long weekend beginning on Thursday, more than 1300 gallons of the new petrol had been sold to customers, including one racing enthusiast who arrived in an English racing car appropriately painted gold. Meanwhile, people all over the Baltimore area were receiving by mail a sample double-page ad for the new fuel and a message from the general manager of manufacturing, Mr J. P. Warner. His message, attached to a questionnaire, advised in part: 'Keep going with Esso Extra and then try the new fuel as soon as it is available. You will be the best judge of which is the buy for you in performance per dollar. Esso gives the motorist the choice of three brilliant best buys.' So went tests in Baltimore and elsewhere. Sales rates were even higher than expected.

By mid-June, Esso revealed top-level information on both past and present timetables for Golden Esso Extra. The company's petrol subcommittee had recommended early in January that octane ratings be stepped up at a faster rate than had been planned. This was based on earlier 'too conservative' forecasts for rising compression ratios and octane trends, which were now expected to continue at least through 1960. Because of the large refinery investments implied by such a move, the Board of Directors, in late January, asked for a review of the problem and for possible alternative technical ways to solve it. At the same time, marketing management asked its people for specific recommendations. By February 7, the third-grade route had been formally recommended to marketing management, which, a week later, passed it along to the Board and began to develop a name for the new product. On February 23, Sunoco announced its move, and Esso's Board of Directors adopted the third-grade proposal on April 18. During the next week, key people from various divisions met to hear the decision and to discuss pricing, timing, and initial market targets. These decisions were made final on April 26, and the press release came out on May 1. (The original plan called for a June 20 announcement, but the date was moved up when Esso 'heard reports that a competitor was planning to buy some gold paint'.) After its tests, GEE was to be fully marketed in the six cities by June 20. By mid-August, the third grade was to be available to 75 per cent of Esso's clientele in an eighteen-state area. Ninety per cent distribution coverage in that area was to be achieved as rapidly as new tanks, pumps, and other special equipment could be installed – no later than the start of 1957.

The Humble Oil & Refining Company, another affiliate controlled by Jersey Standard, was to offer 'Golden Enco Extra' in its Texas and New Mexico sales area with about the same timetable.

Esso's Rationale and an Audacious Invitation

Esso's market estimates and forecasts, based largely on the extrapolation of recent history and supplemented by information supplied by their 'man in Detroit', laboratory and road tests, and other information sources, were soon made available to the public.

According to Esso, 22 per cent of all 1956 cars and 5 per cent of all cars then on the road needed a super-premium. By the following year, available average premiums would fail to satisfy 40 per cent of new cars built. The spread between high- and low-compression ratios and related octane offerings continued, and Esso predicted an even wider range between 1956 and 1961. By 1961, they said, a premium then capable of satisfying 95 per cent of all cars would fail to satisfy 50 per cent of all new cars coming off assembly lines.

The average premium RON had been forecast at 96 for 1956,

but it began to look like it would hit 97. The average premium was expected to pass 100 by 1965 and the highest-octane fuel was expected to reach 103 by 1961.

Esso, therefore, perceived its problem in these terms – how can we produce more high octane motor fuel without incurring huge increases in costs and prices? With existing technology, the industry had little difficulty up to an octane number of 90 or so. But beyond that point, refining costs increased geometrically with arithmetic increases in RON. For the sake of illustration, it was approximately three and a half times more costly to squeeze out one more number between 99 and 100 octane than it was between 96 and 97. Basic refinery economics made 100 RON fuel impractical on a large scale.

Therefore, reasoned Esso, it was essential to move to a three-grade petrol system. The company embarked on a crash programme, four years ahead of schedule, in order to beat competition to the punch and to realize greater profits through production economies via three grades. Such a venture, according to Esso, was in everyone's best interests.

First of all, the motorist would gain something. Projected regular and premium grades would be just fine for many motorists for years to come. However, if a two-grade system were retained and all premium RONs were increased to a level satisfying only a relatively small percentage of high-requirement automobiles, premium prices would have to rise. This would, in effect, penalize many users of premium gas that needed lesser RONs. These drivers would be caught in the middle of the two-grade squeeze, unable to use regular but required to pay more for unnecessary octane numbers. Esso people said that as much as 85 per cent of all premium users would pay for quality they didn't actually need. A third grade would deliver requisite quality to those motorists who had to have it and could pay about three cents more per gallon and would free other premium users from overbuying octane numbers. This would lower fuel costs for the average motorist. Esso estimated that a three-grade system could save motorists several hundreds of millions of dollars each year and perhaps as much as a half-billion dollars annually by 1961.

Even the non-motoring public, said Esso, stood to benefit. A three-grade pattern would improve the overall petrol yield from a barrel of crude and hence make for more efficient utilization of natural oil resources.

Three grades would also pave the way for technological advances in the automotive industry. It would release car makers from the need to restrict engine power and efficiency to conform to average available fuel quality.

According to Esso, a three-grade petrol system would benefit more than Esso itself, motorists, the general public, and the car manufacturers. It would, said Esso, also be in the best interest of the entire petroleum industry to shift over to three grades. The ability to adjust the range of octanes produced and offered for sale among three rather than between two grades would provide increased competitive power as well as greater consumer satisfaction. Getting down to numbers, President Hope claimed that the oil industry as a whole would have to invest three billion refinery dollars between 1956 and 1961 to offer necessary octane ratings for top-premium fuel under a constantly upgraded two-grade plan. A three-grade system would satisfy top 1961 octane requirements with a total investment of but 1·6 billion dollars for the industry. Perhaps 20 to 25 per cent of refining savings would have to be invested in new pumps, storage tanks, and delivery methods. In short, Mr Hope extended an invitation to the entire industry to trade-off a 1·4-billion-dollar refinery saving for a mere 300-million-dollar expenditure on marketing.

John A. Millar, Esso's General Manager of Marketing, put it bluntly. 'God knows we don't have all the brains, but as we see it the three-grade system is the best course. We'll be making gasoline much more economically than the competition if they don't take the multi-grade course. Any company that wants to make a profit ought to follow this.' Mr Millar continued. 'I wouldn't want them [competitors] to think we were trying to tell them what to do. Sure we wanted to beat them to the punch. But we didn't want to catch them totally unprepared. We thought it better to come out this far ahead – six or seven weeks – and tell them what we are going to do.'

Although Sun had made the first big move in 1956, Esso was making an open bid for leadership and hoping the entire industry would follow its move to three grades.

Waiting for the Bandwagon

Just two weeks after Esso's May 2 announcement, the *Oil & Gas Journal* ran a piece headlined 'Esso Move May End Two-Grade Gasoline Marketing'. Gulf Oil announced that it was doubling a recently placed order for new reforming capacity at its Philadelphia refinery. A number of smaller firms planned fast increases in high-octane capacity, including some additions of catalytic reforming processes. A spokesman for the Sun Oil Company said, 'Esso had confirmed our belief that something had to be done, and I applaud them for it.'

But it quickly became clear that many oil companies either would not or could not accept Esso's invitation to the three-grade club. Shell came out with a new additive and increased the octane rating of its premium, called it 'Super Shell with TCP', and priced it a cent above Esso Extra and two cents below Golden Esso Extra. Many other firms (Sinclair, Socony Mobil, Tidewater, Pure Oil, etc.) stuck with two grades, some boosting premium RONs and most going up a bit on price.

Esso's move on the heels of Sun's experiment brought about more hurried top-level conferences that any other oil marketing development in years. 'The whole thing has a lot of people knocking their heads together,' one major petroleum executive remarked. In June, *National Petroleum News* reported that marketers were looking for answers to these basic questions: What's my competition doing? Is a higher octane necessary now? If so, what's the best way to supply it, by upgrading premium or the multi-grade route? *NPN* caught the flavour of greatly mixed attitudes in the collected comments of many major oil company officials. The following are typical:

1. 'We'll have to meet it head on with a third grade; I am more or less convinced of that. I don't see how the industry can miss doing something. This year's premium gasolines do not take care of all cars.'

2. 'I think Esso overshot the market on this. We believe our present premium will handle 98 to 99 per cent of all new cars. We won't need 100 octane for several years yet.'

3. 'We don't think over 5 per cent of the cars require higher octane fuel than the going premium grades. It is just not worth it to revamp your whole set-up back to the refinery for that small market.'

4. 'We're taking a hard look for competitive reasons, not because of our customer needs. We're trying to prepare ourselves to move into the multi-grade field if competition makes us.'

5. 'We're in a good position to hold off and watch the battle between Golden Esso and Super Shell. We've lost nothing so far by waiting so we're inclined to drag our feet a little longer. We'll probably make a decision by the end of the year.'

6. 'It's not economical to keep raising the octane rating of premium because a lot of people don't need it. We've always hesitated to take the lead because it is too costly. We would rather be right than first.'

7. 'Sun and Esso have fought for years. Sun goes down to Florida and pulls its stunt; then Esso comes along and says they'll be double-damned if they'll let 'em get away with that. So now it looks like we are all faced with another costly marketing problem.'

8. 'I think Esso's figures that one out of five cars need higher octane are unrealistic. If they get that 20 per cent of the new cars, they're going to be in big trouble, octane-wise, because they can't refine it – not that much of it. I think they realize that, putting up that 3-cent price barrier.'

As others ruminated, Sun and Esso moved boldly ahead with their new programmes.

Marketing a Super-premium

Golden Esso Extra was introduced with an octane rating of 100 to 101, compared to 97 for Esso Extra and 94 for regular Esso. A three-cent price differential separated the three brands from each other. Under stable price conditions, this would yield a dealer margin of four cents per gallon on regular, six cents on premium, and six to eight cents per gallon on super-premium.

Considering the magnitude of the distribution job to be done, Esso executed its programme in a hurry. Golden Esso Extra was to be vended through a separate gold and white pump at filling stations. New pumps, storage tanks, and added delivery systems required an investment of over thirty million dollars, with the conversion cost per station averaging five to seven thousand dollars. All converting jobbers and dealers wanting it were financed by Esso. In this connection, it may be noted in passing that the pump supplier, Gilbert and Barket Manufacturing Company, was a wholly owned Esso subsidiary.

An advertising and promotion budget of between ten and twelve million dollars was devoted to support the new three-grade system's first year. Major media included single-page and double-page newspaper ads, outdoor posters, radio, and TV – all extolling Esso's 'Three Brilliant Gasolines' but emphasizing the introduction of new Golden Esso Extra. At the station level, the new pump, a display piece in itself, was revealed at elaborate unveilings. Plastic pump signs, banners, pole signs, and driveway display panel posters communicated to the public at its point of purchase. Dealer incentive contests were launched whereby prize points, redeemable for valuable merchandise, could be earned on the basis of the number of gallons of GEE sold. Service station personnel received training materials and lectures. Motorists were also given free samples of the new fuel in selected areas.

Meanwhile, Sun had experienced some technical problems with its new blending pumps but went on to improve and extend them throughout all of its nineteen-state marketing area with advertising support stressing the theme 'Choose the exact octane strength your car needs – pay only for the octane your car needs'.

Their curiosities aroused, consumers responded by trying the super-premiums. So eager were reporters of the *Esso Dealer*, a house organ, to report on consumer and dealer reactions to GEE, that they sought out comments of managers of dealer-owned stations in which the super-premium was first marketed. The reporters were to relate many stories of 'marked enthusiasm' for the new product, recorded in testimonials such as these:

1. Louis D. Skolfield, New Orleans station manager: 'Believe it or not, we actually had some days in which we sold more Golden

Esso Extra than Esso or Esso Extra. Yes, sir, I'm sure we have another great product.'

2. Mr Howard Smith, a Memphis manager: 'Those first newspaper ads really started bringing people into our station. Two of my first-day customers returned that same week and told me they had been on extended motor trips and that they had not only improved their miles per gallon, but that their cars had much more pep.'

3. Russell R. Rinehart, Washington, D.C., said, 'I have never known so much public enthusiasm for a new Esso product in all my 32 years with the company, in spite of the exceptionally good results from the many new and improved products in the past. Customers tell us they have seen our advertising and have talked about it with their friends.'

4. 'We don't try to sell it – just explain it,' reported Baltimore station manager E. S. S. Conner, Jr. 'People with cars that might need Golden Esso Extra, for the most part, are asking for it. Others are curious and would like to rejuvenate their old cars.'

5. Boston station manager Charles R. Aldrich was quoted as saying, 'The advertising programme on Golden Esso Extra really seems to have hit the public with a bang. They start asking questions before we have time to even say hello. Some of our customers with new cars estimate as much as 50 per cent better performance.'

6. The story was similar in Elizabeth, New Jersey, according to Joseph T. Kelly. 'Many of our customers are remarking that Golden Esso Extra has improved the general performance of their cars. The comments from the new car dealers are interesting; it seems that Golden Esso Extra is the answer to a good many of their problems with pinging and sluggishness.'

From the beginning, both Esso and Sun recognized that but a small segment of the motoring public would accept the highest-octane super-premiums. Yet, Esso hoped that GEE might eventually account for as much as 15 or 20 per cent of that company's total volume. By November of 1956, Esso reported the following picture:

1. Total premium and super-premium sales had increased more than 4 per cent over the preceding year.

2. Sales of GEE represented about 10 per cent of total gallonage.

3. Of those trying GEE for the first time, some 18 per cent had been using a competitive brand.

4. One of three customers who tried it was sticking with it.

5. New-car drivers were buying the bulk of the new brand – 71 per cent drove 1956 or 1957 cars.

6. Sixty-one per cent of GEE triers were drivers of expensive cars, and six out of every ten of these kept on using it.

7. Improved public opinion for Esso was reflected in surveys that showed the public credited the firm with being the first to offer that type of improved product.

At year end 1956 was looking good for GEE, and prices were holding. It wasn't a particularly good year for Shell, whose overall petrol volume was up just a little more than a half per cent over 1955. Sun's volume was up over 5 per cent. Yet, Gulf and Texaco both closed out 1956 with greater percentage gains, compared to 1955 volume, than either Esso or Sun – somewhere in the vicinity of sixteen per cent up.

ROLLER COASTER YEARS: THE END OF THE FIFTIES

The years 1957, 1958, and 1959 were a time of dizzying ups and downs and turnabouts for cars and for fuels.

Cars

Detroiters entered 1957 with confident sales forecasts and still-rising compression ratios, but the year was to close out on a less than optimistic note. An early indicator of possible trouble appeared in the form of criticism of the power race by champions of driving safety. By July a sharp dip appeared in the stock market, and murmurs of a possible depression or recession soon circulated. Car sales were definitely starting to slip during August. Small cars were selling well enough to occasion conversation despite still-small market shares. (The 'official' position of most car makers then was that the small car was but a fad appealing to a slight portion of the market.) As demand fell off, most car manufacturers felt the pinch of excess capacity. Whether inexorably compelled by long production lead-time, or for other reasons, Detroit brought out still more powerful 1958-model cars in the

177

autumn of 1957. That autumn will also be recorded as the time of the introduction of the Edsel.

As Detroit continued its 'big car' talk, a sharply painful economic recession hit the American economy in 1958. Yet, while Edsel floundered, Ford experienced surprising success with its new four-passenger Thunderbird. At the same time, Romney's Rambler was starting to move pretty well, and the sale of imported cars was definitely growing. One now began to hear guarded comments that the 'small car' market caught the attention of Detroit as soon as it had passed the 'attractive enough' level of 5 per cent share of total market. Apparently, Detroit now saw a new route to prosperity in market segmentation and future product proliferation. But, as they speculated on a car for every purse and prospect – young or old, conservative or racy, masculine or feminine, saver or spendthrift – 1958 car sales plummeted to their lowest level since production had recovered after World War II. In 1958, 4·7 million new units were sold.

And then came 1959, the second best year in car history with sales of 6·5 million cars. In part, this was due to a growing belief that we had finally learned to control recessions. Russia's Sputnik also played a part – technology was no longer viewed as a limiting factor anywhere and the grapevine said that petrol internal combustion engines would be relegated to the scrap heap in a few years as gas turbines, solar, electric, and diesel-powered vehicles took over. The year 1959 was one of fear mixed with hope for the motoring public and those seeking to serve them. Hope for a better future was balanced against a wait-and-see stance on the part of the buyer.

What better environment could there be for the introduction of small cars by the Big Three? American Motor's Romney, after introducing the Rambler in 1950, feeling a flush of success in 1957, and recording sales of 186,000 units in 1958, was predicting a multi-billion-dollar market for 'compact' cars within two or three years and a take-over of half the entire car market by 1965. U.S. compact cars – Corvairs, Falcons, Valiants, and others – were widely introduced in the autumn of 1959. As early as August, *Business Week* predicted that Ramblers, Studebaker

Larks, imports, and the first Big Three compacts could total 1·2 million units by year end. Before November 1, *Fortune* reported that Volkswagen was six months behind on its orders and that all imports together would account for sales of 600,000 new cars.

By the end of 1959, it appeared that top compression ratios would continue to rise, that average compression ratios would drop, that 1960 might just turn out to be the best sales year in car history, and that future prospects for the coming decade of the sixties were exceedingly bright for makers and marketers of cars in America.

Petrols

While cars were in the lead car, fuels were in the caboose of the 1957–1959 roller coaster. At the start of 1957, total petrol demand continued to increase, but at a decreasing rate.

Aeroplanes needing high-octane fuel were slowly giving way to kerosene-burning jets. With hope in their hearts, many of the major oil companies watched Detroit as the car people continued to push up compression ratios in 1957. Additive enthusiasts reluctantly moved to higher octanes. Anti-additive supporters re-examined their positions. Most of the bigger two-graders improved regular or premium grades – or both – by combining additives and refinery octanes. Every important oil company was concerned about 'premium' fuel. When the 1958 new cars came out in the autumn of 1957, half of them carried manufacturers' recommendations for premium fuel and some 16 per cent needed the highest available RON for top performance. The *average* premium petrol on the market passed 98, and numerous premiums were offered by two-graders at 99 to 100 octane. Octane requirements of 110 or more were still predicted for 1960. In 1957, despite or because of changes in aircraft and other oil markets and the early warnings of a possible recession ahead, super-premium automotive petrols appeared to have a bit of an edge over lower-rated fuels.

Sunoco expanded its blends. In April of 1957, Gulf Crest had been introduced as a new third-grade high-RON fuel. By the summer, no less than a dozen 100-or-higher-octane motor fuels were on the market, according to a U.S. Bureau of Mines survey, and nine were being offered as a third grade. Golden Esso Extra, although somewhat off-target, was still moving upward towards a new peak by the end of that year.

The 1958 recession and the off-year for cars further slowed the growth rate of motor fuels. Petroleum production had started to outpace demand. Oil companies riveted their attention on market shares. Their ad campaigns, in the aggregate, were enough to confuse the most intellectual of consumers. The octane race continued well into the autumn, when an article in the November 7 issue of *Petroleum Week* was headlined, 'Ads Talk Octane But Who's Racing?' Most promotion dropped appeals based upon power, high octanes, and additive and began to stress economy, thrift, value. Ready prognosticators said that super-premiums were due for a dive and that they would soon become white elephants. And, indeed, Esso and Humble were running into certain difficulties. Golden Enco Extra, in the Texas and Gulf Coast markets, wasn't doing too well. Humble's net income dipped for the second year. Esso's crude-oil prices had risen significantly, forcing a price increase on Golden Esso Extra early in 1958. Under stiffened competitive conditions, the new prices didn't hold and GEE began to slump. Advertising support for Golden was all but eliminated long before New Year's Eve.

In 1959, petrol marketers felt the impact of forces already experienced by the motor companies in 1958. The recession had made motorists more sensitive to petrol price levels. Excess capacity led many refiners to sell off surpluses to small independent marketers who sold it to consumers under private brand names at discount prices. When the new compact cars came out in the autumn, many operated satisfactorily on regular or even sub-regular fuels, and Detroit pressured the oils less for higher-octane premiums than for high-RON regular petrols. During the first five months of 1959, the relative growth in demand for regular was twice as great as for premiums. Regular sales were up 4·9 per cent over the corresponding period in 1958; premium sales recorded a 2·1 per cent gain.

The multi-grade petrol picture was especially murky. In

October of 1959, a VP of one of the top ten oil companies was quoted as saying, 'I think the super-premium grade was a big mistake. The trend today is away from the higher-octane fuels. I certainly would consider it unwise to start marketing a higher-octane gasoline this year.' Yet, premium petrol sales (premiums plus super-premiums) were still growing at a slow but steady pace.

Golden Esso Extra faced a difficult problem. Crude-oil costs had been rising at the same time that petrol prices to wholesalers, dealers, and motorists had to be cut. If GEE were to become profitable, something had to be done in the middle – to cut the costs of refining. By June 1959 Esso had found a new process for making high-octane gas at substantially reduced cost from the same octane pool level it had before. In September it was announced that the previously separate Esso, Humble, Carter, Oklahoma, and Pate affiliates of Jersey Standard would be reorganized and consolidated under the Humble name as one unified domestic arm of the parent concern. The purposes of this move were to achieve greater management and operating efficiency quickly through such means as the reduction of duplication and, eventually, to market all Jersey Standard products in the U.S. under a single, nationwide brand name. The first aim was achieved. As of this writing, the second has yet to be attained, since the U.S. government frowns on the move.

While still backing GEE, Esso was in a profit squeeze. By late November or early December of 1959, Esso's newly elected president, O. V. Tracy, noted that the company was keeping its eyes on the sale of compact cars and said, 'Gasoline consumption per car is less and the demand for premium gasoline may be reduced.' Executive vice-president, Robert H. Scholl, stated that while there might be less need for increasing petrol octane numbers in the future, the trend to smaller cars had not affected Esso's sales of premium fuel because, 'Esso's buyers are probably more quality conscious' than buyers of competitive products.

THE KALEIDOSCOPIC SIXTIES

While 1960 didn't break the still-standing 1955 record for auto
sales, it was a new 'second-best' year for the industry. Quanti-
tatively off on the right foot, the decade opened on a number of
qualitative questions.

Economy, Power, Variety – or What?

By many numeric standards (number of cars on the road; number
of cars with more than 10:1, more than 9:1, more than 8:1 compression ratios, etc.) 1960 was justifiably viewed as a 'more than
ever before' year. It was also a time for considering whether it was
a 'less than ever' year. While few new cars with less than 8:1
compression ratios were marketed after 1959, the end of the old
horsepower race was freely forecasted. As far as the public was
concerned, nothing very dramatic came out of Detroit in 1960 or
1961. The 1961 model-year was down sharply from the year
before but, by autumn, Detroit still predicted a seven-million-unit
sales year as a sure thing for 1962.

At first, the car market seemed bifurcated. Then it appeared to
spread out and splinter into twigs and branches. By early 1962,
the fastest-growing car categories were in the less than 9:1 and
the more than 10:1 compression ratio classes. The middle grades
weren't doing well at all; small cars were doing better than the big
ones in the market place. This was also the point at which Chrysler
began to promote the idea that high-priced, gas-turbine cars would
be on the market within five or six years – a notion met with
guarded scepticism by both GM and Ford. While the horsepower race seemed to be breaking out all over again and domestic
compacts became less appealing to many motorists, the 1963
model-year marked the end of limited-alternative automotive
production and the fresh acceptance by Detroit of market segmentation by offering more choices for everybody. A trend
towards sportier models began as Ford's Thunderbird was
challenged by Buick's Riviera, the Chevrolet Corvette, Pontiac's
Grand Prix, Studebaker's Avanti. The market became so fragmented that one count of 1964 models showed 323 different types

and styles. This trend was accentuated by the fabulously successful Mustang. By 1968, Mustang alone was offering a dozen different 'power teams' – six engines and six transmissions to choose from. For two-thirds of these power packages Ford recommended premium fuel.

Petrols in Turmoil

Petrol marketers entering the sixties faced a disturbing set of circumstances. Although compact cars were still holding down premium RONs, there had been a general improvement in petrol qualities over the years. This added to costs. The growth rate of demand continued to slow down* and motorists exhibited increasingly split loyalties to motor fuel brands along with an already well-developed price sensitivity. Between 1955 and 1960, spare petrol refining capacity in the industry had risen from virtually nothing to about 15 per cent. Corporate objectives shifted more and more from straight profit maximization to holding or improving market shares by inducing brand-switching away from rivals. Even supermarket chains and mail-order retailers got into the act. By 1960, independents had deeply penetrated the market with retail prices traditionally two cents under those of their suppliers. In some areas twenty per cent or more of total gallonage went through discounters' pumps. By 1961, independents held a 50 per cent share of market in San Antonio. The stage was set for a good old-fashioned Texas showdown.

It was there that Gulf Oil decided to realign its product and price lines and launch a programme quickly hailed as 'brilliant' strategy by many majors. At the time, Gulf was offering three grades – super-premium 'Gulf Crest', premium-grade 'No-Nox', and regular 'Good Gulf'. In July of 1961 all this was revamped in San Antonio. Top-RON Crest was dropped from the line-up. The premium-grade was up-graded and redesignated as 'New-No-Nox'. 'Good Gulf' was unaffected. The third Gulf pump was now

---

* During the period 1947–1955, total petrol demand grew at an annual rate of over 6 per cent. From the mid-fifties to the mid-sixties sales gains had been reduced to around 3 or 3·5 per cent per year.

to vend a new sub-regular 'combat grade' of 91-RON fuel* priced at a level to meet discounters head-on. It was called 'Gulftane'.

Sun Oil's first response was to add *two* new sub-regulars to its blender, Sunoco 180 and 190, also priced to meet and/or beat independents. The private brands then recountered by cutting back *their* prices two cents a gallon to preserve the traditional spread between majors and independents. The whole industry now started to buzz with comments about market chaos and wide-open price wars.

Humble Oil, with a big stake in the Texas market, had experienced rougher going with GEE there than it had in the East. But it had no desire to get involved with sub-regulars and price disturbances. Apparently, Humble *was* interested in Gulf's 'New No-Nox'. By mid-1961, Humble was selling regular Esso † (94 RON), premium-grade Esso Extra (from 97 to 99 octane, depending on area), and Golden Esso Extra (100 to 102 RON). In the autumn, it was announced that this line would be rearranged in three areas – Pittsburgh, Norfolk/Newport News, and eleven Texas markets – on a test basis. Regular Esso would be held at the same octane and the same price. Golden Esso Extra was to be suspended. Esso Extra would hold its price while boosting octane to just under 100. A third product, 'intermediate in quality and price' and dubbed 'Esso Plus', was to be slotted-in between Esso and Extra at a level of 97 octane. A two-cent spread was to separate each of the three grades, and the beefed-up Esso Extra would be fully competitive with all premiums. Esso Plus could thus be used to 'trade up' regular-grade users to an 'economy premium'. Tests continued well into the spring of 1962. Results were to determine the fate of Humble's super-premium – Golden Esso Extra – in other markets.

* For comparative purposes, it is well to note that, nationwide, regular fuel averaged 92·8 RON, while average premiums, including super-premiums, were about 99·2 octane. As for Detroit's fuel recommendations for new cars, a new low for premiums was reached in 1961. Whereas almost 50 per cent of 1958 cars called for 1958 premium, only 23·5 per cent of 1961 models called for 1961 premium fuel.

† For convenience, the name 'Esso' is used throughout this section. Actually, Humble marketed under the 'Enco' name in Gulf Coast markets and under the 'Esso' name in the East.

In the meantime, although sharp price competition had forced the withdrawal of a number of sub-regulars, and although the *Wall Street Journal* was soon to report that marketers on the low end of the octane scale were beginning to fear they had guessed wrong and that premiums would once again begin to grow, Gulf was already moving nationally with its new line by mid-1962. Humble gradually phased GEE out of its line and expanded the new assortment to the twenty states in which it had a three-grade system. During a widely publicized speech in the fall of 1962, Mobil Oil's president commented that 'there is no more technical need for sub-regular grades of gasoline today than there was for a super-premium gasoline yesterday'. No matter how many shared the view, it was patently evident that Gulf and Humble had handed down 'a death sentence' for super-premiums. They were clearly on the way out before the end of 1962.

The newly apparent vulnerability of sub-regulars and super-premiums suggested both problems and opportunities to oil marketers of every caste. Product changes and price changes were vigorously mixed with name changes and claim changes as the sixties soared on. This was to be a decade of nimble jockeying for market share.

As to advertising appeals, 'we've gone through them all', said industry promoters in October of 1963, according to *Printers' Ink* magazine. Power, sexuality, technology, whimsey, and imagery finally settled 'into a period of almost Teutonic technical-mindedness'. Corporate name changes blossomed as if firms were afraid of some uncertain ancestry – Socony Mobil, on the occasion of its centennial year, in 1966, dropped the 'Socony'; Calso (Standard of California) became Chevron; Indiana Standard thought it right to rename itself 'Amoco'. Amoco offered a 'Final Filter'. We all were told that 'Megatane' was superior to octane as a measure of motor fuel quality. Shell advertised 'nine ingredients' with special emphasis on something called 'Plat-formate'. During 1960 and 1961, restless accounts representing advertising billings of almost fifty million dollars were shifted among advertising agencies.

As Shell brought in new people and Humble reorganized, the

'additive *versus* octane' debate came to an end. Oil marketers, by the mid- to late-sixties, were candidly admitting that *all* motor fuels were blends of additives and octanes. Quick starts, clean burning, greater mileage, and a myriad of other qualities were as important as octane, so it seemed. Few motorists could tell one fuel from another – unless they heard pinging. Yet, most major oil companies began to state that additives and octanes had ceased to become an either–or issue and were now some sort of combinatorial problem. One of the industry's great debates and sacred cows thus came to a timely end.

In the meantime, Sinclair was busily digging up dinosaurs for the 1964–1965 World's Fair in New York. Humble resurrected a feline that had slept for a quarter-century in promotional files and urged us all to put a tiger in our tanks – multilingually in a number of countries.

The middle to late sixties produced a confusing sort of apparent stalemate. Motorists were induced or seduced into buying cars made 'just for you'. Credit cards, stamps, tigers' tails, glassware, sweepstakes, lotteries, and other bonuses persuaded us to choose one brand over another. Mr Nader's followers urged the body politic towards more car safety. The U.S. Bureau of Mines, HEW (the Department of Health, Education, and Welfare), and others sounded social alarms for more lead-free fuels to diminish air pollution.

Economic imperatives seemed to emphasize automotive variety together with petrol up-grading and differentiation. Social imperatives stressed safety, clean air, and the diminution of pollution in general. For cars and their fuels, the sixties were ending, and their makers contemplated the mysterious future of the seventies.

LOOKING BACKWARD AND FORWARD

After almost a decade and a half of super-premiums and multi-grade petrols, the industry continues to evaluate and discuss its past and future. Many debates cluster around three inter-related questions:

  1. Why didn't more oil companies accept Esso's invitation to climb aboard the super-premium three-grade bandwagon?

2. Just how successful, or unsuccessful, were Golden Esso Extra, blending pumps, and three-grade marketing systems?

3. What questions or answers, derived from the experience of the past fifteen years, seem to be most important to the industry in the decade ahead?

Rejected Invitations

It has already been recorded that Sun and Esso attracted a number of followers but that most of the industry did *not* introduce a super-premium or depart from two-grade marketing. Lack of unanimity in such a complex industry shouldn't really be surprising. With some thirteen thousand producers, one hundred and fifty refiners and even more brands, twelve thousand wholesalers, and well over a third of a million retailers – many of which are completely independent – it is to be expected that no two companies are, and never were, in identical strategic situations. Each firm had its own ambitions, limitations, and alternatives. What attracted some marketers to super-premiums, three grades, or blenders sharply repelled others. Many were either unable to unwilling to play follow-the-leader.

In the first place, no two petrol marketers were equally 'marketing oriented'. In the second place, each had unique problems and opportunities. Let us consider these in reverse order. From the marketing point of view, each company had a private perspective on forecasts, market position, product mix, pricing, distribution, and promotion.

Every year, Du Pont, the Ethyl Corporation, car manufacturers, and petroleum marketers peer into misty crystal balls overlaid with statistics or consult oracles to predict a future which no mere mortal can rightfully claim to foresee with any degree of clarity. A wide variety of forecasting methods are employed to yield an even greater variety of forecasted results. In late 1955, Sun, Esso, and some others apparently foresaw a sharp increase in the demand for premium motor fuels. Yet, a Midwestern oilman then claimed that Golden Esso Extra was a 'dead duck' three months after it came out because there was 'just no demand for it'. Conservative firms, small and large, made conservative

187

forecasts or used the low-end estimates of others to justify cautious approaches to oil exploration, production, refining, and/or marketing. The optimists leaned the other way. If corporate actions are based on decisions, and if decisions are based on guesses or predictions, it is small wonder that oil marketers with widely varying prognosticating procedures and outputs foresaw the future in quite different terms and then acted in different fashions.

With or without reliable and uniform sales forecasts, the oils also had in fact uniquely different market positions to defend or to expand from. No oil company precisely duplicated another's geographic market coverage, and octane requirements have always varied by region and climate. Eastern markets – with shorter drives, variable temperature, more high-powered cars – and mountainous markets call for higher octane fuels than non-Eastern or prairie-state areas. Beyond geography, motor fuels are by no means synonymous in commercial significance with other crude-oil by-products. Home heating oils, although of declining importance to the industry, were profitable segments in which some were entrenched. Some saw salvation in jet fuels rather than high-octane markets. In car fuels, each company had a different measured or assumed degree of brand loyalty and market penetration in each octane classification. By 1955, Sun was strong in regulars and sub-regulars. Esso probably had the highest premium-to-regular ratio in the industry and stood to lose the most if premium-grade car fuels chanced to slip. Strength in one by-product market signified weakness in another for most oils. Each oil marketer made an independent set of decisions with reference to which segments it chose to defend most vigorously and which was most vulnerable to its own potentiality for aggressive attack by direct or indirect means.

No two firms had similar market-penetration patterns in the multiple markets for crude-oil products nor equally profitable product mixes. In addition, marketers, test-tube researchers, and engineers still quarrelled over different hypotheses and theories about the precise nature of the relationship between compression ratios, octane requirements, and the potentialities of additives.

No conclusive reconciliation on these sub-issues is yet in sight. Any ultimate umpire will be a richly deserved candidate for the industry's equivalent to a Nobel peace prize.

No two firms operated through precisely the same distribution channels. And, as every beginning student of marketing knows, channel differences can be and often are of crucial importance to product success. A petrol marketer with a high percentage of company-owned or controlled service stations, with a rich proportion of volume flowing through direct rather than jobber channels, and with more flexibility in the sheer logistical problems of storage and physical supply is in a better position to make a marketing change-over all the way to the final point of purchase by motorists than another supplier would be without such advantages. In this respect, Esso was in a much more favourable position for marketing changes than Shell, Sinclair, Mobil, and many others were at the time GEE was first introduced.

In 1955–1956, some firms saw Esso's invitation as a kind of sucker trap into which they refused to be lured. Quite early in the game, such companies had expressed fears over the possible return of what some referred to as 'the depression Ghost'. During the great depression of the 1930s, many petrol marketers had gone to three grades – a premium, a regular, and a sub-regular price-fighting brand. Since petrol prices are resolutely wedded to petrol RONs, many feared that widespread adoption of a three-or-more-grade marketing system could bring a return to depression-era price wars. This turned out to be a not altogether unjustified fear, as Gulf and Sun can now unquestionably attest.

Few consumers or petrol retailers know much about petrol qualities, and their edification comes, if at all, only at the expense of much effort and money. Therefore, each oil marketer also had privy notions about the best way to promote motor fuels. Even without such a variety of marketing viewpoints, it should have been seen that industry-wide change-overs to super-premiums, third grades, and multi-grades were of low-order probability. An evaluation of technological and financial differences between companies, quite apart from marketing factors, might logically have led to the conclusion that more than a Sun or an Esso would be needed to lead the entire industry towards marketing three or more grades of motor petrol at one time or even over some reasonable time period.

Every large oil company has, at any given moment, an almost infinite number of possible alternatives to pursue with a finite budget. Before the well, between well and pump, and after the pump are numerous areas of possible investment. Capital-budgeters are persistently pressed to make terribly difficult defensible recommendations from among alternatives such as these: How should the corporate pot be split between exploration, development, refining, and marketing? How much money should go into reorganization and managerial improvements? Are chemicals and petrochemicals better investments than other petroleum products? If the emphasis is to be on automotive fuels, should we add more TEL, introduce other additives, upgrade refinery output, increase the number and calibre of service stations, or what?

Marketing and financial factors are merged with production considerations in arriving at such crucial decisions and programmes within individual firms in a highly competitive industry. What about crude position? By the mid-fifties, for instance, Shell was almost exclusively preoccupied with exploration and development problems carrying higher priorities than those in refining and marketing. Hung up on high-priced U.S. crude and quota-controlled Venezuelan imports, Shell had little opportunity really to emphasize refining or marketing until about 1960. On the other hand, Jersey Standard's domestic problems in the early to late fifties centred less on crude supplies than on refining and marketing. Esso, with unusually deep penetration into higher-octane motor fuel markets, lagged in top-RON refining capacity by 1955, and found itself in an increasingly difficult position to retain premium-fuel leadership without major investments in refining and marketing.

Although this brief catalogue of alternatives and factors affecting their selection or rejection barely scratches the surface of a much more complex and compelling reality for individual decision-makers, it may suggest reasons why Esso could have been more attracted than Shell or someone else towards dumping the two-grade petrol system and towards introducing super-premium motor fuels. It implies more than it expresses why some said 'Yes' and others 'No' to Jersey Standard's RSVP to join its Esso in a high-RON race.

Was GEE a Failure?

The golden super-premium is widely held to have been a clear misfire. Among the conclusions of all nay-sayers, one is that GEE was 'no gain for Jersey'. Extravagantly unwarranted opinions that Golden was a 'twenty-million-dollar loser' have also been voiced. At any point on the broad scale of estimated losses, arguments supporting the evaluations can be classified under two main headings that might be labelled the 'rejected invitations' and 'no demand' hypotheses.

Many hold that the mere fact that most companies didn't follow Humble beyond the magical 100-RON mark makes for a *prima facie* case against GEE and other super-premiums. On the surface, at least, such a baldly stated theory of the omniscient majority can be summarily dismissed. Yet, with major qualifications, grains of merit may be found around and beneath the hypothesis. In the rough-and-tumble world of petrols, product leadership by big companies is more apparent than real. Maybe Esso did get out in front a bit too far in octane numbers and prices to bring in a winner. To whatever extent automotive engineers consider fuels as constraints on engine designs they would be more likely to consider average offerings rather than extreme motor fuel qualities within relevant octane requirement ranges.

The second hypothesis is that GEE failed because there never was a real need for it. Many non-followers held that position at the time of the 1956 Esso–Humble announcement. In 1960 a Du Pont survey showed 1·3 per cent of respondents reporting purchases of super-premiums. Sixty per cent of those same respondents reputedly bought the products because of high prices which *implied* high quality that could not otherwise be recognized in demonstrable car performance improvements.

Although the hypothesis has never been tested to the satisfaction of research purists, substantial evidence suggests that actual need for octane ratings over 100 did not represent more than 1 per cent of total motor petrol needs at any time during the 1956–1962 super-premium era. Gulf Oil publicly stated the same conclusion in 1961. By inference, one might conclude that Esso arrived at the same point in 1962. Most critics doubted from the beginning that going after such a tiny market sliver could be justified on economic or strategic grounds. Esso was said to have over-stretched refining capacity in an unnecessary crash programme representing an overly sensitive reaction to Detroit in a vain effort to protect an imaginary 'image' of premium-grade leadership. A wish-fulfilling prophecy of 5 to 10 per cent market share, backed by more than a hundred million dollars of capital expenditure by less than ten marketers, made some unmeasured contribution towards capturing about 2 per cent of total petrol sales – twice the level justified on the basis of 'real' need.

Humble Oil & Refining Company officials object to these viewpoints. They resolutely refuse to dub GEE a 'failure', substituting phrases such as 'qualified success' instead. Humble does admit to having met with greater problems in the South than it did up North. But company spokesmen claim that GEE volume never fell below 5 per cent of total Esso–Humble petrol sales, that it averaged out around 7 to 8 per cent, and that at no time did it represent a financial loss. By adding GEE to the two previous products in the petrol line-up, subsequent gains in the overall premium-to-regular ratio are said to have resulted in a more profitable product mix.

To add more thorns to an already prickly brier patch, remember that we are not dealing with one issue but with two or more. A distinction must be drawn between *products* and the *distribution systems* through which they are vended. Super-premium petrols have ostensibly been off the market since 1962, but we still have service stations with blending pumps, three pumps, and two pumps. Which system is best?

To state that General Motors, Ford, or Chrysler could theoretically produce cars all year long without duplication is to cite a well-worn cliché. Yet, this hackneyed expression contains conceptual and strategic values for petrol marketers. With increasing product variety coming out of Detroit, some two-grade petrol marketers *are* finding it difficult to match fuels to cars. Automotive product differentiation begets petrol product differentiation. Three-graders and multi-grade blenders appear to be in more favourable positions to satisfy a greater number of needs than two-graders.

Yet, petrol variety has some upper limit, set not by technology but by customers. Despite highly developed skills in blending at refineries, bulk plants, and service stations, multiple grades cause confusion at both dealer and consumer levels. If one accepts the psychological proposition that people find it difficult to make choices, or often prefer to avoid choices, that the difficulty is compounded in proportion to the number of alternatives from which those choices must be made, and that the middle ground is easier to take than extremes, then one must also conclude that two-graders offer motorists the simplest decision-making situation, that blending pumps unduly complicate the matter and invite 'trading down', and that three-graders (assuming one product is regular and the remaining two are premiums) invite 'trading up' at least to the middle grade.

Before clouding the issue further, it must be admitted that no definitive conclusion has yet been discovered to establish once and for all whether super-premiums and vending systems associated with them were or will prove out to be successes or failures. Nobody knows. Precise yardsticks for measurement of results were never established or made public before the events took place. With respect to GEE, a Humble executive has said, 'We are not unhappy but could have been happier.' Since 1964, a benevolently smiling tiger has cast a rosy glow over Esso. Two-grader Shell elected to add more and better stations to its distribution system rather than increase product variety and hasn't done badly at all in the sixties.[13]

For an individual refiner, one barrel of a given type and variety of crude oil will, after refining, end up in countless end products, uses, and markets. With joint-costs and other factors making it all but impossible to link causes to effects in this industry, conclusions drawn over issues discussed in this chapter can be no more than private opinions. The prudent view may be a split decision: Super-premiums were misfires of minor consequence; three-grade systems are likely to prove out as successes for those firms using them. Each of us must come to an independent conclusion, bearing in mind the relativity of terms like 'success' and 'failure' and other points sketched out in Chapter I.

Babe Ruth set records for strike-outs as well as home runs. Companies described in other chapters may find solace in that fact. Oil companies are still in there swinging, and the books will have to be kept open for some time before we know on which side of the ledger to post final records on petrols and their marketing systems.

Problems and Prospects

The oil industry will face great problems and fresh opportunities in the coming decade. Pessimistic industry commentators have compiled a long and gloomy list of difficulties. Without dwelling overly long on morbid subjects, let us consider just three of these items.

It has been declared that the days are numbered for motor petrols. Chrysler has said for years that the gas turbine is just around the corner, and many have believed it. Free-piston engines, fuel injection, and electric, solar, and atomic-powered vehicles are seen as distinct possibilities. Cars may no longer need petrol in their diets – kerosene, peanut oil, batteries, and a huge number of alternate energy sources may soon be substituted.

Conservationists and medical interests may someday outlaw the sale of all leaded petrols. When and if this eventually comes to pass, a capital investment of up to three billion dollars could be involved in an industry-wide conversion to lead-free fuels if octane levels are maintained.

Regulatory policies will continue to contribute to industry instability. The federal government's crude-oil import control programme, for example, is so constructed as to provide many refiners with a strong incentive to refine more end products than are actually needed in diverse markets every year. This, coupled with other contributing factors, leads to persistent imbalances between supply and demand, induces oils to emphasize tactical rather than strategic aspects of the business, and helps explain why oil marketers often seem to be zigging when they ought to be zagging.

More constructively oriented optimists claim that such problems can easily be met. Oil companies can work in closer co-operation with Detroit to make better petrol-powered engine designs as a hedge against a take-over by substitute fuels. Oils can, and already have, worked to develop mechanical automotive accessories to take care of pollutants resulting from evaporation or imperfect combustion of leaded hydrocarbon fuels. Political lobbying may be made more effective to ease regulatory policies and permit petroleums to become more marketing oriented. While optimists regard the problems of pessimists as opportunities, realists see the optimists' recommendations as temporary measures at best.

In the no-man's-land (or everyman's domain) between optimism and pessimism one can perceive visceral feelings that survival and success may lie somewhere embedded in the precept that, 'in the valley of the blind, the one-eyed man is king'.

Outside the industry, it is widely held that the consuming public is blind. Motorists have no real means for judging how good or bad motor fuels are, and dealers are of little or no help to them.* This point was succinctly put by *Consumer Reports* in March of 1963: 'the industry and consumers face the classic marketing situation for which quality standards are the classic solution . . . the consumer has no adequate basis for an informed

---

* The author happens, for many reasons, to buy most of his petrol from Humble. In March 1969, I asked a number of Esso servicemen just what the differences were between 'Plus' and 'Extra'. Not one could explain them to me. I do know that my car knocks on 'Plus' but not on 'Extra' – should I have my car's ignition retarded and try 'Plus' again? – am I over-buying octane numbers? To whom must I turn for answers? By late 1969, the Justice Department and the FTC were contemplating a legal requirement that octane ratings be posted at all service station pumps. Therefore, by the publication date of this book, this situation might well have been clarified.

choice'. In this respect, petrol marketers find themselves in the same rocking boat as those selling such products as anti-freeze (see Chapter II) and tyres. There are countless measures of fuel quality, intramural quarrels over relevant yardsticks, high costs, and dubious benefits to marketers from a new educational programme with a high potentiality for failure. No ordinary motorist really knows, although he is told and often suspects, that all petrols are created equal. If there really are significant differences between motor fuels, it would seem that refiners with the best fuels would seek to demonstrate that fact. But to demonstrate it would not be easy. An entirely new dictionary would be needed to translate product attributes from the language of producers to the lingo of laymen. The translation problem would probably require a massive collaborative effort between all automobile manufacturers, petrol marketers, the American Petroleum Institute, the American Society for Testing and Materials, the Bureau of Mines, the Department of Commerce, a battery of linguists, technologists, and general semanticists.

Such an effort to correct consumer blindness is not likely to be forthcoming nor would it be likely to be wholly successful if attempted. Marketing, thus deprived of an opportunity to demonstrate intrinsic product differences in petrols, is emasculated to the point where extrinsic brand names, advertising, prices, promotional deals, distribution efficiency, and service-station convenience, courtesy, and attraction must carry the day for petrol marketers.

If motorists cannot be cured of blindness, perhaps some petrol marketer can become king of that particular valley by opening one or more of its own eyes.

If actions are based on decisions, and if decisions are based on predictions, then oil marketers might conclude that survival and success may lie in the direction of improving their own forecasts. Current thinking about future events more often than not proves to be wrong. The mid-fifties forecasts of Gulf, Humble, and others unquestionably *did* prove to be wrong. Can't that be corrected? Compelling arguments can easily be marshalled for an affirmative answer. Individual oil marketers *can* balance refinery capacity and refinery runs with market needs – *provided* market needs can be estimated with a reasonable degree of accuracy and provided that many companies are ready to refine less than maximum legal quantities of petrol. While the oils' technological changes do actually come about because of competitive and other environmental pressures and, as even Humble admits, 'without particular regard to the existing supply and demand situation' it might yet be questioned whether the investment of manpower, facilities, time, and money in better forecasts is the real answer for solving the oils' problems and capitalizing upon future opportunities.

At the moment, the future of oils seems linked to Detroit, to which petrol makers try to make adaptive responses with some time lag. But Detroit has made a number of human misjudgements. It is burdened with long lead times, has had to gamble with styles, cannot pre-test its models with consumers, has found historically based projections unreliable and econometric models frustrating, and has learned that fortuitous timing holds the key to success – despite all we hear of fashion theory, concept testing, diffusion processes, taste-maker theory, and important results from the Survey Research Center of the University of Michigan. Linked to Detroit and its unenviable forecasting record, oils seem to be not only vulnerable but to be getting less than their money's worth in maintaining men in Detroit for intelligence purposes. Better liaison with an uncertain Detroit is no viable answer to long-run prayers of oilmen.

While petrol marketers are encouraged to develop better forecasting techniques, it appears that they still have a long way to go.[14] Even recent improvements in input–output analysis, sophisticated as they may be and possibly steps in the right direction, are not yet practical for much industry use.[15] Current and past attempts at forecasting may even have hindered instead of helped forward planning. As Jay W. Forrester has said in his book *Industrial Dynamics*, 'It is quite reasonable to expect that forecasting methods will be one of the factors creating system instability and that they can accentuate the very problems they are presumed to alleviate . . . the forecasting process can affect not only the series of events being forecast but can affect the future forecasting procedures themselves. A forecast which is too high leads to certain production and inventory crises which create greater forecasting caution in the next year. This conservatism can bias future forecasts downward with the result that they undershoot.' Whether over or under, forecasts do tend to bring about their own self-fulfilling prophecies and to convert the future into predetermined history.

In the final analysis, the key to survival and prosperity in the oil business does *not* lie in better forecasts. Available techniques cannot handle the enormous range of variables (economic, political, technological, competitive, institutional, demographic, sociological, and others) that must be estimated for strategic planning purposes. Furthermore, strategic intelligence decays at a much faster rate than tactical information; the latter data, therefore, provide inputs for forecasting models which can then grind out no more than short-term predictions. The complexity of the industry also makes it all but impossible to use the so-called 'range principle' ('minimum, maximum, and most likely' estimates of forecasted values) to provide needed flexibility for corporate-level contingency planning.

Finally, the fact of the matter is that nobody without occult powers can really foresee the future. As Peter Drucker has put it, and the italics are his, '*Long-range planning is necessary precisely because we cannot forecast.*' Drucker also correctly says that, 'it is not the "facts that decide"; people have to choose between imperfect alternatives on the basis of uncertain knowledge and fragmentary understanding'.[16]

The *future* of the petroleum industry depends on the quality of long-range strategic planning (not the same thing as forecasting) that is accomplished *today*. While it is beyond the scope, purpose, and possibilities of this chapter to describe fully how the industry should go about it,[17] the broad outlines of long-range strategic planning can be sketched in brief outline with a broad brush.

A starting point is to consider customers, both present and potential. Lord Keynes observed, 'In the long run, technological change is simply a matter of demand.' The oil industry clearly reveals short planning horizons when it freely admits that its technological change comes about from competitive pressures without particular regard for demand conditions. Drucker has stated that there is only one real business purpose, 'to create a customer'. Theodore Levitt has charged the industry with 'selling what we make' instead of 'making what will sell', indicated that oils were doomed because they were not adequately exploiting the desires of motorists, and urged oilmen to consider themselves as being in 'the energy business'.

The critical question is *what* customers – and *when*. Petroleum has countless uses and users. As more than one observer has noted, Mr Levitt may have shown as much or more myopia in proclaiming his vision than can justly be attributed to executives in the petroleum businesses he vilified. The language of Keynes and Drucker strongly and properly hints that petroleum marketers must be oriented to *multiple* markets and to *future* markets. To accept too literally the advice of Levitt and go chasing after fuel cells and batteries as petrol substitutes may, as others have already observed, lead the oils down the road to disaster rather than up the trail to survival and prosperity. Oil executives will have to make assumptions as to the future, make difficult entrepreneurial decisions today about countless future market targets, and then set priorities and timetables for their exploitation. The most difficult decision of all will be the one concerning what role motor fuels will be assigned in the petroleum companies' product mixes for the seventies and whether automotive motor fuel markets can be allowed to dry up in the face of encroaching substitutes for petrol.

Members of the petroleum industry also face the task of balancing private assumptions about future markets with assessments of their own individual capabilities for change. They will, in Druckerian terms, have to define just what businesses they really are in today and hope to be in tomorrow. Although each major oil company in a conglomeration of entrepreneurial enterprises, the observation of one steel company president may have relevance to that painful process of definition. He has asserted or implied that petroleum companies are and will be in the business

o

of producing, up-grading, and exploiting crude oil to the fullest extent of crude's potential. Today, the industry probably has less spare capacity for making petrol than it does for making other petroleum end products. It is also probable, prior comments about petrol qualities notwithstanding, that the long-term upper limits to product variety and customer satisfaction for the entire range of crude oil by-products will be set by technology rather than users' concern over latent or manifest need.

It may be that aggressively entrepreneurial companies with the greatest technical prowess for squeezing more and better things out of crude have a leg up on the others. Some are saying that Shell and a few others now occupy such a strategic position and stand ready to challenge rubber companies, plastics outfits, agricultural and industrial chemicals producers, and others in entirely new markets with superior technology. But this brings us dangerously near to forecasting.

What is more to the point is that petroleum firms must hustle to innovate and bring about a sound marriage between markets and technology – innovation not only in terms of new products, but innovation in marketing methods for yet-to-be-defined markets, organizational innovation to get necessary long-range strategic planning done, innovation in terms of capital budgeting, innovation in entirely new marketing and distribution mechanisms, and innovation in every other critical aspect of business management.

Any fair historical survey of petroleum's past shows that the industry has rather consistently come up with both diagnostic and prescriptive know-how, that it has demonstrated a capacity for change ranging from filling the lamps of China to protecting Chinese cabbages in America, and that it has a deeply ingrained propensity for survival even while upheaval affects the markets it serves. This author is more optimistic than many another over the industry's chances for not only surviving but prospering during the decades ahead. That some oil companies will also fall victim to mismarketing of many varieties may also be accepted as a foregone conclusion for the seventies.

CHAPTER VII

Part 1: Messages from Misfires

A great deal of human misery, whether in marriage or marketing, stems from making mistakes from which we either fail to learn anything at all or from which we learn only too well the wrong lessons. A woman may view a broken romance through embittered eyes and conclude that *all* men are no good, instead of trying to discover how to succeed through failure. In business, 'all too often people in marketing are getting pinned down with a steely stare by top management and asked questions like these –

'*How come* we struck out on three products in a row?

'*How come* sales aren't up to forecast?

'*How come* we spent so much in advertising for such a puny result?

'Finally, *how come* we aren't making any money around here? And the reason we are being asked questions like that, surprisingly often, traces to *our* forgetting the ABC's.' [18]

But mismarketing is not just something to be mourned over. Messages from misfires can add greatly to the planning, organizing, operating, and controlling efficiency of many concerns. 'There must be attitudes of calculated risk-taking, of willingness to make a few mistakes for the sake of many successes. The only way to avoid all mistakes is never to do anything new or different, to create, to grow. The winner is the company that is willing to make mistakes – but organizes to keep them fewer and less severe than those of competitors.' [19]

'I think,' said one agency VP, 'that the greatest single challenge for marketing men can be stated quite simply: How can we bring home more successes – fewer failures?' And a General Foods executive has remarked: 'We just keep trying to improve our batting average. Isn't that what the business game is all about?' Boosting the batting average can be even more important to marketers than to ballplayers. In his book, *Business and Society*, Joseph W. McGuire made this crisp comment: 'It may not be correct to state, as did the unfortunate Mr Charles E. Wilson, that "what is good for General Motors is good for the country", but it is probably accurate to remark that, in the aggregate, business activities are so central to our well-being that every time these activities decline the heart of society skips a beat.' A nation's heart murmurs are too often caused by mismarketing – frequently by some of the largest companies.

In 1964 General Foods was called before the Federal Trade Commission to justify the company's actions in a case involving GF's acquisition of a smaller firm producing S.O.S. soap pads. The government's concern was with the preservation of competition; its fear was that a very large firm could use superior marketing power to injure smaller producers of scouring pads if the take-over were allowed. As part of the defence, attorneys for General Foods were understandably anxious to demonstrate that GF was by no means so all powerful as to be immunized against mismarketing. Mr Mortimer himself cited an impressive list of product failures suffered by his company (including Gourmet Foods, a baby-food line, a ketchup, Kool-Shake, and others) to demonstrate that it was continually vulnerable to misfires.

As the chapters of this book attest, mismarketing in *many* big companies has affected America's cardiac condition – sometimes imperceptibly and sometimes not. It is now tempting to assemble a lengthy catalogue of concrete reasons why marketing programmes have failed. But since no two of us could likely agree on the list, here are just a few broad generalizations designed to provoke interest and constructive thinking about some of the major factors behind mismarketing.

(1) *Confusing Tactics with Strategy*

A classic dilemma has centred around our persistent inability to distinguish between marketing tactics and strategy. After the

Philco take-over, Ford's Mr Beck may have been addressing himself to this point by saying that, 'Whenever you get to a spot where you run a company to conserve cash, it's not a question of whether you're going to fail, but how soon.' While many people, Ford's and others, were too harshly critical of some pre-Fordian Philco managers, it seems inescapably clear that Philco was never quite certain whether its 'Instant Dividend' was a strategic or a tactical operation. Some readers may discern a similar confusion in the cases of the anti-freeze makers and the oil companies. While the distinction is often difficult, it is always essential to make it. The more intimately a marketing activity impinges upon the survival power of a particular firm, the more strategic it is to that company. We are again dealing with a slippery set of dualistic and relative concepts. But to prevent or reduce the incidence of mis-marketing, strategic considerations must clearly be assigned higher priorities and given more rigorous administrative attention than the merely tactical or operational aspects of marketing.

(2) *Failing to Define One's Business Adequately*

To a substantial degree, the apparent confusion of marketers between strategy and tactics could be lessened if those at the top faced squarely the question of what their businesses have been, are now, and should be in the future. At least as long ago as 1954, Peter Drucker said, 'that the question is so rarely asked – at least in a clear and sharp form – and so rarely given adequate study and thought, is perhaps the most important single cause of business failure'. As Theodore Levitt and others argued so force-fully a half decade later, neglect in defining business purpose *adequately* has resulted with terrifying frequency in mismarketing in America and elsewhere. Having experienced for themselves the bitter taste of failure, and chastened by many an outsider, mar-keters increasingly listen and learn from constructive critics in and out of their respective firms. Since its experience with Gourmet Foods and less widely publicized marketing misfires, for example, General Foods has vastly improved upon its understanding of its own corporate uniqueness as applied to marketing. And several petroleum companies have been individually moved to reconsider whether they are in 'the energy business', 'the business of producing and up-grading crude oil', or something else. To the extent that more top executives wrestle with these issues those under them will learn to translate their answers into effective marketing action. Marketers will then be freed to utilize the ever-growing body of literature on business and marketing strategy[20] to improve the batting averages of their individual businesses.

(3) Undercounting or Underestimating Those Concerned

Many individuals and groups (consumers, retailers, wholesalers, trade associations, trades unions, various governmental bodies, watchdog groups, stockholders, and a *host* of others) have a vital stake in the marketing practices of individuals, companies, nations, and multi-national groups.[21] In this book, we have borne witness to highly emotional and sometimes propagandistic wars waged by numerous parties to marketing activity – perhaps especially in the case of the Instant Dividend, but to a lesser extent in the anti-freeze, beer, food, and petrol stories. We can also find in other historical marketing sources numerous examples of furious and more protracted conflict between multiple parties over changes or innovations – early and bitter reactions against supermarket chains, somewhat more recent debates about the 'legitimacy' of the discount house, perennial expressions of emotion over legalized resale price maintenance (whether labelled 'fair trade', 'quality stabilization', or something else). Marketing misfires have helped to impress upon us the necessity of looking at marketing from a multi-partied viewpoint. Worldwide reactionary and revolutionary forces operating as we enter the seventies may place even greater significance on understanding the many-faceted nature of modern marketing. Past mismarketing has *already* forced us to seek new philosophies and methods of commercial conflict resolution.

Furthermore, literally *every* case in this book suggests that we nearly always undervalue the importance of trade channels in the planning and execution of marketing operations. It is quite likely that trade channel problems and opportunities, after three or more decades of relative neglect, will provide a primary focal point for marketing problems and opportunities in the decades ahead.

And we still haven't said much about competition. The 'Instant Dividend' story added to an already huge fund of awareness that there are very few new marketing ideas that can't be copied. But, readers may also be interested to note that Lever Brothers moved into the fancy foods field in 1966 quite largely on the basis of a strategy precisely formulated on a platform of trying to avoid previous errors made by General Foods in the same field. It is not now pertinent to inquire whether Lever is always successful, although it most assuredly is not. But two mini-messages from marketing misfires (neither new nor startling but nevertheless important) might be inserted here. First, there may be just as important marketing opportunities open to emulators as there are to innovators. Second, rivals can and do (with increasing frequency and sophistication) monitor and learn from the mistakes (and successes) of others.

Let us not miss the larger point. If marketers don't stress a broadly based sociometric approach to truly multi-partied marketing in the seventies, it will be because they haven't learned or applied the ABC's of mismarketing discovered and rediscovered by examining marketing's generally shiny but somewhat tarnished past. Hopefully, it is now axiomatic that marketers will retain their hard-learned orientation to the consumer while tempering it with a much more fundamental understanding of broader social and environmental forces relevant to their daily work.

(4) *Underestimating Dangers in Frontal Assault*

Marketing failures have often resulted from head-on attacks against the entrenched positions of stronger marketing rivals. Liddell Hart and other experts on military strategy have long extolled the merits of the 'indirect approach' and demonstrated the frequent futility of direct lines of attack, but marketers seemingly ignore the lessons of both military and marketing history here. Neither 'Telar' nor 'Dowgard' could push 'Prestone' from its perch. 'Rheingold' ran into trouble in Los Angeles partly because that was an area newly full of unusually eager, intense, and tough competition. Other such cases abound. General Foods withdrew a baby-food line largely because the position of Gerber and other brands had been fatefully under-estimated, just as Swanson and other companies forced GF out of the frozen pie business. About twenty years ago, according to Spencer Klaw,[22] Lever Brothers suffered a twenty-four-million-dollar loss over a six-year period on its 'Surf' brand of detergent in a losing attempt to buck P&G's 'Tide' and Colgate's 'Fab'. Rather than exploit lines of least resistance, many marketers still misfire by engaging the enemy on his own ground or his own terms, instead of exploiting his weaknesses, avoiding decisive engagement when that seems prudent, outflanking him, or using other forms of indirect marketing manoeuvre. As the number and forms of competition increase in the years ahead, the need for innovative and adaptive *indirect* marketing will be felt even more keenly than it has in the past.

(5) *Mismarketing Through Faulty Communications*

Most men who earn a living through marketing have high regard for their skills as communicators. But records show they still have a bit to learn. In this book, we have seen errors made by both internal and external transmitters and receivers of marketing messages. Advertising *media* have inappropriately related to markets. And the impressions or *messages* carried in promotional vehicles of all sorts have also proved to be troublesome contri-butors to marketing mistakes. Consumers simply hadn't compre-hended how really permanent their anti-freezes were, why or how octane or megatane ratings and the presence or absence of 'Platformate' influence the performance of their cars, why one beer was supposedly better than another, whether an 'Instant Dividend' plan benefited them or not. Dealers and distributors who have failed to understand 'what's in it for them' have been written off as recalcitrant or ignorant. But faulty communications transmitted by marketers themselves were a key factor in many of these histories. Marketing men have often fallen into semantic traps without even trying. Super-sophistication, including the employment of bulging bags of research tools for pre-testing and post-testing communications effectiveness plus discourses over whether or not 'the medium is the message', may have diverted marketers from the basics of effectively informing and persuading prospects. Some marketers are expert at avoiding the modern and pressing admonition to tell it like it is. Purveyors of real estate, swimming pools, insurance, banking facilities, and many other goods and services have demonstrated a special ineptitude for marketing communications. The next decades will offer great challenges to apply hard-won lessons from the past in order to sustain and enhance the social image of marketing as a profession and to improve the batting averages registered on the fresh scorecards of individuals and corporations engaged in that endeavour.

(6) *Off-target Marketing*

Customers are created by delivering benefits and satisfactions on which people place some economic value. Needs and wants are as heterogeneous as the individuals who have them. It is therefore difficult to draw a sharp bead on the best market segments to shoot for in a given marketing situation. Philco failed to clarify who could benefit most from its Instant Dividend until quite late in the game. With Gourmet Foods, GF belatedly tried to redirect a strategy originally aimed at an ill-defined and overly segmented market. Some anti-freeze manufacturers badly over-estimated the number of motorists with a caretaker attitude towards automobile cooling systems. Rheingold learned that Los Angelenos were quite different from New Yorkers and had to be approached on different terms. Mismarketing has often been a consequence of failing to zero in on the right category of consumers – defined in terms of such variables as geography, demographic factors, and insights from the classification systems of behavioural scientists. But the decade of the sixties witnessed an unprecedented increase in our knowledge of consumers. That growth, coupled with the individual businessman's awareness of past errors and a knowledge of the particular constraints his own firm's uniqueness places on target marketing, ought to bring home more successes and fewer failures in the seventies.

(7) Unbalancing the Marketing Mix

Studies of marketing failures have exposed the 'fallacy of the One Fatal Flaw'. It is as futile to seek a single reason for a misfire as it is to search for a lone key to commercial success. Marketers must think in terms of the *syndromes* of mismarketing to determine if individual elements of a marketing programme have been internally consistent or working at cross-purposes. Success or failure often hinges on interrelationships between all the forces at an executive's disposal. The ideal pattern, perhaps, is an orchestrated harmony of marketing factors, custom-assembled for correctly specified target markets and tuned-in to all environmental and other boundary conditions. Of course, this calls for more art than science – an extremely high order of executive judgement.

In his 1948 study of manufacturers' marketing costs, Harvard Professor James Culliton described the business executive as 'a "mixer of ingredients", who sometimes follows a recipe prepared by others, sometimes prepares his own recipe as he goes along, sometimes adapts a recipe to the ingredients immediately available, and sometimes experiments with or invents ingredients no one else has tried'. Quite properly, I believe, this makes the Director of Marketing's job sound somewhat more like that of a Cordon Bleu chef than a lab scientist's. Culliton's associate, Neil Borden, later expanded upon and popularized the notion of 'the marketing mix'[23] – which results from the blending of product planning, pricing, branding, packaging, displaying, distributing, selling, advertising, servicing, and other activities into an internally consistent and mutually reinforcing whole. At the conceptual level, all astute marketers now use this term or its equivalent as a part of their working vocabularies and understand that the mixture must constantly be kept in proper balance. From the point of view of marketing research and practice, we have also made a bit of progress in making the concept operational. For example, Gordon E. Miracle[24] and others have contributed towards clarifying just how product characteristics influence marketing in areas such as distribution channels, promotion, product policy, and pricing. Some attention, you may recall, was devoted to such relationships in the case of Philco's merchandising operation. But marketing specialists, and perhaps to some lesser extent the generalists, are quite likely to continue to construct the unbalanced mixes that have so often contributed to mismarketing in the past . . . unless, of course, they dust off available books on marketing history and learn to profit from lessons outlined in them.

(8) *Inflexibility in Planning and Execution*

In Chapter I, 'failure' was viewed as a relative term with many meanings, but we have been using the word in the sense of falling short of expectations or of not achieving objectives at acceptable cost. Yet, Simon, Smithburg, and Thompson's classic book *Public Administration* notes that, 'Most human planning probably results in failure if we measure it by comparing the results achieved with the results originally intended by the planners.' The operative word is *originally*. Early marketing planning is never based on hard facts but on various premises, forecasts, and assumptions involving limited knowledge, piecemeal data, and imperfect concepts. Still, as one fellow expressed it, men have 'planned conquest with painstaking detail built on the bedrock of meticulous and irrefutable logic'. The plans have too often then been rigidly and unwaveringly adhered to, without *any* modification, in their actual execution. Planning overkill and organizational rigidity seem to be an increasingly important factor in mismarketing in today's world of accelerating change.

This is no argument against planning itself, for sound diagnosis is the basis for good prescription and subsequent success in any field. It is an argument for more *flexibility* in administrative planning, organizing, executing, and controlling. Flexible, innovative, and imaginative planning places greater emphasis on the possibility of unforeseeable events and allows that the impossible can sometimes occur. Public administrators and military people have traditionally stressed contingencies to a greater extent than businessmen. But marketers have been showing signs of change. In *The Creative Organization*, Gary A. Steiner argued for more 'administrative slack; time and resources to absorb errors'. To some extent, modern techniques of planning and monitoring hold promise in this connection – the development of variant forms of PERT (Programme Evaluation and Review Technique), the use of models for simulating market behaviour in advance of action, the employment of Bayesian procedures for dealing with decisions under uncertainty, and real-time computer arrangements to provide on-stream feedback of marketing intelligence. These developments, with which marketers must be familiar, have potential for helping to prevent mismarketing in its incipient stages by indicating how and when to make timely adjustments to plans and activities that can convert projected failure into solid success. But the new tools are not enough. Part of the requirement is attitudinal. High-level executives must act like entrepreneurs instead of 'organization men' and develop a risk-taking ethos within their marketing set-ups. In the final analysis, the most important single element in marketing is probably still just plain old-fashioned guts.

Nothing in this book's conclusions have been offered as universal truths or as the only maxims for a marketing primer. There is still but one laboratory in which thoughts about marketing can be infallibly proved right or wrong – the world market place itself.

Still, there is, as John Brooks put it, a certain 'grandeur' in failures. It comes from what we learn by examining them. Do-it-yourselfers might find the last section of this book of some value in performing private post-mortems on other marketing misfires for the purpose of contributing even more towards boosting the batting average in marketing.

Part 2: On Exploring Marketing Misfires

If this book has at all succeeded in making its intended point, both practical business executives and students in colleges and universities can benefit from the *ex post facto* analysis and synthesis of marketing misfires. Chapter I intimated that such a task might be easy. This is a half-truth.

Business history – hot, cold, or lukewarm – is not unlike other forms of past-telling. Our world has yet to witness an unerring forecaster or a perfectly objective historian. Twenty-twenty hindsight is, contrary to cliché, about as rare as a crystal ball with no fog.

SOME PROBLEMS WITH POST-MORTEMS

Marketing misfires raise special problems for the researcher. Some of these difficulties can inhibit research, and they may explain why marketing failures haven't received more formal study. Some can be overcome or mitigated if we are fully aware of them. Three problems to consider are (1) availability of data, (2) quality of data, and (3) questions of causality.

Availability of Data

There are reasons why it can be quite difficult to marshal information on marketing misfires. In the first place, companies may guard data for competitive reasons. No company likes to expose a weakness or an 'Achilles Heel' to alert rivals who may just be waiting to perceive a chink in the firm's armour upon which to capitalize. Second, marketers are fully aware of the promotional and public relations value of the 'success story' and equally cognizant of the potential negative effect that 'failure stories' may have on customers, dealers, employees, stockholders, bankers, and other corporate publics. This may lead to obfuscation, covering up, and keeping mum in the face of outside inquiries concerning past marketing mistakes. Third, failures may be embarrassing to those directly responsible for them, and the resurrection of a painful past may even undermine the morale and self-confidence of those company employees not directly responsible but nevertheless 'associated' with a company's errors. For such reasons, companies may refuse to release key data or even to discuss the marketing failure under consideration.

Also, after some failures, staffs change – and business, not terribly good at recording its own history, may not have the answers. Nobody may *know* why the failure happened.

Quality of Data

Assuming that the researcher can collect a sufficient *quantity* of data on a marketing misfire, a further problem arises in that the data may be of poor *quality*. The analyst may make errors in collecting data (e.g. by failing to understand properly or assess the significance or relevance of particular kinds of information). Nobody can be 'completely objective' in observing and reporting marketing events, and errors of interpretation are particularly difficult to measure, predict, or control. To the extent that post-mortem information rests as much on *opinion* as on *fact*, errors may creep in because of unconscious biases on the part of the observer or reporter, deliberate attempts to distort information, or honest 'point-of-view' errors. *Assumptions* are also sometimes needed to plug gaps in a network of facts. Because of these kinds of factors, the quality of the available information can vary widely from one source to another.

Laymen, interested but uninformed, unqualified by previous training and experience, or with some private axe to grind, are sometimes not averse to coming forward quickly with answers to explain a marketing fiasco; at first blush, they often sound simple – even obvious – and certainly reasonable from the 'common sense' standpoint. Actually, however, these 'answers' can be superficial half-truths or even grossly incorrect; under close scrutiny, the common explanations often turn out to be at least partly mythical. The detached observer who poses as an 'expert' on these matters frequently *knows* little of which he may be speaking. Furthermore, the man-on-the-street may exhibit a counterpart to the 'American love of the underdog' philosophy. Having been weaned on stories of David and Goliath and Jack the Giant Killer, the detached observer may actually *hope* inwardly for programme failures in a large company. John Brooks has pointed out that the failure of a big company sometimes sets off an 'orgy of gloating hindsight in the press'.

Advertising executives, media representatives, and trade papers in the promotional area may also view marketing failures through imperfect lenses because of vested interest and strategic position, for advertising has some severe and not always rational or informed champions and critics. Thus, when marketing misfires are under discussion, there is some tendency either to place all the blame on faulty advertising or to absolve the advertising function of any responsibility. In most failure cases, neither of these extreme positions reveals the whole truth.

Company executives personally associated with a marketing misfire may – deliberately or otherwise – attempt to 'excuse' themselves or their functional areas from responsibility via covert rationalization or overt buck-passing of the responsibility to other individuals and to other elements of the marketing effort.

Questions of Causality

Assuming the researcher can get enough data of acceptable quality, he still faces the hurdle of assessing complex cause-and-effect relationships in the marketing area. Without being unduly modest, we must admit that we really *know* very little about the specific reasons for 'total programme' marketing successes or failures – our measurement tools and instruments cannot often predict or explain precisely why particular results derive from a given *pattern* of marketing effort. We must often fall back very heavily on personal judgement when imputing causality. Yet, the fact we will never know with certainty what caused a marketing failure does not release us from the responsibility of making informed guesses. In doing this, we ought to be alert to the fact that some marketers have a proclivity for citing single 'causes' of failure, whereas in most cases there are *countless contributing factors* leading up to the final disastrous result.

The designer may say 'The fault lies with the marketing research boys' at the same instant that the director of marketing research attributes the 'real' cause to faulty product design. In a particular case, both may be partly correct, but because they are 'component-centred' due to their different roles in the company, they may be biased and may shrug off factors that seem 'insignificant' from their individually parochial perspectives.

It has been estimated that the Edsel team made four thousand separate decisions on styling questions alone. Certainly it is just as unlikely that one single error on any single one of these matters spelled doom as it is unlikely that the best choice was made in all four thousand instances. The full explanation of marketing failures thus requires the tracing of complex 'means–end chains' to reproduce the total fabric of cause-and-effect. As a minimum, research must strive to uncover as many different reasons as possible and then somehow to weigh them in terms of their individual and collective contributions to the marketing failure.

If we are to overcome problems such as these, the research attack must be pre-planned and properly executed with these difficulties in mind. As a primary research objective, we must take pains to get enough data of sufficiently good quality to offer a reasonably well-substantiated explanation of what *caused* the misfire under examination. Failing this, one can easily learn the wrong things from a post-mortem study and suffer, not learn, from the experience.

MISFIRE STUDIES AS A LEARNING EXPERIENCE

Both student and teacher can be stimulated by taking a closer look at misfires. To either or both, these thoughts are offered as possible guidelines for educational purposes:

Know What Is Required

Sometimes a boss will delegate an assignment with the statement, 'Find out what you can about such-and-such.' He cannot be more specific than this because he himself doesn't really know what to expect; if he knew the findings in advance, he would have no need to make the assignment in the first place. Therefore, one cannot expect specific detail on what is required. However, by describing what an autopsy is and by noting why it is assigned, the requirements may be clarified a bit.

An autopsy involves the inspection, dissection, appraisal, and reconstruction of some past stream of events which has culminated in a marketing failure. It is a written, documented case history of a misfire treated systematically, comprehensively, and in considerable depth. The autopsy should not merely be descriptive but should attempt to uncover and evaluate the causes of failure in order to reveal new insights, criteria, procedures, or guidelines for future marketing decision-making in the affected company and for improving our knowledge of marketing in general. The autopsy must be research-based, not grounded purely in the guesses, hunches, personal assumptions, and private hypotheses of the investigator. It provides an opportunity to test the utility of concepts and procedures developed in marketing courses, although classroom concepts should never be forced into the analysis where they are not fully applicable to the factual reality of the case under investigation.

Select Cases Carefully

Depending upon circumstances and preferences the student may be asked to select his own autopsy cases, to pick out his choices from a prepared list of alternatives, or to carry out a predetermined case assignment without option. In the writer's experience group projects have generally produced better results than individual ones, perhaps because they represent a pooling of views and may generate more competition among students.

The scope of the assignment may be narrow or broad, depending upon the skills, backgrounds, interests, and needs of the students. The case should be selected to stimulate the imagination and satisfy student curiosity to the maximum extent in order to sustain motivation. Wherever possible, those cases should be explored that will make a potential contribution towards advancing marketing knowledge in some relatively unexplored area of marketing management. Ease of research, of course, is another criterion, and those cases that have been most widely discussed in the accessible marketing literature are usually easiest to examine.

Lasting historical interest and educational value are prime criteria for choice, hence, cases that are likely to become dated quickly should be avoided. It has proved more instructive to use 'cool' cases rather than 'hot' ones, i.e. current or very recent cases. A case that has had time to cool off can be studied from a sounder and more reflective perspective and very likely will produce better judgements. Such cases are less 'sensitive' from the competitive and public relations standpoints, they are less embarrassing to the companies affected, and they are less distorted than the hot cases subject to the 'orgiastic' commentary following on the heels of a major marketing failure. It should be noted here that it is exceedingly difficult to appraise a failure which appears to be 'in process'.

Marketing students are more likely to get maximum benefits from (*a*) total programme rather than partial programme failures, (*b*) failures registered by large, successful companies rather than small, little-known firms, and (*c*) the typical or basic case rather than the exotic, exceptional, or merely intriguing sort of case.

Adopt a Proper Frame of Mind

The motive and intent of the serious student of marketing should not be to criticize or to point the finger of shame at an individual or a company. Quite the contrary! The key question is not *who* was wrong, but *what* went wrong. If one has some private axe to grind, he should get rid of it or, failing that, follow the dictates of personal integrity and get himself excused from working on the particular project. To avoid a preconceived stand, the student should view the assignment as 'research to *know*' rather than 'research to *show*'. A real effort is sometimes needed to produce maximum objectivity in the mind and heart of the researcher. It is also important to be forward-looking rather than backward-looking. It is far more constructive to say that in the *future* the company should do such-and-such than it is to say that in the *past* the company should have done thus-and-so. What is past is past. It cannot be undone. It is essential that one approach an autopsy with a constructive – not a destructive – attitude.

How to Find the Data

Since the evaluation of a misfire will depend, at least in part, on the quantity and quality of the research reflected therein, it is imperative that the student know how to begin to marshal his data.

First, the student must determine what kinds of data are likely to be needed, and second, he must have some notion as to where to find them. One will certainly want attitudes, opinions, and personal observations as well as statistical and other facts in order to develop his complete story. Data will be needed on the company itself, the ultimate and intermediate markets in which and through which it attempted to get its marketing work done, and other external or environmental information reflecting the competitive situation, industry structure and practices, legal considerations, and so on. As quickly as possible one should establish the time period during which the failure was generated and unfolded in order to 'home in' on published sources of data more easily. In short, it will probably be necessary to examine data available from both inside and outside the company, from both general and specific sources, and in both published and unpublished form. Different data sources will yield varying kinds and qualities of data, so many sources must be tapped to do a thorough job on a marketing post-mortem.

The student should get acquainted with the generally available published data at an early stage of the research. There is a wide range of marketing books, periodicals, and statistical sources from which one can glean information of a normative, or bench mark character. Several good lists and bibliographies are available to lead one to these sources without too much waste time or motion.[25]

These general sources, however, will seldom if ever completely suffice. Creative research cannot be reduced to a routine; it demands more than the tapping of conventional resources. Originality, imagination, and initiative provide the real pay-off.

The best background data on a company or an industry is often found in financial rather than marketing references, *per se*. Annual reports, stock prospectuses, Moody's Industrials, Standard & Poor's Directory, and articles from financial journals such as *Forbes*, *Barron's*, *Investor's Reader*, the *Commercial and Financial Chronicle*, *Financial Analyst's Journal*, or the *Magazine of Wall Street* may all prove valuable.

General reference works, which can be found in virtually any library, such as *Readers' Guide to Periodical Literature* or the Public Affairs Information Service, are all sources the student should consult.

The daily or weekly news-type sources of current marketing events, advertising news, and trade happenings are often especially useful in reconstructing what happened in a particular time period during which a marketing misfire occurred. By reading a series of news items in such publications as *Advertising Age*, *Printers' Ink*, *Business Week*, the *Wall Street Journal*, and *The New York Times*, one can sometimes get almost a blow-by-blow account of events as they were transpiring.

Trade associations are sometimes fruitful sources of data. Various 'corporate publics' may also provide useful data on occasion, especially the dealers, distributors, or other customers of the company. Personal visits to local stores or a few chats with housewives in the neighbourhood may reveal usable hypotheses during the early stages of an informal investigation or background analysis of a marketing misfire.

Firms that supply goods and services to the company under investigation (advertising agencies, market research firms, management consultants, industrial designers, packaging consultants, raw material and equipment suppliers, and others) can sometimes be tapped for data otherwise unavailable from published sources. These firms and individuals are especially likely to point out reasons for failure which are *not* closely related to their own specialties. Because such professional people protect the confidentiality of their client's information, it is usually necessary to get a clearance from the company before speaking or writing to these outside agencies. Two additional tips: (1) sometimes a marketing failure results in a severed relationship with the professionals, and in such cases it might be advisable to interview both the agency having the account before the failure and the new agency; and (2) sometimes one can tap competitive suppliers who have never had the company as a client or customer.

Executives and other personnel in the affected company, of course, may be contacted directly by letter, telephone, or personal visit. They are particularly good sources for uncovering possible circumstances allegedly beyond the control of the company that may have contributed to the failure.

To illustrate more concretely how misfire research involves marshalling data from many sources, we can cite the case of a student who did a superlative job on a difficult case involving an Ohio manufacturer of specialty mushroom products. The highly specialized nature of the problem made research difficult. Yet, the student was able to piece together valuable data from the following scattered sources: discussions with a competitive manufacturer in Brooklyn, an executive of a large food company, and local retail store operators; published reports on the mushroom market from the Agricultural Marketing Services division of the U.S. Department of Agriculture, the New York State Department of Agriculture, a college research bureau, the American Mushroom Institute, the National Canners Association, and *Parent's Magazine*; a Dun & Bradstreet report on the company; general articles from *Business Week, Printers' Ink,* and *Fortune*; and more specialized trade papers such as *Food Field Reporter, Progressive Grocer,* and *Chain Store Age.*

Exploiting the Sources

Some advance thought should be devoted to the issue of how all of these data sources can be best exploited. If key sources are left untapped the quality of the autopsy (and, hence, its educational value) will suffer. Three tips on tapping sources are offered here for consideration.

First, one should begin the background research as early as possible. If the student waits until he is pressed for time in meeting due dates for the final report of his study, he simply will not have the time to do the kind of research needed to back up sound conclusions.

Second, the student should be prepared to do as thorough a research job as he is capable of doing. The research job on a misfire is a BIG one – often too big for a single student to do properly in the time available to him. Whenever a group of students are assigned to one project, there is a possibility of splitting up the data-gathering chore. Students should feel perfectly free to share raw data with other members of the class and even to discuss the significance of the information that is developed – provided that each student assumes full responsibility for his own analysis. The matter of organizing for data collection may be left up to the students themselves. Some individuals work best on a 'lone wolf' basis, others may prefer to team up with one or two friends, some may exercise their leadership talents by attempting to organize the whole class and get a highly efficient division of labour for the data-gathering activity, especially if the project is big enough to permit this approach. Regardless of how the work is organized, it is important that students harass busy executives as little as possible – perhaps one or two students could undertake personal interviews for the group while others concentrate on published materials.

Third, review the earlier section on 'Some Problems with Post-mortems' then try to overcome the difficulties by being good research strategists and tacticians. One question to think about is the proper *sequence* for tapping sources. The aim should be to exhaust all the available data in as revealing and efficient a manner as possible. In most cases, perhaps, a strategy of attack something like the following will be most appropriate: Start by plumbing the available published data – and do not stop looking if one article appears to have all the answers. One should get as much background data as possible to serve as a base for shaping further assumptions, hypotheses, and research objectives. When this has been done one may turn to whatever direct observational work may be indicated, e.g. store visits to observe the merchandise. Next, one might interview available people such as customers and dealers who were not directly responsible for the marketing failure under investigation. The last step might be to talk to personnel in the company identified with the failure and to its competitors. This is a 'save your gunpowder' approach which helps one learn 'what to believe' as the project develops; it will save the time of busy interviewees; and it puts one in a position to know clearly what information is needed so that doors won't be closed or interviews quickly terminated because of lack of preparedness or sense of direction. Finally, of course, skill and tact are necessary in eliciting information in personal interviews. A skilful interviewer, for example, might succeed in showing an executive that a failure study can actually be a public relations plus instead of a handicap when it is handled in a proper way.

Interpreting the Data

It is difficult to give constructive advice on how to evaluate data, for no two people would be likely to find the same mental processes comfortable, and because close attention to detail and reading between the lines is required. However, the central problem can be stated as one of 'converting *data* into *information*'.

One point to consider is *relevance*. Wholly irrelevant data can be completely discarded at the start. More difficult to establish is the *significance* (that is, both meaning and importance) of various bits of raw data. There are many different kinds of data, and different types will be accorded different values and weights in the overall analysis. The overall interpretation and evaluation are likely to be more sound if one keeps the following points firmly in mind.

1. The quality of data varies from one source to another; therefore, one way to appraise data is to 'consider the source' very carefully.

2. Symptoms should always be distinguished from causes, and causes from effects.

3. Distinguish between facts, attitudes, and opinions; and evaluate each kind of data separately.

4. Separate the data chronologically when feasible, e.g. 'before the event' opinions may be less valid than 'after the event' opinions.

5. Clearly recognize – and label – which impressions, assumptions, and hypotheses are privy to you and which can be traced to someone else.

6. Draw upon whatever concept or insights may have been developed in texts, lectures, or case discussions that might provide 'handles' for dealing with the data.

Having reached the point where one feels that he has done enough research and analysis to put together a fairly realistic overall appraisal of why the company failed to achieve its marketing objectives, the final phase of the autopsy involves the preparation of a written report.

Preparing the Report

There are many ways of putting together a good report on a marketing failure. Perhaps the nature of the data and preferences of individual students will be the determining factors. Nevertheless, it may be instructive to comment on the organization and format of such reports.

In experimenting with the autopsy case as a teaching method, I have found that students have followed one of three basic formats with some success:

1. The Chronological Narrative
2. The Question-and-Answer Format
3. The Components-of-Marketing-Strategy Approach.

Regardless of specific format, all reports require some kind of reconstruction of past events. However, the chronological narrative attempts to relate events precisely as they happened in historical time sequence. There are some problems in using this approach, such as gaps in available data, unavailability of good records by which to pin down events to the dates or periods in which they occurred, and the fact that many events have a habit of unfolding simultaneously – thus requiring the use of the 'flashback' technique to tell the story properly. These problems are not always enough to inhibit the approach. For instance, the news type of published sources sometimes follows commercial events quite closely as and when they occur. A rough calendar of events can sometimes be constructed by following such sources.

The chronological approach clearly has some strong merits to recommend it. It usually results in an interesting story that is 'alive' to the reader. It reveals the evolutionary dynamics (key aspects of timing, critical turning points, etc.) as no other method can. It usually facilitates an examination of the organizational, co-ordinative, and programming dimensions of complex marketing campaigns. And it permits close study of 'means-ends' chains, cause and effect networks, and the dynamic interrelationships among various parts of the marketing mix as they unfold through time.

The question-and-answer format facilitates an examination of the marketing failure within some rationally construed decision-making framework. For example, sub-headings of some student reports have been artfully arranged around questions such as these:

1. *What were the company's intentions?* The reply would include an explicit statement of the firm's decision and plan of action against the backdrop of specific objectives.

2. *Why was the particular decision or plan of action chosen?* (Needed to clarify the situation out of which the problem or opportunity arose and including an examination of the reasonableness of the decision.)

3. *What was done?* Required: a full description of what the company actually did and whether or not these activities accorded with plan – plus something on the 'why' or 'why not'.

4. *What were the results?* This would include both good and bad results, both unexpected and expected fruits of the action – appraised from the point of view of the company as a whole and from both short-term and long-term perspectives. Concrete unit and dollar

223

sales figures, estimates of dollar profits or losses, market-share position data, and similar numerical information – supplemented by qualitative strategic considerations – would be included here.

5. *Why weren't expectations met?* This would involve a dissection of possible contributing conditions and factors leading to the failure, beginning with the origins of the downfall and culminating in some array of all known causal elements in probable descending order of importance.

6. *What lessons were learned from the post-mortem?* This would include two basic kinds of lessons: general insights into the nature of marketing management of interest to the student, and specific lessons of present or future use to the company involved – what can be done now to salvage whatever is possible after actions have begun to reveal their flaws, things to do and not to do under similar circumstances in the future, and so on.

A third format, the components-of-marketing-strategy approach, simply involves the choice of report sub-heads corresponding to major subdivisions of marketing management used in the basic course. For instance, the report might be organized around such sub-headings as:

1. Environmental Analysis – Competition, market structure, etc.
2. Company Analysis – Resource strengths and limitations, objectives, the generation of strategies.
3. Elements of the Marketing Plan
   a. Market Targets
   b. Product Strategy
   c. Distribution Strategy
   d. Pricing
   e. Promotional Campaign and Tactical Evolution
4. Organization, Implementation, and Follow-up on the basic plan.

Such an approach has the merit of assuring comprehensive coverage of most of the topics covered in marketing management and demonstrates to the instructor how competent the student is in applying them to a concrete setting. However, it has the disadvantage of sometimes encouraging a rather mechanistic application of classroom concepts.

No doubt there are other formats that might be productive, and many types of problems other than those described above. It will be well worth our while to explore various approaches to the study of marketing misfires because of the important potential of this type of study in improving competitive efficiency in marketing.

Appendix and Notes

APPENDIX

Source Materials

No author can claim that he is fully aware of every information source tapped during the long process of research and writing. The problem of acknowledgement is especially troublesome for writers of history and biography . . . and marketing history is no exception.

More than one hundred persons gave of their time to provide important information in personal interviews – executives and alumni of companies directly involved in the cases, their past and present advertising agencies, their competitors, retailers, and wholesalers vending their products and carrying out their programmes, trade association personnel, ultimate consumers – both pleased and otherwise, and numberless others less directly involved with the misfires.

It was with more than a little trepidation that I finally submitted drafts of chapters to executives of most of the companies concerned before revising the manuscript for final publication. My fears were soon quelled. Cynics and critics of American business should be informed that many of our marketers will admit and discuss their failures, some in more detail than their victories. It is a tribute to American businessmen that they possess this self-assurance. Few businessmen in other countries seem to have what it takes to see the positive values inherent in confessing and analysing past misfires. Perhaps that is precisely why the American marketing batting average, and the health of our economy, is as good as it is. Almost all executives and companies connected with these cases have openly co-operated to make my narratives more accurate than they might otherwise have been. I appreciate their attitudes and actions.

I must especially thank Professor Taylor W. Meloan and others at the University of Southern California for permission to adapt most of the material contained in my original essay, 'Autopsies of Marketing Failures', which appeared in 1964 in USC's publication, *Competition in Marketing*. That essay became the principal basis for Chapter I and the closing sections of this book.

Some seventy-five graduate students prepared term papers on the subject of marketing misfires at my suggestion and under my guidance while I was on the faculty of the Graduate School of Business at Columbia University. I wish I could personally thank each of them for the fresh perspectives they brought to these studies.

While I am indebted to so many for the raw materials, it has proved impossible to acknowledge individually all sources used in the production of this book. This is due in part to the extensive, varied, individualistic, fragmented, overlapping, and frequently conflicting or contradictory observations made by or in diverse sources.

Although I have inserted some footnotes, they have been used sparingly and only where absolutely essential. Ostentatiously detailed documentation would often have detracted rather than contributed to accuracy and would almost certainly have intruded upon and diminished whatever freshness and readability remain in these tales. Some specific citations follow.

I have tried to maintain an accurate master list of every reference to which I am directly or indirectly indebted, yet I am quite aware that I may have unintentionally omitted notes on important sources.

I drew on more than 800 articles in some seventy periodicals in producing this book. The specific periodicals are:

Advertising Age
Advertising Agency Magazine
American Brewer
American Economic Review

Barron's
Brewing Industry
Brewing World
Broadcasting
Business Horizons
Business Week
Canner/Packer
Chemical Week
Colliers
Commercial & Financial Chronicle
Consumer Bulletin
Consumer Reports
Dun's Review and Modern Industry
Editor and Publisher
Electrical Merchandising Week
Electronic & Appliance Specialist
Engineering News
Financial World
Food Engineering
Food Field Reporter
Forbes
Fortune
The Gallagher Report
Gourmet
Home Furnishings Daily
Harvard Business Review
The Investor
Investment Dealers Digest
Journal of Advertising Research
Journal of Commerce
Journal of Marketing
Madison Avenue
The Magazine of Wall Street
Michigan Business Review
Modern Brewery Age
Modern Packaging
National Petroleum News

Netherlands-American Trade
Newsweek
The New Yorker
The New York Herald Tribune
The New York Times
The New York World-Telegram
The Oil and Gas Journal
Pageant
Perth Amboy News
Petroleum Week
Popular Science
Printers' Ink
Progressive Grocer
Sales Management
The San Francisco Chronicle
Sponsor
Super Market Merchandising and The Discount Merchandiser
Supermarket News
Survey of Current Business
Telefood
Television Age
Tide
Time magazine
U.S. News & World Report
The Value Line
The Wall Street Journal

Approximately 175 other secondary sources were also consulted: books, monographs, pamphlets, research reports, published speeches, standard business reference works, and in-company documents, memoranda, annual reports, house organs, and press releases.

If I have contributed anything at all to these stories, it has been by way of synthesizing and interpreting some of the events and forces that lie behind some of the little known but nevertheless important chapters of American commercial history to help marketers of the 1970s and beyond to profit from the basic mistakes of their predecessors.

Notes on Sources

1. Among the notable exceptions to this is Richard Austin Smith's provocative book, *Corporations in Crisis*, Doubleday & Company, Inc., Garden City, New York, 1963.

2. John Brooks, *The Fate of the Edsel & Other Business Adventures*, Harper and Row, New York, 1963. See also: William H. Reynolds, 'The Edsel Ten Years Later', *Business Horizons*, Autumn 1967, pp. 39–46.

3. All of the quotations and many of the points in the section on the costs of marketing failure have been taken from *Sales Management*, July 15, 1960, pp. 17–18.

4. From a *Reader's Digest* condensation of 'On the Far Side of Failure', an article by Mr Gordon originally appearing in the July 1961 issue of *Future*, a publication of the U.S. Junior Chamber of Commerce.

5. See J. P. Napier, 'How to Reduce the Cost of "Point-of-View" Errors', *The Neilsen Researcher*, November 1957, pp. 2–6.

6. Readers interested in the then-current viewpoints on packaging and its relation to the Gourmet Foods line and how it was promoted in the early stages may wish to consult: Alice B. Ecke, 'Did GF Find a Market for its Gourmet Foods?', *Sales Management*, June 20, 1958, pp. 62–66.

7. See Theodore Levitt, 'Marketing Myopia', *Harvard Business Review*, July–August 1960, pp. 45–56. For additional conceptual background, see Gordon R. Conrad, 'Unexplored Assets for Diversification', *Harvard Business Review*, September–October 1963, pp. 67–73.

8. For capsule summaries of Ford's first years with Philco, see both 'Henry Ford and His Electronic Can of Worms', *Fortune*, February 1966, and 'Philco-Ford: The Balance Sheet', *Forbes*, March 1, 1967, pp. 54–55.

9. 'One Product, One Price, One Market: The Policy That Built Schaefer', *Sales Management*, March 15, 1941, pp. 14 ff.

10. 'More Than Ads Sell Rheingold', *Business Week*, September 21, 1957, pp. 70 ff.

11. In preparing this section, I have drawn on several sources, but most heavily on 'Hamm Brewing Builds to National Brand by '70', *Advertising Age*, January 16, 1961, p. 3.

12. For one educated guess as to the future of the industry, see Ann and Ira Horowitz, 'Profiles of the Future: The Beer Industry', *Business Horizons*, Autumn 1967, pp. 5–19.

13. *See* Joseph Poindexter, 'The High-Octane World of Shell', *Dun's Review*, October 1967, pp. 40 ff.

14. See Robert D. Entenberg and Albert L. Menard, Jr, 'Future Octane Number Requirements for Future Market Demand', *Journal of Marketing*, January 1966, pp. 28–32.

15. 'Input–Output', *Sales Management*, November 5, 1965, pp. 43 ff.

16. Peter F. Drucker, 'Long-range Planning', *Management Science*, April 1959, pp. 238–249.

17. Readers wishing to pursue the matter further might consult: (1) E. Kirby Warren, *Long-Range Planning: The Executive Viewpoint*, Prentice-Hall, Inc., Englewood Cliffs, New Jersey, 1966; or (2) Seymour Tilles, 'How to Evaluate Corporate Strategy', *Harvard Business Review*, July–August 1963, pp. 111–121.

18. Hans L. Carstensen, Jr, and Norman H. McMillan, 'New Products: Boon or Bust', *Madison Avenue*, November 1961, pp. 26 ff.

19. 'Successful Products Depend on Taking Chances', *Printers' Ink*, October 26, 1962, p. 76.

20. A sampler of good sources includes: (1) Lee Adler, *Plotting Marketing Strategy*, Simon and Schuster, New York, 1967; (2) H. Igor Ansoff, *Corporate Strategy*, McGraw-Hill Book Co., New York, 1965; (3) Luck & Prell's *Market Strategy*, Appleton-Century-Crofts, New York, 1968; and (4) Tilles' 'How to Evaluate Corporate Strategy', *Harvard Business Review*, July–August 1963.

21. For a random assortment of both general and specific treatments of the marketer's environment, see Francis Joseph Aguilar, *Scanning the Business Environment*, The Macmillan Company, New York, 1967; William H. Newman and Thomas L. Berg, 'Managing External Relations', *California Management Review*, Spring 1963, pp. 81–86; and Thomas L. Berg, 'Union Inroads in Marketing Decisions', *Harvard Business Review*, July–August 1962, pp. 67–73.

22. See Spencer Klaw, 'The Soap Wars: A Strategic Analysis', *Fortune*, June 1963, pp. 123 ff.

23. Neil H. Borden, 'The Concept of the Marketing Mix', *Journal of Advertising Research*, June 1964, pp. 2–7.

24. Gordon E. Miracle, 'Product Characteristics and Marketing Strategy', *Journal of Marketing*, January 1965, pp. 18–24.

25. For instance, see Steuart Henderson Britt and Irwin A. Shapiro, 'Where to Find Marketing Facts', *Harvard Business Review*, September–October 1962, pp. 44 ff.

Index

AB (Appliance Bonus) Plan of Lob-law's, 104, 121
Additives *vs.* octanes battle in petrol industry, 160–61, 162–63, 179, 186
Advertising Age, 33, 71, 96*n*, 109, 115, 117, 119, 123, 218
Age of customer, as factor in fancy foods market, 51, 52
Air pollution and leaded petrols, 186, 194, 195
Alcohol, use of, as anti-freeze, 14, 15, 16, 17, 25, 44
Alternative courses obscured by marketing failures, 5, 7
American Petroleum Institute, 159
Analose, of Bristol-Myers, failure of, 10
Anti-freeze: history of, 13–24; use of alcohol as, 14, 15, 16, 17, 25, 44; ethylene glycol as, 15, 17–19 (*table*); application of term 'permanent' to, 15, 18, 23, 24, 25, 210; proliferation of private-label brands during the 1950s, 18, 21, 38; and aggressive marketing techniques, 19; 'do-it-yourself' trend in market, 20–21, 22, 39; marketing outlets for, 21; market factors during the fifties, 21–22; market, and anticipation of air-cooled engines, 22; consumer re-use of, 22–23, 24, 27, 39; educational campaign against re-use of anti-freeze, 23–24; and market-share battle of Union Carbide, Dow, and Du Pont, 25–39; post-mortem and aftermath of mismarketing of, 39–45, 204, 207
Appliance-tape plans. *See* Instant Dividend Plan (ID) of Philco
A&P stores, and tape deals on appliances, 104

Availability, as criterion of fancy foods, 48
Aviation high-octane gas, 158, 179

Bailey, G. O., 59
Ballantine beer, 140, 153
Baltimore, tests in, of customer reaction to GEE, 168–69
Bankruptcies, corporate, mismarketing as factor in, 3–4
Barron's, 93
Barth, Louis, 51
Beck, Charles E., 118, 129, 203
Beer: market goes flat after WW II, 133–35; age as factor in consumption of, 134, 134*n*; personal income, relation of, to beer consumption, 134, 134*n*; volume of beer substitutes, relation of, to beer consumption, 134, 134*n*; shifts from 'on-premise' consumption of, to home consumption, 135; packaging of, 135; 'quality labels', 135; distribution changes as a result of increase in take-home buying, 135–36; marketing advantages of national-brand brewers over small local, 136; and intense competition for bigger shares in market, 136–37; levelling off of beer market by 1953, 140; legal battles in California over methods of distribution of, 148*n*. *See also* Brewing industry; Rheingold beer
Better Business Bureau (BBB), investigations of Philco's ID by, 113–16 (*tables*), 121
Blench, Ronald, 59, 62
Blue Sunoco petrol of Sun Oil Company, 160, 167
Boolhack, Nathan, 109

235